ECONOMIC ISSUES, PROBLEMS AND PERSPECTIVES

RECOVERY AFTER RECESSION

SELECT RESEARCH AND ANALYSES

ECONOMIC ISSUES, PROBLEMS AND PERSPECTIVES

Additional books in this series can be found on Nova's website under the Series tab.

Additional E-books in this series can be found on Nova's website under the E-book tab.

GLOBAL RECESSION - CAUSES, IMPACTS AND REMEDIES

Additional books in this series can be found on Nova's website under the Series tab.

Additional E-books in this series can be found on Nova's website under the E-book tab.

ECONOMIC ISSUES, PROBLEMS AND PERSPECTIVES

RECOVERY AFTER RECESSION

SELECT RESEARCH AND ANALYSES

DREW SYMMES
AND
AMANDA ZULPO
EDITORS

nova publishers
New York

For permission to use material from this book please contact us:
Telephone 631-231-7269; Fax 631-231-8175
Web Site: http://www.novapublishers.com

Library of Congress Cataloging-in-Publication Data

ISBN: 978-1-62417-777-4

Published by Nova Science Publishers, Inc. † New York

CONTENTS

PREFACE

This book provides select research and analyses pertaining to the economic recovery and sustaining U.S. economic growth in a post-crisis economy.

Chapter 1 – The 2007-2009 recession was long and deep, and according to several indicators was the most severe economic contraction since the 1930s (but still much less severe than the Great Depression). The slowdown of economic activity was moderate through the first half of 2008, but at that point the weakening economy was overtaken by a major financial crisis that would exacerbate the economic weakness and accelerate the decline.

Economic recovery began in mid-2009. Real gross domestic product (GDP) has been on a positive track since then, although the pace has been uneven and slowed significantly in 2011. The stock market has recovered from its lows, and employment has increased moderately. On the other hand, significant economic weakness remains evident, particularly in the balance sheet of households, the labor market, and the housing sector.

Chapter 2 – Congress in recent years passed a number of bills intended in part to jump-start a recovery in the labor market from the recession that began in December 2007. Members are interested in the labor market's response to these measures to help them decide how well the legislation has worked and whether additional job-creation legislation may be warranted in light of the pace and composition of job growth since the recession's end in June 2009. Accordingly, employment data from the U.S. Bureau of Labor Statistics is analyzed in this report from December 2007 to September 2012 (the latest month for which data were available at the time of the report's preparation).

A "jobless recovery" prevailed across firms in the private nonfarm sector until March 2010. That is to say, the number of private-sector jobs generally continued to fall until nine months into the recovery. The recovery was jobless until October 2010, 16 months into the recovery, across all employers in the public and private sectors of the nonfarm economy. At that point, net job growth in the overall economy began not because public-sector employment started to rise but because it fell more slowly while private-sector employment continued to grow. Given the pace of job growth during the recovery, a few more years will likely elapse before the approximately 7.5 million jobs lost during the recession are recouped.

Chapter 3 – The U.S. economy has grown slowly since the deep recession in 2008 and 2009, which was triggered by a sharp drop in house prices and a subsequent financial crisis. During the three years following the recession (that is, the third quarter of 2009 through the second quarter of 2012), the economy's output grew at less than half the rate exhibited, on average, during other recoveries in the United States since the end of World War II. All told, between the end of the recession and the second quarter of 2012, the cumulative rate of growth of real (inflation-adjusted) gross domestic product (GDP) was nearly 9 percentage points below the average for previous recoveries. Researchers continue to grapple with understanding the roles that steep declines in house prices and financial crises play in slowing the growth of output.

In the current recovery, both potential GDP, a measure of the underlying productive capacity of the economy, and the ratio of real GDP to potential GDP have grown unusually slowly. Because potential GDP is an estimate of the amount of real GDP that corresponds to a high rate of use of labor and capital resources, it is not typically affected very much by the up-and-down cycles of the economy; in contrast, because the ratio of real GDP to potential GDP depends on the degree of the economy's use of resources, it captures cyclical variations in real GDP around its potential level. In the first 12 quarters after the last recession, both potential GDP and the ratio of real GDP to potential GDP grew at less than half the rate that occurred, on average, in the aftermath of other recessions since World War II (see Figure 1). Disaggregating the unusually slow growth in output since the end of the last recession, the Congressional Budget Office's (CBO's) analysis shows that that pace is mostly owing to slow growth in the underlying productive capacity of the economy and to a lesser extent, to slow growth in real output relative to that productive capacity.

Chapter 4 – Testimony of Douglas W. Elmendorf given on November 15, 2011 before the Senate Budget Committee.

Chapter 5 – This paper studies the behavior of recoveries from recessions across 59 advanced and emerging market economies over the past 40 years. Focusing specifically on the performance of output after the recession trough, we find little or no difference in the pace of output growth across types of recessions. In particular, banking and financial crisis do not affect the strength of the economic rebound, although these recessions are more severe, implying a sizable output loss. However, recovery does change with some characteristics of recession. Recoveries tend to be faster following deeper recessions, especially in emerging markets, and tend to be slower following long recessions. Most recessions are associated with a slowing, if not outright decline in house prices, but recessions with large declines in house prices also tend to have slower recoveries. Long recessions and those associated with poor housing-market outcomes can lead to sustained output losses relative to pre-crisis trends. Consistent with microeconomic studies showing permanent income loss to job-losing workers during recessions, we find that the sustained deviation in output from trend is associated with a reduction in labor input, especially linked to declines in employment and labor-force participation following recessions. On net, our results imply that the output/employment gap following a severe, long recessions is considerably smaller than is typically assumed by standard macro models, which in turn may have substantial implications for macroeconomic policy during recoveries.

In: Recovery after Recession: Select Research and Analyses ISBN: 978-1-62417-777-4
Editors: Drew Symmes and Amanda Zulpo

Chapter 1

ECONOMIC RECOVERY: SUSTAINING U.S. ECONOMIC GROWTH IN A POST-CRISIS ECONOMY*

Craig K. Elwell

SUMMARY

The 2007-2009 recession was long and deep, and according to several indicators was the most severe economic contraction since the 1930s (but still much less severe than the Great Depression). The slowdown of economic activity was moderate through the first half of 2008, but at that point the weakening economy was overtaken by a major financial crisis that would exacerbate the economic weakness and accelerate the decline.

Economic recovery began in mid-2009. Real gross domestic product (GDP) has been on a positive track since then, although the pace has been uneven and slowed significantly in 2011. The stock market has recovered from its lows, and employment has increased moderately. On the other hand, significant economic weakness remains evident, particularly in the balance sheet of households, the labor market, and the housing sector.

Congress was an active participant in the policy responses to this crisis and has an ongoing interest in macroeconomic conditions. Current macroeconomic concerns include whether the economy is in a sustained recovery, rapidly reducing unemployment, speeding a return to normal output and employment growth, and addressing government's long-term debt problem.

In the typical post-war business cycle, lower than normal growth during the recession is quickly followed by a recovery period with above normal growth.

This above normal growth serves to speed up the reentry of the unemployed to the workforce. Once the economy reaches potential output (and full employment), growth returns to its normal growth path, where the pace of aggregate spending advances in step with the pace of aggregate supply. There is concern that this time the U.S. economy will either not return to its pre-recession growth path but perhaps remain permanently below

* This is an edited, reformatted and augmented version of a Congressional Research Service publication, CRS Report for Congress R41332, from www.crs.gov, prepared for Members and Committees of Congress, dated October 12, 2012.

it, or return to the pre-crisis path but at a slower than normal pace. Problems on the supply side and the demand side of the economy have so far led to a weaker than normal recovery.

If the pace of private spending proves insufficient to assure a sustained recovery, would further stimulus by monetary and fiscal policy be warranted? One lesson from the Great Depression is to guard against a too hasty withdrawal of fiscal and monetary stimulus in an economy recovering from a deep decline. The removal of fiscal and monetary stimulus in 1937 is thought to have stopped a recovery and caused a slump that did not end until WWII. Opponents of further stimulus maintain that the accumulation of additional government debt would lower future economic growth, but supporters argue that additional stimulus is the appropriate near-term policy. There is concern that the "fiscal cliff," the confluence of various spending cuts and tax rate increases that are scheduled to occur at the beginning of 2013 unless policies are changed, could have an adverse effect on the economic recovery.

In regard to the long-term debt problem, in an economy operating close to potential output, government borrowing to finance budget deficits will in theory draw down the pool of national saving, crowding out private capital investment and slowing long-term growth.

However, the U.S. economy is currently operating well short of capacity and the risk of such crowding out occurring is therefore low in the near term. Once the cyclical problem of weak demand is resolved and the economy has returned to a normal growth path, mainstream economists' consensus policy response for an economy with a looming debt crisis is fiscal consolidation—cutting deficits. Such a policy would have the benefits of low and stable interest rates, a less fragile financial system, improved investment prospects, and possibly faster long-term growth.

BACKGROUND

Severity of the 2008-2009 Recession

The 2008-2009 recession was long and deep, and according to several indicators was the most severe economic contraction since the 1930s (but still much less severe than the Great Depression). The slowdown of economic activity was moderate through the first half of 2008, but at that point the weakening economy was overtaken by a major financial crisis that would exacerbate the economic weakness and accelerate the decline.[1]

When the fall of economic activity finally bottomed out in the second half of 2009, real gross domestic product (GDP) had contracted by approximately 5.1%, or by about $680 billion.[2] At this point the output gap—the difference between what the economy could produce and what it actually produced—widened to an estimated 8.1%. The decline in economic activity was much sharper than in the nine previous post-war recessions, in which the fall of real GDP averaged about 2.0% and the output gap increased to near 4.0%. However, the recent decline falls well short of the experience during the Great Depression, when real GDP decreased by 30% and the output gap probably exceeded 40%.[3]

As output decreased the unemployment rate increased, rising from 4.6% in 2007 to a peak of 10.1% in October 2009, and remaining only slightly below that high into 2011. The U.S. unemployment rate has not been at this level since 1982, when in the aftermath of the 1981 recession it reached 10.8%, the highest rate of the post-war period. (During the Great Depression the unemployment rate reached 25%.) This rise in the unemployment rate translates to about 7 million persons put out of work during the recession. Another 8.5 million workers have been pushed involuntarily into part-time employment.[4]

The recession was intertwined with a major financial crisis that exacerbated the negative effects on the economy. Falling stock and house prices led to a large decline in household wealth (net worth), which plummeted by over $12 trillion or about 20% during 2008 and 2009. In addition, the financial panic led to an explosion of risk premiums (i.e., compensation to investors for accepting extra risk over relatively risk-free investments such as U.S. Treasury securities) that froze the flow of credit to the economy, crimping credit supported spending by consumers such as for automobiles, as well as business spending on new plant and equipment.[5]

The negative shocks the economy received in 2008 and 2009 were, arguably, more severe than what occurred in 1929. However, unlike in 1929, the severe negative impulses did not turn a recession into a depression, arguably because timely and sizable policy responses by the government helped to support aggregate spending and stabilize the financial system.[6] That stimulative economic policies would have this beneficial effect on a collapsing economy is consistent with standard macroeconomic theory, but without the counterfactual of the economy's path in the absence of these policies, it is difficult to establish with precision how effective these policies were.

Policy Responses to the Financial Crisis and Recession

Both monetary and fiscal policies as well as some extraordinary measures were applied to counter the economic decline. This policy response is thought to have forestalled a more severe economic contraction, helping to turn the economy into the incipient economic recovery by mid-2009. These policies likely continued to stimulate economic activity into 2012.

Monetary Policy Actions

To bolster the liquidity of the financial system and stimulate the economy, during 2008 and 2009 the Federal Reserve (Fed) aggressively applied conventional monetary stimulus by lowering the federal funds rate to near zero and boldly expanding its "lender of last resort" role, creating new lending programs to better channel needed liquidity to the financial system and induce greater confidence among lenders. Following the worsening of the financial crisis in September 2008, the Fed grew its balance sheet by lending to the financial system. As a result, between September and November 2008, the Fed's balance sheet more than doubled, increasing from under $1 trillion to more than $2 trillion.

By the beginning of 2009, demand for loans from the Fed was falling as financial conditions normalized. Had the Fed done nothing to offset the fall in lending, the balance sheet would have shrunk by a commensurate amount, and some of the stimulus that it had added to the economy would have been withdrawn. In the spring of 2009, the Fed judged that the economy, which remained in a recession, still needed additional stimulus. On March 18, 2009, the Fed announced a commitment to purchase $300 billion of Treasury securities, $200 billion of Agency debt (later revised to $175 billion), and $1.25 trillion of Agency mortgage-backed securities.[7] The Fed's planned purchases of Treasury securities were completed by the fall of 2009 and planned Agency purchases were completed by the spring of 2010. At this point, the Fed's balance sheet stood at just above $2 trillion.[8] (Further monetary policy actions taken to accelerate the pace of economic recovery are discussed later in the report.)

Fiscal Policy Actions

Congress and the Bush Administration enacted the Economic Stimulus Act of 2008 (P.L. 110- 185). This act was a $120 billion package that provided tax rebates to households and accelerated depreciation rules for business. Congress and the Obama Administration passed the American Recovery and Reinvestment Act of 2009 (ARRA; P.L. 111-5). This was a $787 billion package with $286 billion of tax cuts and $501 billion of spending increases that relative to what would have happened without ARRA is estimated to have raised real GDP between 1.5% and 4.2% in 2010 but increased real GDP by a smaller amount in 2011 and will increase 2012 GDP by an even smaller amount.[9]

In terms of extraordinary measures, Congress and the Bush Administration passed the Emergency Economic Stabilization Act of 2008 (P.L. 110-343), creating the Troubled Asset Relief Program (TARP). TARP authorized the Treasury to use up to $700 billion to directly bolster the capital position of banks or to remove troubled assets from bank balance sheets.[10]

Congress was an active participant in the emergence of these policy responses and has an ongoing interest in macroeconomic conditions. Current macroeconomic concerns include whether the economy is in a sustained recovery, rapidly reducing unemployment, speeding a return to normal output and employment growth, and addressing government's long-term debt problem.

IS SUSTAINED ECONOMIC RECOVERY UNDERWAY?

Evidence indicates that the economy, as measured by real GDP growth, began to recover in mid-2009. However, the pace of growth has been slow and uneven with a pronounced deceleration evident during 2011. During 2009 and 2010, growth had been sustained by transitory factors, such as fiscal stimulus and the rebuilding of inventories by business. Economic growth in 2010 showed signs of being generated by more sustainable forces, but the strength of those forces continues to be uneven, and a slowing of growth during 2011 prompted concern about the recovery's sustainability.

- For the second half of 2009 and through 2010 real GDP (i.e., GDP adjusted for inflation) increased at an annualized rate of 3.0%. However, during 2011 growth slowed to 1.6% and that weakening has continued in 2012, with real GDP in the second quarter of 2012 increasing only 1.7%. In comparison to previous economic recoveries, growth at 3.0% is relatively weak, but is fast enough to at least make slow progress at reducing the large output gap and at reducing unemployment. However, growth at less than a 2% annual rate may not be fast enough to close the output gap or keep the unemployment rate from rising. Through 2010, much of the economy's upward momentum was sustained by the transitory factors of inventory increases and fiscal stimulus. However, sustainable recovery would depend on more enduring sources of demand such spending by consumers and businesses reviving and providing continued momentum to the recovery. While business investment spending has been relatively brisk during the recovery, consumer spending was relatively tepid. Weak consumer spending along with the rapidly fading effects of fiscal stimulus and weaker growth in Europe raises concern about the sustainability of U.S. economic recovery.[11]

- Credit conditions have improved, making getting loans easier for consumers and businesses, loosening a constraint on many types of credit supported expenditures. The Fed's survey of senior loan officers indicates that, on net, bank lending standards and terms continued to ease during 2012 and that the demand for commercial and industrial loans had increased.[12]
- The stock market has rebounded and interest rate spreads on corporate bonds have narrowed. The Dow Jones stock index had plunged to near 6500 in March 2009 but by mid-September 2012 had regained about 97% of its lost capitalization. Spreads on investment-grade corporate bonds, a measure of the lenders' perception of risk and creditworthiness of borrowers, have fallen from a high of 600 basis points in December 2008 to less than 100 basis points in 2012.[13]
- Manufacturing activity has shown steady improvement. Through August 2012, output had increased 3.8% over a year earlier and capacity utilization has risen from a low of 64% in mid-2009 to 77% by August 2012. (A capacity utilization rate of 80% - 85% would be typical for a fully recovered economy.)[14]
- Since mid-2009, non-farm payroll employment has increased by about 3 million jobs. Monthly gains have been consistently positive since late 2010, but often not at a scale characteristic of a strong recovery. Recent months have seen employment gains steadily falling, down from 275,000 workers in January 2012 to 114,000 workers in September 2012.[15]
- The housing sector has recently shown evidence of improving health. Private new housing starts increased at an annual rate of near 750,000 units in July 2012, up from less than 400,000 units during the recession (but still far short of the pre-recession highs of over 2 million units). Also, house prices have begun to increase, on average, up about 4% over the first half of 2012.[16]
- China, Asia's other emerging economies, and Latin America are growing rapidly, which is transmitting a positive growth impulse to the United States by boosting demand for U.S. exports. Also, the dollar is very competitive from a historical perspective, adding support to U.S. exports.

On the other hand, growth is well below the historical norm for U.S. economic recoveries as persistent sources of economic weakness continue to dampen economic activity.

- In the third quarter of 2011, the economy had regained its pre-recession level of output. But it took 15 quarters to accomplish this as compared with 5 quarters on average in previous post-war recoveries. However, since potential GDP has also continued to grow for these 15 months, the output gap has only narrowed from about 8.1% to 6.1%.[17]
- Consumer spending, the usual engine of a strong economic recovery, remains tepid, generally slowed by households' ongoing need to rebuild substantial net worth lost

during the housing crisis and the recession, continued high unemployment and underemployment, and a surge in energy prices in the first half of 2012.

- Employment conditions, despite improvement, remain weak. The unemployment rate, which had peaked at 10.0% in October 2009, fell slowly but steadily, reaching 8.3% by January 2012. Since then, however, little improvement has occurred, with the unemployment rate only slightly lower at 7.8% in September 2012.[18] Moreover, a considerable share of that improvement is not the result of workers finding jobs, but by discouraged workers leaving the ranks of the officially unemployed by leaving the labor force. Such a high rate of unemployment after more than three years of economic recovery is unusual and a source of concern. Another measure of labor market conditions, the employment to population ratio, which is not affected by changes in labor force participation, shows a labor market that is essentially "treading water." During the recession that ratio fell from 63% to 58% and it has remained near that low through three years of economic recovery.[19]
- The housing market, while showing signs of revival, is likely to continue to fall short of its typical contribution to economic recoveries. Mortgage loan foreclosures are still high, house prices are still weak in many regions, and millions of mortgage holders are "underwater," with the market values of their houses below the amount of their mortgages. Beyond the direct effect on economic activity through lower rates of new construction, housing market weakness has a strong negative indirect effect on the balance sheets of households and banks. The sharp fall in household net worth caused by the fall of house prices has been an important factor dampening current consumer spending and the pace of overall economic recovery.
- Growth in the UK and the Euro area has been weak and fiscal austerity measures to stem the growth of public debt have likely pushed the region back into recession, slowing growth further. Slower growth in this region, a major U.S. export market, has likely transmitted a contractionary impulse to the United States, slowing the pace of the U.S. recovery in 2012 and will likely continue to do so into 2013.[20]

THE SHAPE OF ECONOMIC RECOVERY

In the typical post-war business cycle, lower than normal growth of aggregate demand during the recession is quickly followed by a recovery period with above normal growth of spending, perhaps spurred by some degree of monetary and fiscal stimulus. The degree of acceleration of growth in the first two to three years of recovery has varied across post-war business cycles, but has been at an annual pace in a range of 4% to 8%.[21] This above normal growth brings the economy back more quickly to the pre-recession growth path, and speeds up the reentry of the unemployed to the workforce.

Once the level of aggregate demand approaches the level of potential GDP (or full employment), the economy returns to its pre-recession growth path, where the growth of aggregate spending is slower because it is constrained by the growth of aggregate supply, which in recent years is estimated to have been at an annual pace of near 3.0%. (A subsequent section of the report looks more closely at aggregate supply.)[22]

There is concern, however, that this time the U.S. economy, without supporting stimulus from policy actions, will either not return to its pre-recession growth path, perhaps remain permanently below it, or return to the pre-crisis path but at a slower than normal pace, or worse, dip into a second recession. Below normal growth would almost certainly translate into below normal recovery of employment, whereas a second round of recession could increase the already high unemployment rate. The next sections of this report discuss problems on the supply side and the demand side of the economy that could lead to a weaker than normal recovery.

Demand Side Problems?

Much of the vigor that occurred on the demand side of the economy in 2009 and 2010 appears to have come from fiscal stimulus and business inventory restocking. Fiscal stimulus and inventory rebuilding are, however, temporary sources of support of aggregate spending. Sooner or later fiscal stimulus falls away. The Congressional Budget Office (CBO) projects that fiscal stimulus peaked in 2010, provided a smaller boost to demand in 2011, and continued to diminish in 2012.[23] Inventory building is a self limiting process that will not go on indefinitely; stock-building was weaker during most of 2011, and despite a stronger turn in late 2011 and early 2012 inventory growth will unlikely continue to have a major positive effect on aggregate demand.

A strong recovery of private sector demand, including consumer spending, investment spending, and exports, is required to sustain an economic recovery that brings the economy quickly back to its pre-recession growth path and unemployment rate. However, there are major uncertainties about the potential medium-term strength of each of these components that could dampen aggregate spending and constrain the economy's ability to generate a recovery period with above normal growth and quickly falling unemployment.

Consumption Spending

Personal consumption expenditures historically constitute the largest and most stable component of aggregate spending in the U.S. economy. During the first three post-war decades, personal consumption spending averaged a 62% share of GDP. However, that share rose significantly over the next three decades, averaging about 65% in the 1980s, 67% during the 1990s, and about 70% between 2001 and 2007. The high level of household spending reached during the 2001-2007 expansion is unlikely to reemerge during the current recovery because it was supported by an unsustainable increase in household debt, a decrease in personal savings, ease of access to credit, and lower energy prices.

Household Debt

In the mid-1980s, after a long period of relative stability at a scale of around 45% to 50% of GDP, the debt level of households began to rise steadily, reaching over 100% of GDP by 2008. Such a substantial rise in the level of household debt was sustainable so long as rising home prices and a rising stock market continued to also increase the value of household net worth, and interest rates remained low, mitigating any rise in the burden of debt service as a share of GDP.

The collapse of the housing and stock markets in 2008 and 2009 substantially decreased household net worth, which had, by mid-2009, fallen about $16 trillion below its 2007 peak of nearly $67 trillion.[24] This near 25% fall in net worth pushed the household debt burden up substantially. Unlike in earlier post-war recoveries, the current need of households to repair their damaged balance sheets has induced a large diversion of current income from consumption spending to debt reduction.[25] That above normal diversion has persisted in 2012 and is likely to be a continuing drag on the pace of economic recovery in 2013.

A substantial rebuilding of household net worth has occurred during the recovery. Through the first quarter of 2011, household net worth has increased by about $12 trillion, reaching about $63 trillion and recovering nearly 75% of what was lost during the recession. This improvement has occurred largely on the asset side of the household balance sheet, primarily due to the rise of the stock market from its low point in early 2009.[26] Traditionally, rising home equity, largely dependent on the path of house prices, has been the major contributor to household wealth. The rapid rise of home prices during the last economic expansion caused an equally rapid rise in home equity. Consumers borrowed against this equity to fund current spending. With the sharp fall of home prices, home equity was reduced substantially, erasing that source of funding. Home prices are only now beginning to rise and the housing market is expected to remain weak for several more years, slowing the pace of households rebuilding their net worth, and continuing to dampen consumer spending.[27]

In addition to diverting more personal income to saving, a continued weak labor market is likely to dampen income growth and, in turn, slow the recovery of consumer spending.

Credit Conditions

Easy credit availability in the pre-crisis economy enabled households to readily borrow against their rising home equity to fund added spending. Financial innovations allowed lenders to keep interest rates low and offer liberal terms and conditions to entice households to borrow. Many believe that credit conditions will remain tighter during the current expansion. Interest rates are still low, but banks greatly tightened the terms and conditions of consumer loans during the crisis and recession and have only slowly relaxed them as the recovery has proceeded. While not likely as important a driver of higher savings as high household debt, tighter credit conditions will make it less likely that households will exploit any increase in their home equity to fund current spending, further constraining consumer spending relative to what occurred during the 2001-2007 economic expansion.

Personal Saving

The U.S. personal saving rate averaged about 10% of GDP consistently through the 1970s, 1980s, and 1990s. Subsequently, the personal saving rate declined sharply, reaching a low of 1.0% by 2005.[28] It is likely that the reduction of household saving was in large measure a consequence of the sizable increase in household net worth associated with increased house prices and stock prices occurring at that time. As wealth rose rapidly, it was less urgent to divert current income to saving.

The sharp reduction of household net worth during the recent recession dramatically changed the financial circumstances of households, reducing the use of debt-financed spending. The need to repair household balance sheets induced households to pay down debt. The poor prospect for the appreciation of house prices has eliminated the ability to use rising equity as a substitute for saving.

In addition, the increase in economic uncertainty in the aftermath of the financial crisis and recession will likely mean that over the medium term, households could continue to be more inclined to save. As the economic decline intensified, the personal saving rate increased, climbing from 3.5% of GDP in 2007 to 6.1% of GDP in 2009.[29] However, since that point the personal saving rate has fallen, averaging about 4.0% in the first half of 2012. The passing of the dire financial and economic circumstances that prevailed in 2008 and 2009 has likely led to some of the recent moderation in households' saving behavior. A lower rate of saving enables higher rates of consumption, but it is uncertain that continued fall of the saving rate will be a substantial source of support for current spending by households.

Energy Prices

A 30% increase in the price of oil from October 2011 through April 2012 has likely adversely affected household budgets and contributed to the slow rate of increase in consumer spending over the same period.[30] In the short run, the U.S. demand for energy is relatively inelastic, with little curtailment of energy use in the face of the rising price. As households and businesses spend more for energy, which is largely imported, they tend to spend less on domestic output, slowing economic growth.[31] Since April 2012, the price of oil appears to have stabilized, and if it remains near the current level, the dampening effect on economic growth is likely to fade. In addition, increasing supplies of shale gas have resulted in lower natural gas prices, which may benefit household budgets.

Slow Recovery of Consumer Spending?

If consumer spending continues its slow paced recovery, then for the U.S. economy to return to its normal pre-crisis growth path, an improved pace of GDP growth will have to come from other components of aggregate demand: investment spending, net exports, or government spending.

Investment Spending

Investment spending is the third-largest component of aggregate spending, historically averaging 17% to 18% of GDP in years of near normal output growth. (Government spending is second largest at about 20%.) Historically, the largest portion of total investment spending is business fixed investment, its share averaging 11% to 12% of GDP in periods of normal growth. The second component of total investment is residential investment (i.e., new housing), averaging 4% to 5% of GDP.

Investment spending is very sensitive to economic conditions and more volatile than consumer spending. This sensitivity is at least in part because investment projects are often postponable to a time when economic conditions are more favorable. Its volatility makes investment spending an important determinant of the amplitude, down and up, of the typical business cycle.[32]

As aggregate spending fell and credit availability tightened in 2008, investment spending quickly weakened. As a share of real GDP, investment spending fell from about 16% in 2007 to about 11% at the economy's trough in 2009. The sharp fall in real GDP from the second quarter of 2008 through the first quarter of 2009 was nearly fully accounted for by the sharp fall of investment spending over this same period. With economic recovery, investment spending was a leading source of economic growth, elevating its share of real GDP to 13.1%

in 2010; it continued to increase strongly over 2011, reaching 13.5% of real GDP. In the first half of 2012, investment spending continued its upward trend reaching 14% of real GDP.[33]

In particular, the *equipment and software* component of nonresidential investment has been the principal source of business spending strength and an important contributor to the pace of the economic recovery. Equipment and software spending increased 14.6% in 2010, contributing nearly a full percentage point to the growth of real GDP in that year. This category of business investment spending continued to be an important source of economic growth in 2011, increasing at an annual rate of 10.4% and contributing 0.7 percentage points to real GDP growth. However, in the first half of 2012 investment spending on equipment and software slowed substantially, advancing at a slower 5% annual rate.[34]

Typically, this same sensitivity also works in the opposite direction. Strongly rising investment spending, responding to improving market demand, reduced uncertainty, and expanding credit availability, often gives an above normal contribution to the rebound of aggregate spending during the recovery phase of the business cycle.

Looking forward, however, some significant constraints on both residential and business investment raise uncertainty about whether investment spending will continue to be a strong contributor to economic recovery, and therefore, whether it could be a component of aggregate spending capable of compensating for a weaker than normal recovery of spending by consumers.

The principal constraint on residential investment has been the large inventory of vacant housing, left over from the 2002-2006 housing boom. It is estimated that the number of vacancies could be more than 2 million units above what would normally be expected at this stage of the business cycle.[35] As discussed above, the housing market has recently shown signs of stabilizing, and residential investment spending has risen strongly in 2012, albeit from a very low base. On balance new house construction is likely to remain relatively weak for the next two years while the inventory overhang continues to be worked down.

The prospect for nonresidential investment is likely to be better than for residential investment, but it is not clear that with economic recovery nonresidential investment will exceed its pre-crisis level. On the supply side, capacity utilization rates have climbed back from record lows of below 70% reached during the recession, but, at about 75% currently, are still only at the lows reached in the 1990 and the 2001 recessions and well short of the 80% to 85% that would typically correspond to operating near or at capacity.[36] On the demand side, business investment in new plants and equipment is most often a response to the expectation of increased demand for the products they produce. The main driver of that demand is consumer spending and, as discussed above, that spending has been tepid, with the not unlikely prospect that it may continue to be weak over the near term if households have made a lasting commitment to increased savings.

Stronger foreign demand could also stimulate investment spending and in theory compensate for the weaker pull of domestic demand, but as discussed more fully below, foreign demand may also be weak. Also, problems in the financial sector have caused sharply reduced activity in commercial real estate, contributing to persistent weakness in business investment spending on structures.[37]

In general, it seems questionable whether total investment spending would provide the offset to a below normal contribution of consumption spending to economic growth over the near term.

Net Exports

The U.S. trade deficit (real net exports) shrank from about 6% of real GDP in 2006 to below 3% in 2009. Since the beginning of the recession in late 2007 through the end of the contraction in mid-2009, net exports made a significant positive contribution to real GDP in an otherwise declining economy. Even as economic weakness abroad caused U.S. exports to fall, imports fell by more, providing a net positive push to current economic activity.[38]

The 3 percentage point swing in real net exports is, however, largely the consequence of the severe economic weakness in the United States over this period. Since mid-2009, the deficit in net exports has increased slightly, reaching 3.2% of real GDP in 2010, but in 2011 the deficit decreased slightly, falling to 3.1% of real GDP; and in the first half of 2012 it again decreased slightly to 3.0% of GDP. This relatively flat performance means that over the course of the current recovery net exports have not had either a substantial positive or negative impact on economic growth. This neutral pattern makes it uncertain that net exports can be expected to boost aggregate spending sufficiently to offset weak consumption over the medium term and help assure a sustained recovery at a pace that steadily reduces unemployment.

Boosting U.S. Net Exports Through a Rebalancing of Global Spending

Increasing U.S. net exports to any degree requires that the trade deficit continues to decrease. For that to happen, trade surpluses of the rest of the world with the United States must also decrease.

To achieve this adjustment of trade flows, a sizable rebalancing of domestic and external demand on the part of the deficit and surplus economies would need to occur.[39]

Because a trade deficit is a consequence of an economy spending more than it produces, rebalancing in this circumstance requires a decrease of domestic spending and increase of domestic saving. In contrast, for overseas trade partners, because a trade surplus is a consequence of an economy spending less than it produces, rebalancing in this circumstance requires an increase of trade partner domestic spending and decrease in trade partner domestic saving.

This rebalancing of spending will put pressure on the dollar to depreciate and foreign currencies to appreciate. A fall in the value of the dollar relative to the currencies of the surplus countries causes the price of foreign goods to rise for U.S. buyers and the price of U.S. goods to fall for foreign buyers. This change in the relative price of foreign versus domestic goods will cause the net exports of the United States to rise, giving the boost in spending needed to potentially offset reduced consumption spending. The change in relative prices would also cause the net exports of surplus countries to fall as more of current output is absorbed by increased domestic spending.

In the United States, as discussed above, some measure of rebalancing seems to be occurring, as evidenced by the increase in the personal saving rate above its pre-recession low. Although there are good reasons to expect this increase to be sustained, there is the possibility that households would eventually revert to their pre-crisis low saving patterns. However, even if household saving remains higher, it is likely that any significant increase in the overall U.S. national saving rate would also require an increase in government saving via smaller federal budget deficits.

Large U.S. budget deficits over the near term are providing a needed boost to weak aggregate spending during the early stages of an economic recovery. With the strengthening of private spending as the recovery matures, large government budget deficits would fade away, causing government saving to rise. What puts this fading away of budget deficits in doubt over the long term is the prospect of having to fund the obligations attached to the rising demand of an aging U.S. population for healthcare, Social Security, and other entitlements. Without policy actions to address these long-term demands, it is not clear how the long-term budget deficits will fall.

Effective global rebalancing arguably also involves sizable adjustments by the largest surplus economies—Germany, Japan, and China. However, there are significant potential constraints on how substantially each of these three economies can "save less and spend more," perhaps limiting any sizable appreciation of their currencies relative to the dollar, and any associated boost in U.S. net exports.

The inability of Germany to move its exchange rate independently from the other Euro area economies reduces its flexibility of adjustment. In addition, the effects of the 2008-2009 recession have left limited room for further fiscal expansion and small ability to lower the household saving rate. In addition, the ongoing sovereign debt crisis in the euro area has dampened growth prospects in Germany, likely weakening the demand for U.S. exports. While its level of debt is not high, recent German policy actions have stressed fiscal consolidation, tending to increase saving and dampen spending.[40] Japan, which does have a very high level of public debt, has little to no room for fiscal expansion and a poor prospect of boosting household spending. Moreover, both Germany and Japan, faced with substantial near-term economic weakness in the aftermath of the global recession, may take steps to avoid the dampening of their net exports that a sizable appreciation of the exchange rate would cause.

China has the largest bilateral trade surplus with the United States and therefore has the potential to have a large impact on U.S. export sales and through that a significant positive impulse on the pace of the U.S. economic recovery. Also, economic growth has remained relatively strong in China through the recent global financial crisis and recession, and aggregate demand is expected to be strong through the next two to three years. What is uncertain, however, is whether a greater share of this spending will be domestic demand, particularly consumption spending by Chinese households.

The very high rate of saving by Chinese households is thought to be a precautionary measure to compensate for a lack of social insurance. It likely also reflects limited access to consumer credit. The difficulty for the near-term task of sustaining economic recovery is that even if policy actions are taken to remove these constraints on consumer spending, households are likely to only gradually change their pattern of consumption and not provide a sharp near-term boost to domestic spending.

Also, a closer look at the sources of increase in China's domestic saving over the last decade reveals that the principal contributor to that growth was Chinese companies, not households. Therefore, changing the saving practices of Chinese companies is likely to be an important aspect of any large increase in China's saving rate. It is argued by some that Chinese companies retain too large a share of their earnings. Better access to credit and changes in the governance rules of Chinese business would likely reduce the business saving rate. But, as with households, even if such policy initiatives are forthcoming, the change in the business saving rate is likely to emerge only gradually.[41]

Even with a successful rebalancing, it is unlikely that China alone can propel a boost in U.S. net exports sufficient to offset weak domestic demand and pace economic recovery.

China's global trade surplus is estimated to be about 10% of GDP. However, China is only about one-third the size of the U.S. economy. Therefore, if China's trade were only with the United States, it would have to reduce its trade surplus by 3% of GDP to affect a 1 percentage point reduction of the U.S. trade deficit. But since, in fact, only about 16% of China's trade is with the United States, it would take a 15 percentage point change in China's trade balance (moving from a surplus equal to 10% of GDP to a deficit equal to 5% of GDP) to reduce the U.S. trade deficit by 1 percentage point. (This assumes that the fall of China's trade surplus is not offset by an increase of other trading partners surpluses.)

Other emerging Asian economies also run trade surpluses, and adding these to the calculation makes the relative scale of rebalancing needed to achieve a given amount of improvement in the U.S trade deficit more feasible. However, all of emerging Asia is only about half the size of the U.S. economy. Therefore, if the U.S. share of the whole region's trade is similar to China's, emerging Asia would need to accomplish a sizable 7 percentage point change in its trade balance to generate a 1 percentage point change in the U.S. trade balance. As with China, for a reduction of the trade surpluses of other emerging Asian economies to happen quickly, their currencies will need to appreciate against the dollar.

All in all, there are reasons to doubt whether U.S. net exports can increase over the near term at a pace sufficient to fully compensate for the prospect of slower than normal growth of other components of U.S. domestic spending.

Supply Side Problems?

The supply side of the economy governs its capacity for producing goods and services. That capacity is a function of the economy's supplies of labor and capital and the level of technology used to turn labor and capital into the output of goods and services. In the short run, the potential supplies of these productive factors are relatively fixed and will determine the economy's potential output. In periods of economic slack, rising aggregate demand can increase the economy's output and employment up to the level of potential output, which corresponds with full employment.

In the long run, as the supplies of capital and labor and the level of technology increase, the level of potential output also increases. Over time the steady rise of potential output will define the economy's long-term growth path (called the "trend" growth rate). When aggregate demand is below potential output the economy can grow faster than trend growth, but when the level of aggregate demand reaches the level of potential output, further growth of output will be constrained to the trend growth rate.

Typically the long-run growth path is thought to be relatively stable and not greatly affected by recessions and the associated short-term fluctuations in aggregate demand. Over the post-war period, the average annual growth rate of potential output for the United States has been 3.4%; however, since the 1970s it has averaged closer to 3.0%.[42]

An analysis by the International Monetary Fund (IMF) examines the question of whether output will return to its pre-crisis trend.[43] It examines the medium-term and long-run paths of output after 88 banking crises over the past four decades in a wide range of countries (including both advanced and developing economies). A key conclusion was that seven years after the crisis, output had declined relative to trend by nearly 10% for the average country. But there was considerable variation of outcomes across crisis episodes.

In other words, such crises not only reduce actual output, but also may reduce potential output (the economy's structural and institutional capacity to produce output). In this circumstance, the economy could return to its trend growth rate, but there is unlikely to be a rebound period of above normal growth to quickly return the economy to its pre-crisis potential output and growth path and, in turn, quickly reduce unemployment. This failure to return to the pre-crisis potential output means that the economy bears the burden of a permanent output loss and the large initial increase in the unemployment rate caused by the crisis could persist even as the economy is growing at its trend rate.

The IMF analysis suggests that the reduction of the post-crisis growth path is likely to be the consequence of decreases of approximately equal size in the employment rate, the capital-labor ratio, and productivity. The adverse effect of the financial crisis on the employment rate is thought to arise from an increase in the "structural unemployment rate," hampering the post-crisis economy's ability to accomplish the needed reallocation of labor from sectors that have contracted permanently to sectors that are expanding.

Because the aftermath of the crisis will likely involve sizable changes in the composition of the economy, it likely also increases the mismatch between the skills of the unemployed and the skills demanded in the post-crisis labor market—job vacancies go unfilled for lack of a worker with sufficient skills for the job.[44] Also, labor force participation rates may fall if the crisis is severe enough to substantially increase the numbers of the long-term unemployed, some of whom may become discouraged from searching for a new job. A crisis-induced fall of house prices and a rising incidence of mortgages with negative equity will also discourage the geographic mobility of workers who are unable to sell their houses.

The adverse impact of a financial crisis on capital accumulation is likely the combined outcome of several factors. Decreased demand for products and heightened uncertainty of potential return dampens the incentive to invest. In addition, the financial crisis could impede the process of financial intermediation for up to several years, as weakened balance sheets, lower collateral values, and elevated risk premiums slow the flow of credit and elevate the real cost of borrowing.

The dampening effect on productivity may occur as higher risk premiums and a generally more cautious approach to spending by businesses diminish the willingness and ability to finance relatively high-risk projects. Expenditures on research and development are typically pro-cyclical and likely to be sharply reduced in times of crisis.

Productivity tends to recover quickly after recessions and thus allows the economy to resume growth at the pre-crisis trend rate. However, the capital and employment losses tend to endure and keep the economy on a lower growth path.

Has the recent financial crisis caused a reduction in the potential output of the U.S. economy and placed it on a lower trend growth path? It is difficult to make a concurrent determination because potential output is not directly observable, and can only be imputed from the economy's actual post-crisis performance. A clear determination of any such permanent output loss is some years in the future.

Although the IMF study gives reasons why the financial crisis possibly could have adversely affected the economy's supply side, the study also finds that there can be some significant mitigating factors that could be particularly relevant for the U.S. economy. First, a high pre-crisis investment share is a good predictor of a large potential output loss. This is a reflection of the high sensitivity of investment to the negative effects of a financial crisis. For the United States there was no sharp increase in investment spending above trend as measured as a share of GDP for the three years prior to the financial crisis, averaging near a typical 16% of GDP.[45]

Second, the IMF study also found that those economies that aggressively apply stimulative fiscal and monetary policies during the crisis tend to have smaller medium-term output losses. As already discussed, the United States has applied quickly and substantially stimulative polices in response to the financial crisis.

Third, countries with fewer labor market rigidities suffered smaller medium-term output losses. U.S. labor markets, as compared to other advanced economies, are relatively free of labor market rigidities, though as mentioned declining house prices may have reduced mobility of some workers who own their own homes.

The Congressional Budget Office (CBO) currently projects U.S. potential output to increase at an annual average rate of 2.2% for the 2011-2016 period, slightly below the 2.4% pace of the 2002- 2010 period. CBO's projected rate of growth of potential output is well below the post-war average of 3.3%. Slower growth of potential GDP is largely the consequence of a projection of significantly slower labor force growth than during the post-war period in the coming decades.

Most of the slow down in labor force growth is related to long-term demographic changes forced by an aging population, however, a protracted recession with growing numbers of long-term unemployed and discouraged workers has also contributed to this labor force dynamic.[46]

Policy Responses to Increase the Pace of Economic Recovery

The momentum of the current economic recovery has been assisted by injections of fiscal and monetary stimulus. But with substantial economic slack remaining and with unemployment still stubbornly high, would further stimulus by monetary and fiscal policy be warranted to sustain economic recovery?

Fiscal Policy Actions Taken During the Recovery

In 2010, many economists argued that another dose of fiscal stimulus was warranted because the effects of the first stimulus package were beginning to fade, and because of evidence that private spending lacked sufficient vigor to sustain a healthy recovery.[47] In this situation, the risk of not applying further fiscal stimulus could be several years of sub-normal growth, or worse, dipping into a second recession.

In response to concerns that the recovery was faltering, Congress passed and President Obama signed in December 2010 the Tax Relief, Unemployment Insurance Reauthorization, and Job Creation Act of 2010 (P.L. 111-312). The essential features of that measure were an extension for two years of the "Bush" tax cuts, a 2 percentage point cut in the payroll tax during 2011, a 13- month extension of unemployment benefits, and allowance for more rapid expensing of business investment in 2011. The CBO estimated that the direct stimulative effect of these revenue and spending changes as measured by the increase in the federal budget deficit would be approximately $374 billion in 2011 and $422 billion in 2012.[48]

A major counterforce to federal stimulus policies has been contraction of spending by state and local governments. Direct expenditures by state and local governments decreased 1.8% in 2010 3.4%% in 2011, and 1.6% during the first half of 2012, having the effect of subtracting from real GDP growth 0.2 percentage points in 2010, 0.3 percentage points in 2011, and 0.2 percentage points in first half of 2012.[49]

Evaluating the Case for Fiscal Stimulus

Fiscal stimulus is not without its critics. The case against more fiscal stimulus comes in three forms, used separately or in combination: one, no further stimulus is needed; two, fiscal stimulus does not work; and three, stimulus increases the budget deficit, makes the U.S. long-term debt problem worse, and dampens economic growth.[50]

In regard to the need for stimulus, the U.S. economy does have strong recuperative powers and it is possible that private spending and economic growth will soon surge without further fiscal stimulus. Events such as improved consumer confidence, lower energy prices, a more normal flow of credit, or faster growth in the rest of the world could separately or in combination induce stronger spending by households and businesses. However, given the severity of the recent recession and, as outlined above, given the current weakness of private spending and the several economic obstacles that households and businesses will probably continue to face over the near term, there remains a significant risk of sub-normal growth for the next several years.

In regard to the ability of fiscal stimulus to boost output and employment, some economists argue that fiscal stimulus only shifts spending, it does not increase spending. In this view, when people see the government running a budget deficit, they anticipate that the government will need to increase taxes in the future to pay off the debt. This anticipation causes households and businesses to increase their current savings to pay for the higher taxes. The increase in saving tends to offset the stimulative effect of the budget deficit.[51] There is little empirical support for this theory, however. Mainstream economic analysis indicates that in circumstances like the present, in which the economy's output is likely constrained by insufficient demand, fiscal stimulus can raise the level of output and employment.[52]

In regard to the long-term debt problem, it is often pointed out that for an economy operating close to potential output, government borrowing to finance budget deficits will draw down the pool of national saving, leaving less available to support private capital investment. Private investment by business and households in education, housing, research and development, and capital equipment that would have otherwise occurred is in theory "crowded out" through higher interest rates bid up by government borrowing. If budget deficits divert national saving from private investment, other things equal, future productivity and income growth may be slowed. However, the U.S. economy is currently operating well short of capacity and market interest rates are generally at or near historical lows, making the risk of such "crowding out" occurring and damaging future economic growth not seem immediate.[53] Another variant of this argument against fiscal stimulus maintains that by increasing public debt, fiscal stimulus undermines household and business confidence and causes them to postpone current spending. In this view, contrary to mainstream economic thinking, shrinking the deficit would, by improving confidence, actually stimulate current spending by consumers and business.[54]

The Short-Term and Long-Term Fiscal Problems

Because the United States faces two macroeconomic problems, two policy responses are, arguably, appropriate: a short-term policy to sustain a cyclical recovery of economic growth and a long-term policy to trim government debt. Conceptually there is no necessary tradeoff between these two objectives. They can be mutually reinforcing: a credible commitment to dealing with the long-term debt problem allays investor uncertainty and increases the near-term incentive to spend, while effectively dealing with the short-term problem of weak aggregate demand puts the economy on a stronger growth path, which boosts tax revenue and eases the long-term debt problem.

Once the short-term problem of weak demand is solved and the economy has returned to a normal growth path, the appropriate policy response for an economy with a looming debt crisis is arguably fiscal consolidation—cutting deficits. Such a policy is thought to have the benefits of low and stable interest rates, a less fragile financial system, improved investment prospects, and possibly faster long-term growth.

To address the government's long-term fiscal problem, Congress passed on August 2, 2011, the Budget Control Act of 2011 (P.L. 112-25). The Budget Control Act (BCA) sets caps on discretionary spending. It also created the Congressional Joint Select Committee on Deficit Reduction, whose task was to propose further policy changes that would lead to $1.5 trillion in further deficit reduction over 10 years.

The joint committee was unable to reach an agreement on how to achieve further deficit reduction. In the absence of an agreement, the BCA established a process for automatic spending reduction. The CBO estimates that the fiscal restraint caused by the expiration of provisions of the 2010 tax act and from enactment of the BCA will decrease real GDP in 2013 by between 1.5% and 3.5%.[55]

The Impending "Fiscal Cliff"

Fed Chairman Ben Bernanke, speaking at an April 2012 press conference, warned about the likely adverse effect on the economic recovery of the "fiscal cliff" the economy could face in January 2013.[56] The fiscal cliff refers to the confluence of various spending cuts and tax rate increases that are scheduled to occur at the beginning of the new year unless policies are changed. The scheduled fiscal events include the end of the extension of the Bush tax cuts, the need for adjustment of the alternative minimum tax (AMT), the end of the Social Security payroll tax cut, reductions in Medicare reimbursement payments, and spending cuts mandated by the "sequestration" process of the 2011 BCA.[57]

Incorporating these policy changes into its most recent projections for the economy, the CBO estimates that this degree of fiscal tightening will lead to real GDP contracting by 0.5% between the fourth quarter of 2012 and the fourth quarter of 2013 and the unemployment rate rising to about 9% in the second half of 2013. These economic conditions would likely be judged as a recession.[58]

Monetary Policy Actions Taken During the Recovery

On November 3, 2010, the Fed announced that it would provide more monetary stimulus by means of the purchase an additional $600 billion of Treasury securities at a pace of about $75 billion per month, and continue the practice of replacing maturing securities with Treasury security purchases. When this second round of monetary stimulus (sometimes referred to as "quantitative easing 2" or QE2)[59] was completed in June 2011, the Fed had increased the size of its balance sheet to more than $2.5 trillion.

The maturity lengths of the securities purchased were mostly between 21/2 and 10 years.[60]

The Fed argued at that time that a second dose of monetary stimulus was needed because economic growth is decelerating and much of what economic momentum existed was being provided by the transitory factors of inventory adjustment and fiscal stimulus. In the second half of 2010, growth slowed to around 2%, a pace barely fast enough to keep the unemployment rate from rising.

Fed Chairman Ben Bernanke indicated that of particular concern was the substantial increase in the share of the long-term unemployed (workers who have been without work for six months or more). Such long-term unemployment tends to convert temporary cyclical unemployment into more intractable structural unemployment.

In addition, the lingering economic slack in the economy had added to deflationary pressure.

Measures of core inflation had been decelerating during 2010, reaching a low of only slightly above 1%.

A continuous decline in the price level is troublesome because in a weak or contracting economy it can lead to a damaging, self-reinforcing, downward spiral of prices and economic activity. Deflation exacerbated the economy's decline during the Great Depression.[61]

To support a stronger recovery, the Fed announced on September 21, 2011, that it would purchase by the end of June 2012 $400 billion of Treasury securities with remaining maturities of 6 years to 30 years and to sell an equal amount of Treasury securities with remaining maturities of 3 years or less.[62] In June 2012, the Fed announced that it would extend this program through the end of 2012.

This program does not expand the size of the Fed's balance sheet. Rather, by changing the composition of its asset holdings toward longer maturities, the Fed is attempting to put downward pressure on longer-term interest rates and increase monetary policy's stimulative effect on economic activity.[63]

On September 13, 2012, the Fed announced a third round of quantitative easing, or QE3. Pointing to slow economic growth and an unemployment rate that has not improved since the beginning of the year, the Fed expressed concern that "without further policy accommodation, economic growth might not be strong enough to generate sustained improvement in labor market conditions."[64] QE3 will increase policy accommodation by purchasing additional agency mortgaged-backed securities at a pace of $40 billion per month, which together with its "maturity extension program" to increase the average maturity of its asset holdings as announced in June, will increase the Fed's holdings of long-term assets by about $85 billion per month through the end of 2012. Moreover, in a significant change from the earlier rounds of quantitative easing, the QE3 mortgage-backed security purchases are open-ended, meaning that the Fed is committing to continuing the program until labor market conditions improve. The Fed also gave further "forward guidance" by announcing that it intends to keep the federal funds interest rates at "exceptionally low levels" through mid-2015.

Evaluating the Case for Monetary Stimulus

The Fed's recent policy initiatives to provide a sucessive rounds of monetary stimulus have been criticized. One concern is an increased risk of inflation. Such a large increase in bank reserves could also lead to a rapid increase in the overall money supply through the "money multiplier" effect, which in normal times might generate inflation. At present, the sizable degree of slack in the economy and banks' heightened tendency to hold reserves rather than lend them out keeps the risk of inflation low.

As noted above, one of the reasons for initiating a second round of monetary stimulus in late 2010 was to counter an incipient deflation problem, which is accomplished by policies that exert upward pressure on the level of prices, that is, policies that generate some degree of inflation. The Fed's second round of monetary stimulus seems to have reduced the deflation risk.

Also, some of the recent increase in broad measures of inflation, such as the consumer price index (CPI), is due to the sharp rise in oil and other commodity prices in the first half of 2011 and again in early 2012. However, such inflation effects are most often temporary and not a source of persistent inflationary pressure. The "core CPI," a measure of inflation that does not include volatile food and energy prices, has remained low. Other indicators also suggest that inflation is likely to remain subdued. First, wages, which are generally the most important determinant of unit production costs, have been stable. Second, longer-term inflationary expectations, as measured by the yields on long-term securities, have not risen appreciably.

However, when the economy returns to more normal conditions, reserves would likely need to be removed to avoid excessive upward pressure on prices. The likely unprecedented scale of the reserves that might need to be drained from the economy has raised concerns about whether the Fed could effectively provide the degree of restraint needed to keep inflation under control.

A second criticism of the Fed's monetary stimulus during the recovery is that it is depreciating the dollar. Although influencing the exchange rate is not a stated goal of the Fed's policy, standard macroeconomic theory would predict, all else equal, that a by-product of monetary stimulus would be a depreciation of the dollar (assuming other countries do not similarly alter their monetary policy in response). A weaker dollar would add to the stimulative effect of monetary stimulus on total spending in the United States by increasing exports and decreasing imports. However, countries such as Germany, Japan, and China that have relied on net exports to propel their economic growth are resistant to a depreciating dollar and have criticized the Fed's actions.

As it turns out, the dollar depreciation that has occurred over the last year is, arguably, not the result of Fed actions, but a correction from the appreciation of the dollar in late 2008 and 2009 that was caused by a flight to safety by foreign investors during the financial crisis. At that time, a strong global demand for relatively safe U.S. Treasury securities bid up the dollar's exchange rate. As financial panic receded, the demand for safety abated, and the dollar depreciated to its pre-crisis level.

A third criticism is that monetary stimulus will have little impact on real economic activity. In the current economic environment, with badly weakened household and business balance sheets placing a premium on improving liquidity, it is difficult for monetary policy to get "traction," stimulating the broader economy by pumping reserves into the banking system. For this reason, the stimulus to the real economy from the Fed's successive rounds of quantitative easing have not been expected to be a "cure-all" for sustaining economic recovery. Moreover, how effective monetary stimulus has been is difficult to judge because there is no ready "counterfactual" state of the economy from which to judge its impact on output and employment. Nevertheless, estimates are possible. Using statistical economic models that incorporate past relations between financial conditions and the economy, it is possible to estimate the impact of monetary stimulus on the economy. For example, one recent study found that the first two rounds of quantitative easing may have increased output by 3% and increased employment by more than 2 million jobs.[65] Other studies have found comparable effects.[66]

A Lesson from the Great Depression

One of the important lessons from the Great Depression is to avoid a hasty withdrawal of fiscal and monetary stimulus in a fragile economy still recovering from a sharp economic decline. Beginning in 1933, the U.S. economy rebounded from its sharp fall into what has become known as the Great Depression. From 1933 to 1936, supported by expansionary fiscal and monetary policies, the U.S. economy grew briskly at an average rate of 9.0% and unemployment fell from 25% to 14%. Economic output had nearly returned to its level in 1929, but the economy was still well short of full recovery. But in 1937, the recovery halted and the economy tipped into a second recession. Most economists believe that the second dip into recession was caused by an unfortunate premature switch to contractionary monetary and fiscal policies in a still-fragile recovering economy.

On the monetary side, in 1936, the Federal Reserve began to worry about inflation. After several years of relatively loose monetary policy, the U.S. banking system had built up large quantities of reserves in excess of legal reserve requirements. The Fed feared, despite little overt evidence of a problem, that should the banks begin to lend these excess reserves, it could lead to an overexpansion of credit and generate an inflationary surge. In an attempt to sop up those excess reserves, the Fed raised the banks' reserve requirements three times during 1936. However, banks were still nervous about the financial panics of the early 1930s and uncertain about the durability of the economic recovery, and consequently wanted to hold excess reserves as a cushion. In response to the higher reserve requirements erasing that cushion, the banks worked to rebuild it by reducing lending, leading to a contraction of credit-supported spending.

On the fiscal side, by 1936, following several years of large budget deficits, the federal government had a strong urge to declare victory and get back to normal policy—specifically, balancing the government budget. The veterans' bonus that was paid in 1936 was not renewed in 1937; in addition, Social Security taxes were collected for the first time in 1937. The overall effect was a fiscal contraction equal to about 3% of GDP.

The double hit of contractionary monetary and fiscal policy in an economy that had still not reached the point in which private demand was capable of fully sustaining economic growth led to a recession. In 1938, GDP fell 4.5% and the unemployment rate increased to 19%.[67]

Economic policy quickly changed course and recovery resumed in the second half of 1938, but the policy error added about two years to the Great Depression, which ended with the step-up in war-time government spending in 1941.

The euro zone countries appear to be re-learning this policy lesson from the Great Depression, at considerable economic cost. Their attempt to impose austerity measures to combat growing government debt, while still in the mist of economic recovery, has pushed the region back into recession.

Economic Projections

Given the unusually large deterioration of the balance sheets of households and businesses, the possible reduction of the U.S. economy's level of potential output, the weakened state of the global economy, and uncertainty about fiscal policy, projections of the U.S. economy's near-term path carry a higher than normal degree of uncertainty. During 2012, most economic forecasters have steadily trimmed their growth projections as it became ever more evident that the economy seemed to be only "treading water," particularity in labor markets. Nevertheless, most forecasters expect the U.S. economic recovery to continue, albeit at a distressingly slow pace.

- In its September 2012 meeting, the Fed's Open Market Committee projected real GDP in 2012 to advance in a range between 1.7% to 2.0% (down from a range of 1.9% to 2.4% in its June meeting) and in 2013 advance in a range between 2.5% to 3.0% (changed from a range of 2.2% to 2.8% in its June meeting). The unemployment rate is projected to be in a range between 8.0% to 8.2% in 2012 (unchanged from its June meeting) and 7.6% to 7.9% in 2013 (compared with a range of 7.5% to 8.0% in the June meeting).[68]
- The IMF's October 2012 projection sees real GDP in the United States increasing 2.2% in 2012 and 2.1% in 2013. (The forecast for 2013 is down 0.1% percentage points from its July 2012 projection though the forecast for 2012 has been revised up by 0.1 percentage points.) Globally, the IMF expects an unbalanced recovery to persist into 2013, with growth of real output in the advanced economies to average 1.5% compared with growth in the emerging developing economies averaging 5.6%.[69]
- Global Insight, an economic forecasting company, is currently projecting real GDP will advance 2.1% in 2012 and decelerate to 1.8% in 2013. The company projects the unemployment rate will be 8.0% and 7.7% in 2012 and 2013, respectively.[70]

End Notes

[1] See CRS Report R40007, Financial Market Turmoil and U.S. Macroeconomic Performance, by Craig K. Elwell.

[2] Real GDP is the total output, adjusted for inflation, of goods and services produced in the United States in a given year.

[3] Data on real GDP are available from the Department of Commerce, Bureau of Economic Analysis, at http://www.bea.gov/national/index.htm#gdp. Size of output gap is based on CRS calculations using Congressional Budget Office estimate of potential GDP, data for which is available at FRED Economic Data, St. Louis Fed, at http://research.stlouisfed.org/ fred2/series/GDPPOT.

[4] Data on unemployment and employment are available from the Department of Labor, Bureau of Labor Statistics, at http://www.bls.gov/.

[5] Data on wealth and financial flows available at the Board of Governors of the Federal Reserve System, at http://www.federalreserve.gov/releases/z1/Current/z1r-5.pdf.

[6] See IMF, World Economic Outlook, October 2009, Chapter 2, at http://www.imf.org/external/ pubs/ft/weo/ 2009/02/ pdf/c2.pdf.

[7] Agency debt and securities are issued by "government sponsored enterprises" (GSEs), such as Fannie Mae and Freddie Mac.

[8] For further discussion of Fed actions in this period, see CRS Report RL34427, Financial Turmoil: Federal Reserve Policy Responses, by Marc Labonte.

[9] See CRS Report R40104, Economic Stimulus: Issues and Policies, by Jane G. Gravelle, Thomas L. Hungerford, and Marc Labonte.

[10] For more information on TARP, see CRS Report R41427, Troubled Asset Relief Program (TARP): Implementation and Status, by Baird Webel.

[11] U.S. Department of Commerce, Bureau of Economic Analysis, National Income and Product Accounts, at http://www.bea.gov/iTable/index_nipa.cfm.

[12] Board of Governors of the Federal Reserve System, Senior Loan Officers Survey on Bank Lending Practices, August 2012, at http://www.federalreserve.gov/boarddocs/ SnLoan Survey/.

[13] Spread of 600 basis points is 6%. Data on spreads found at http://www.bloomberg.com/apps/ quote?ticker= .TEDSP%3AIND.

[14] Board of Governors of the Federal Reserve System, Statistical Release G.17, September 2012, at http://www.federalreserve.gov/releases/g17/.

[15] Bureau of Labor Statistics, Labor Force Statistics from the Current Population Survey, September 2012, at http://www.bls.gov/cps/.

[16] U.S Census Bureau, New Residential Construction In August 2012, joint release, September 19, 2012, at http://www.census.gov/construction/nrc/pdf/newresconst.pdf and S&P Case–Shiller 20-City Home Price Index, available at http://www.standardandpoors.com/ indices/sp-case-shiller-home-price-indices/en/us/ ?indexId=spusacashpidff—p-us.

[17] CRS calculation from Bureau of Economic analysis data for real GDP and CBO estimate of potential GDP both available from Federal Reserve Economic Data (FRED), St. Louis Federal Reserve Bank, at http://research.stlouisfed.org/fred2/.

[18] For the calculation of the unemployment rate, a person without a job is not counted as unemployed or in the labor force unless he or she is actively looking for employment.

[19] Bureau of Labor Statistics, Labor Force Statistics from the Current Population Survey, September 2012, http://www.bls.gov/cps/.

[20] International Monetary Fund (IMF), World Economic Outlook, October 2012, at http://www.imf.org/ external/pubs/ft/ weo/2012/02/index.htm.

[21] Department of Commerce, Bureau of Economic Analysis, at http://www.bea.gov/ national/ index.htm#gdp.

[22] The long-term growth of aggregate supply is determined by the growth in the supplies of capital and labor and on the growth in production technology used to turn capital and labor into goods and services.

[23] The Congressional Budget Office, The Budget and Economic Outlook: Fiscal Years 2012 to 2020, January 2012, at http://www.cbo.gov/publication/42905.

[24] Board of Governors of the Federal Reserve System, "Flow of Funds Accounts," Table B.100, June 2012, at http://www.federalreserve.gov/releases/z1/Current/z1r-5.pdf.

[25] See Evan Tanner and Yassar Abdih, "Rebuilding U.S. Wealth," Finance & Development, IMF, December 2009 at http://www.imf.org/external/pubs/ft/fandd/2009/12/tanner.htm.

[26] Board of Governors of the Federal Reserve System, "Flow of Funds Accounts," Table B.100, June 2012, at http://www.federalreserve.gov/releases/z1/Current/z1r-5.pdf.

[27] The standard model of consumer spending used in economic analysis assumes that consumers seek to avoid large swings in their living standards over the course of their lifetimes. Thus as incomes rise and fall both in the short and long term, individuals are expected to vary their saving rate in order to minimize the effect on their consumption. If consumers seek to maintain a fairly stable level of consumption over their entire lives, then the level of consumption at any given point in their lives will depend on their current wealth and some expectation about their income over the rest of their lives. See Annamaria Lusardi, Jonathan Skinner, and Steven Venti, "Saving Puzzles and Saving Policies in the United States," National Bureau of Economic Research, Working Paper 8237, April 2001.

[28] See CRS Report R40647, The Fall and Rise of Household Saving, by Brian W. Cashell.

[29] U.S. Department of Commerce, Bureau of Economic Analysis, National Income and Product Accounts, Table 5.1, http://www.bea.gov/national/nipaweb/SelectTable.asp?Selected=N.

[30] U.S. Energy Information Administration, Petroleum; Weekly Spot Price, July 2012, at http://www.eia.gov/ dnav/pet/hist/LeafHandler.ashx?n=PET&s=RCLC1&f=D.

[31] Research indicates that a $10 increase in the per barrel price of oil sustained for two years is likely to reduce real GDP growth relative to base-line by 0.2 percentage points in the first year and 0.5 percentage points in the second year. See U.S. Energy Information Administration, Economic Effects of High Oil Prices, 2006, http://www.eia.gov/oiaf/aeo/ otheranalysis/aeo_2006analysispapers/efhop.html.

[32] Ibid., Table 1.1.5.

[33] Department of Commerce, Bureau of Economic Analysis, National Income and Product Accounts, Table 1.1.5, athttp://www.bea.gov/national/index.htm#gdp.

[34] Ibid., Table 1.1.5, at http://www.bea.gov/national/index.htm#gdp.

[35] U.S. Census Bureau, Housing Vacancies and Home Ownership, at http://www.census.gov/ hhes/www/ housing/hvs/ historic/.

[36] Data for capacity utilization are available at Board of Governors of the Federal Reserve System, Industrial Production and Capacity Utilization, Table G17, http://www. federalreserve.gov/releases/g17/.

[37] Bureau of Economic Analysis, National Income and Product Accounts, Table 1.1.5, at http:// www.bea.gov/national/ index.htm#gdp.

[38] Department of Commerce, Bureau of Economic Analysis, National Income and Product Accounts, Table 1.1.6, at http://www.bea.gv/iTable/iTable.cfm?ReqID=9&step=1.

[39] On global rebalancing, see for example, Olivier Blanchard, "Sustaining Global Recovery," International Monetary Fund, September 2009, "Rebalancing," The Economist, March 31, 2010, at http://www.imf.org/external/pubs/ft/fandd/ 2009/09/index.htm, and Board of Governors of the Federal Reserve System, Vice-chairman Donald L. Kohn, Speech "Global Imbalances," May 11, 2010, at http:// www. federalreserve.gov/newsevents/speech/ kohn20100511a.htm.

[40] OECD, Restoring Public Finances, Country Notes: Germany, 2010, at http://www.oecd.org/gov/ budgeting andpublicexpenditures/47840777.pdf.

[41] Of course, for these reforms to translate into a shift in China's trade balance, that nation must be willing to allow its' exchange rate to rise relative to the dollar, causing a decrease in the price of foreign goods relative to domestic goods, and exerting downward pressure on China's trade surplus. From July 2005 to February 2009, China abandoned its dollar peg, allowing the yuan to appreciate by 28% (on a real trade-weighted basis) However, faced with weakening export sales due to the global financial crisis China for the last 10 months has re-pegged the yuan to the dollar. China's export-led growth model, relying on a high saving rate (to keep internal demand low) and a low exchange rate pegged to the dollar (to keep external demand high), has been very successful and, despite the possible advantages of reforms to boost domestic demand, it is uncertain whether China would move substantially away from this model.

[42] CBO, Key Assumptions in Projecting Potential Output, August 2012, at http://www.cbo.gov/ publication/43541.

[43] P. Kannan, A. Scott, and M. Terrones, "From Recession to Recovery: How Soon and How Strong?," in World Economic Outlook, April 2009, pp. 103-138. International Monetary Fund. Also see Davide Furceri and Annabelle Mourougane, The Effect of Financial Crisis on Potential Output: New Empirical Evidence from OECD Countries, OECD Economics Department, Working Paper no. 699, May 2009.

[44] Employment in construction, financial services, and some types of manufacturing may remain depressed for some time, requiring some who lose their jobs in those sectors to seek employment in other sectors. See also CRS Report R41785, The Increase in Unemployment Since 2007: Is It Cyclical or Structural?, by Linda Levine, which suggests that most of current U.S. unemployment is cyclical.

[45] Department of Commerce, Bureau of Economic Analysis, National Income and Product Accounts, Table 1.1.6, at http://www.bea.gov/iTable/iTable.cfm?ReqID=9&step=1.

[46] The Congressional Budget Office, Budget and Economic Outlook: An Update, August 2012, Table 2-3, at http://www.cbo.gov/doc.cfm?index=12316.

[47] Lawrence H. Summers, "Reflections on Fiscal Policy and Economic Strategy," Speech at the Johns Hopkins School of Advanced International Studies, May 24, 2010, at http://www. whitehouse.gov/administration/eop/ nec/speeches/ fiscal-policy-economic-strategy. Other economists have also concluded that further stimulus is called for. See, for example, Brad DeLong "The Worst -of-Both-Worlds Fiscal Policy," June 18, 2010, http://delong. typepad.com/sdj/ 2010/06/worst-of-both-worlds-fiscal-policy.html; and "The Case for More Stimulus" Interview with William Gale of the Brookings Institution, June 2010, at http://www.theatlantic.com/ business/archive/2010/06/the-case-for-morestimulus/57776/.

[48] Congressional Budget Office, CBO Estimate of Changes in Revenue and Direct Spending for the Tax Relief, Unemployment Insurance Reauthorization, and Job Creation Act of 2010, at http://www.cbo.gov/ftpdocs/ 120xx/doc12020/sa4753.pdf.

[49] Department of Commerce, Bureau of Economic Analysis, National Income and Product Accounts, Tables 1.1.1 and 1.1.2, at http://www.bea.gov/iTable/iTable.cfm? ReqID= 9&step=1.

[50] See for example, Derek Thompson, "The Case Against More Stimulus," The Atlantic, June 2010, at http://www.theatlantic.com/business/archive/2010/06/the-case-against-more-stimulus/57774/, and "Here's Why Fiscal Stimulus Won't Work," The Atlantic, February 2010, at http://www.theatlantic.com/business /archive/2010/02/hereswhy-government-stimulus-does-not-work/36466/.

[51] This theory is called "Ricardian equivalence." It is named after the nineteenth-century economist David Ricardo who first made the argument. For further discussion see N. Gregory Mankiw, Principles of Economics (Ft.

Worth, Dryden Press, 1998), p. 556, and Robert J. Barro, "Are Government Bonds Net Wealth?" Journal of Political Economy, vol. 82, no. 6. (November-December, 1974), pp. 1095-1117.

[52] See CRS Report RL31235, The Economics of the Federal Budget Deficit, by Brian W. Cashell; Alan J. Auerbach and William G. Gale, "Activist Fiscal Policy to Stabilize Economic Activity," working paper, September 29, 2009, available at http://elsa.berkeley. edu/~auerbach/activistfiscal.pdf; and Robert E. Hall, "By How Much Does GDP Rise If the Government Buys More Output?" Brookings Papers on Economic Activity, fall 2009, pp. 183- 250. On the probable simulative impact of alternative fiscal measures see CBO, Policies for Increasing Economic Growth and Employment, March 2010, at http://www.cbo.gov/ftpdocs/ 112xx/doc11255/02-23-Employment_Testimony.pdf, and J. Bradford DeLong and Lawrence H. Summers, "Fiscal Policy in a Depressed Economy," The Brookings Institution, March 2012.

[53] For discussion of the long-term debt issue, see President Obama's National Commission on Fiscal Responsibility and Reform, at http://www.fiscalcommission.gov/.

[54] For further discussion of this issue, see CRS Report R41849, Can Contractionary Fiscal Policy Be Expansionary?, by Jane G. Gravelle and Thomas L. Hungerford.

[55] For more information on the BCA, see CRS Report R41965, The Budget Control Act of 2011, by Bill Heniff Jr., Elizabeth Rybicki, and Shannon M. Mahan; and the Congressional Budget Office, Budget and Economic Outlook: An Update, August 2011, p. 38, at http://www.cbo.gov/doc.cfm?index=12316.

[56] Board of Govenors of the Federal Reserve System, Press Conference, at http://www. federalreserve.gov/ mediacenter/ files/FOMCpresconf20120425.pdf.

[57] For more information, see CRS Report R42362, The Federal Budget: Issues for FY2013 and Beyond, by Mindy R. Levit, and CRS Report R42485, An Overview of Tax Provisions Expiring in 2012, by Margot L. Crandall-Hollick.

[58] CBO, The Budget and Economic Outlook: Fiscal Years 2012 to 2022, August 2012, at http://www.cbo.gov/ publication/43539. See also CRS Report R42700, The "Fiscal Cliff": Macroeconomic Consequences of Tax Increases and Spending Cuts, by Jane G. Gravelle.

[59] On the policy of quantitative easing, see CRS Report R41540, Quantitative Easing and the Growth in the Federal Reserve's Balance Sheet, by Marc Labonte; and CRS Report RL30354, Monetary Policy and the Federal Reserve: Current Policy and Conditions, by Marc Labonte.

[60] Board of Governors of the Federal Reserve System, Federal Open Market Committee, http://www. federalreserve.gov/monetarypolicy/fomccalendars.htm.

[61] For further discussion of deflation, see CRS Report R40512, Deflation: Economic Significance, Current Risk, and Policy Responses, by Craig K. Elwell.

[62] Board of Governors of the Federal Reserve System, press release, September 2011, at http://www.federalreserve. gov/newsevents/press/monetary/20110921a.htm.

[63] Board of Governors of the Federal Reserve System, press release, June 2012, at http://www.federalreserve.gov/ newsevents/press/monetary/20120620a.htm.

[64] Board of Governors of the Federal Reserve System, press release, September 13, 2012, at http://www.federalreserve.gov/newsevents/press/monetary/20120913a.htm.

[65] Hess Chung, Jean-Phillippe Laforte, David Reifschender, and John C. Williams, "Have We Underestimated the Likelihood and Severity of Zero Lower Bound Events," Journal of Money Credit and Banking, February 2012, pp. 47- 82.

[66] See for example, Jeffrey C. Fuher and Giovanni P. Olivei, "The Estimated Macroeconomic Effects of the Federal Reserve's Large-Scale Treasury Purchase Program," Public Policy Briefs, April 2011, Federal Reserve Bank of Boston; and Micheal Kiley "The Aggregate Demand Effects of Short-Term and Long-Term Interest Rates," Finance and Economics Discussion Series 2012-54, Board of Governors of the Federal Reserve System, Washington DC.

[67] For further discussion of the recession of 1937, see Christina D. Romer, "The Nation in Depression," Journal of Economic Perspectives 7 (spring 1993), pp. 19-39; Milton Friedman and Anna D. Schwartz, A Monetary History of the United States, 1867-1960 (Princeton, NJ: Princeton University Press, 1963); Francois R. Velde, "The Recession of 1937—A Cautionary Tale," Economic Perspectives, Federal Reserve Bank of Chicago, fourth quarter 2009, pp. 16-36.

[68] Board of Governors of the Federal Reserve System, Minutes of September 2012 FOMC Meeting, Projection Materials, at http://www.federalreserve.gov/ monetarypolicy/ fomccalendars.htm.

[69] International Monetary Fund, World Economic Outlook, October 2012, Table 1.1, at http://www.imf.org/ external/pubs/ft/weo/2012/02/index.htm.

[70] Global Insight, U.S. Economic Outlook, August 2012.

In: Recovery after Recession: Select Research and Analyses ISBN: 978-1-62417-777-4
Editors: Drew Symmes and Amanda Zulpo

Chapter 2

JOB GROWTH DURING THE RECOVERY*

Linda Levine

SUMMARY

Congress in recent years passed a number of bills intended in part to jump-start a recovery in the labor market from the recession that began in December 2007. Members are interested in the labor market's response to these measures to help them decide how well the legislation has worked and whether additional job-creation legislation may be warranted in light of the pace and composition of job growth since the recession's end in June 2009. Accordingly, employment data from the U.S. Bureau of Labor Statistics is analyzed in this report from December 2007 to September 2012 (the latest month for which data were available at the time of the report's preparation).

A "jobless recovery" prevailed across firms in the private nonfarm sector until March 2010. That is to say, the number of private-sector jobs generally continued to fall until nine months into the recovery. The recovery was jobless until October 2010, 16 months into the recovery, across all employers in the public and private sectors of the nonfarm economy. At that point, net job growth in the overall economy began not because public-sector employment started to rise but because it fell more slowly while private-sector employment continued to grow. Given the pace of job growth during the recovery, a few more years will likely elapse before the approximately 7.5 million jobs lost during the recession are recouped.

The two industries hardest hit by the recession—manufacturing and construction—have been recovering at very different rates. In 2011, manufacturing employment surpassed its level at the recession's end. In 2012, construction employment remains over 400,000 jobs below its level in June 2009. Some of the states with the most depressed housing markets as well as manufacturing-dependent states have been especially slow to recover (e.g., Arizona, California, Florida, Indiana, Michigan, Nevada, and Ohio).

During the recession, women lost relatively fewer jobs than men in part because the construction and manufacturing industries predominantly employ men. During the recovery, women have gained relatively fewer jobs than men in part because women are

---

* This is an edited, reformatted and augmented version of a Congressional Research Service publication, CRS Report for Congress R41434, from www.crs.gov, prepared for Members and Committees of Congress, dated October 16, 2012.

a substantial presence in the occupations (e.g., teachers) that account for much of the local and state government workforces.

The oldest and youngest workers have fared quite differently since December 2007. Workers aged 55 and older experienced job growth during the recession and recovery. The youngest age group (16- to 19-year olds) experienced the largest percentage declines in employment during the recession and recovery.

The employment of Hispanic workers returned fairly quickly to its level at the recession's start, despite the ethnic group's concentration in the hard-hit construction industry. Hispanic employment also is concentrated in the leisure and hospitality industry group, which had recouped all its job losses by early 2012.

The lower a worker's educational attainment, the worse they typically fared. As of September 2012, workers with less than 12 years of schooling or with a high school diploma at most did not regain all the jobs they lost since the recession's onset. In contrast, employment among workers with postsecondary education was higher in September 2012 than in December 2007.

INTRODUCTION

Congress passed several bills meant in part to promote and accelerate a recovery in the labor market from the Great (2007-2009) Recession. One of the bills, the American Recovery and Reinvestment Act of 2009 (ARRA; P.L. 111-5), required the Council of Economic Advisers and executive branch agencies to estimate the number of jobs dependent on some or all of the act's provisions. Although such estimates are available, the methodologies used to estimate the number of jobs created or maintained have been criticized.

In addition, ARRA was not the only job creation bill enacted into law in recent years.[1] Congress did not include a requirement to estimate job growth associated with the Hiring Incentives to Restore Employment (HIRE) Act of 2010 (P.L. 111-147), for example.

Members of Congress nonetheless remain interested in the labor market's response to these measures to help them decide how well the legislation has worked and whether additional job creation as well as retraining legislation may be warranted in light of the pace and composition of job growth during the ongoing recovery. This report provides a snapshot of the current situation in the labor market to better inform policymakers with regard to further assisting the unemployed, such as workers laid off from industries that may have permanently downsized employment (e.g., construction).

One way to assess the extent and nature of the recovery in the labor market is to compare employment data from the recession's end in June 2009 (i.e., the trough of the business cycle) with more recent data gathered in surveys that the government regularly conducts. Accordingly, to determine the extent of job growth thus far in the recovery, this report examines the number of jobs from the trough of the business cycle to September 2012 (the latest month for which data were available at the time of the report's preparation). To provide historical context, the timing and strength of job growth during the current recovery is compared with the prior 10 recoveries. Data for September 2012 are compared with December 2007, as well, to discern how close the number of jobs has come to its level at the recession's onset (i.e., the peak of the business cycle). Lastly, employment data by job and individual characteristics for December 2007, June 2009, and September 2012 are analyzed to ascertain how different sectors and demographic groups have fared during the recession and recovery.

SLOW JOB GROWTH OVERALL, LED BY THE PRIVATE SECTOR

The Business Cycle Dating Committee at the National Bureau of Economic Research announced that the 11th recession of the postwar period ended in June 2009, but job growth typically does not commence until a recovery has been underway for some time.[2] Initially, some had hoped that the deep 2007-2009 recession would not be followed by a "jobless recovery" such as occurred after the immediately preceding recessions in 1990-1991 and 2001, when employers kept shedding jobs for a very long time after their end. The hope was instead for a quick and strong rebound such as occurred after the severe recessions of 1973-1975 and 1981-1982. Neither these nor the other U.S. recessions of the postwar period were precipitated by a financial crisis, however. The evidence from other countries that experienced recessions associated with financial crises instead suggests a slow recovery for the United States, and as discussed below, this has been the reality.[3]

A jobless recovery prevailed until October 2010, 16 months into the recovery, across all employers in the nonfarm economy. At that point, net job growth began *not* because public-sector employment started to rise but because it fell more slowly while private-sector employment continued to grow. As shown in *Figure 1,* the number of jobs on all employers' payrolls fell between June 2009 and March 2010. After briefly rising, it resumed declining through September 2010. Job growth during the first half of 2010 was fueled in part by the Census Bureau's temporarily hiring workers to help conduct the decennial count of the U.S. population. Since then, declining employment has occurred at state and local governments due to budget difficulties. (Additional discussion of employment trends in government and other industries appears later in the report.)

Although aggregate employment began to rise after September 2010, the monthly increase in jobs has been too small to have had much of an effect on the U.S. unemployment rate. A commonly cited rule-of-thumb is that in order to keep pace with population growth a net increase of roughly 125,000 jobs per month is needed to keep the unemployment rate unchanged.[4] In 2011, about 150,000 net jobs per month were added on average, and in the first nine months of 2012, an average of about 130,000 private- and public-sector jobs were added each month.[5]

A jobless recovery prevailed across firms in the private-nonfarm sector until March 2010. As shown in *Figure 1*, sustained job growth did not begin until nine months from the latest recession's end in June 2009. Despite the number of jobs at private-sector firms in September 2012 being almost 3.1 million above its level at the recovery's start, the recent pace of job growth at these employers means a few more years will likely elapse before the almost 7.7 million private-sector jobs lost during the Great Recession are recouped.

Employment rebounded at firms in the private sector more quickly during all but two of the prior 10 recoveries of the postwar period. As noted above, private-sector employment began to steadily rise at nine months into the current recovery. In contrast, employment in the private sector did not start a sustained increase until 12 months into the recovery from the 1990-1991 recession, and until 21 months into the recovery from the 2001 recession.

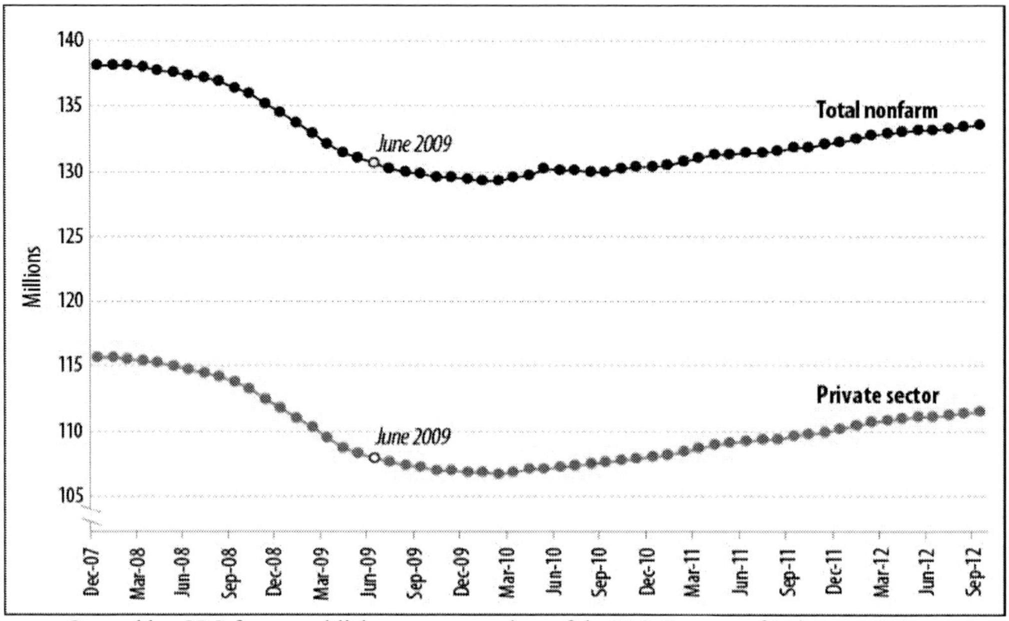

Source: Created by CRS from establishment survey data of the U.S. Bureau of Labor Statistics.

Figure 1. Employment Trends During the December 2007-June 2009 Recession and Subsequent Recovery.

Private-sector employment rebounded more strongly during all but one of the prior 10 recoveries. As shown in column 7 of *Table 1,* employment at private-sector firms in September 2012 was 3.3% above its level at the recovery's start. In contrast, at a point comparable to September 2012 (39 months from the 2001 recession's end), private-sector employment was up only 1.3% from its level at the outset of the recovery from the 2001 recession.

Although total nonfarm employment started to steadily rise earlier (12 months) into the recovery from the 1990-1991 recession compared with the current recovery (16 months), it began to trend upward much later (22 months) into the recovery from the 2001 recession. As shown in column 7 of *Table 1*, overall employment in September 2012 was 2.3% above its level at the recovery's start. In contrast, at 39 months after the 2001 recession's end, employment across all employers was only 1.4% higher than at the outset of the recovery. The *less* sluggish pace of job growth during the current recovery compared with the recovery from the 2001 recession may be partly related to differences in the stimulus legislation enacted to mitigate the two recessions.[6]

The last two columns of *Table 1* show how much employment must increase from its level in September 2012 to recoup all the jobs lost since the beginning of the Great Recession. In September 2012, total nonfarm employment was 4.5 million jobs below its level 57 months earlier at the recession's start and private-sector employment was 4.1 million jobs below its level in December 2007.

In contrast, total and private sector employment at 57 months from the start of all prior postwar recessions exceeded or more nearly approached their pre-recession levels. For example, compared with September 2012's 3.2% shortfall from total nonfarm employment in December 2007, overall employment at 57 months from the beginning of the 2001 recession was 1.7% above its level at the recession's outset. Compared with September 2012's 3.6% shortfall from private-sector employment in December 2007, private-sector employment at 57 months from the beginning of the 2001 recession was 1.2% higher than at the recession's outset.

Some had looked to the 2001 recession and subsequent jobless recovery, when the rate of increase in productivity growth also uncharacteristically rose, to gauge how long it might be before all jobs lost since December 2007 are recouped. The rate of increase in productivity growth usually does not rise during recessions, but it did so during and for some years after the 2001 recession; it did so again during and immediately after the 2007-2009 recession. (An increasing productivity growth rate enables businesses to produce the same amount of goods and services with fewer workers.) After the annual rate of change in nonfarm business productivity had diminished to a decade-low of 0.6% in 2006, it measured 2.3% in 2009 and 4.1% in 2010.[7] Partly due to similarly high rates of increase it took 47 months (until February 2005) from the 2001 recession's start before all job losses were recouped and 50 months (until May 2005) before private sector job losses were recouped. However, in November 2011—47 months from the latest recession's start—all jobs lost during the 2007-2009 recession had not been recouped. Similarly, by February 2012 (50 months from the latest recession's start), the private sector had not fully recouped all the jobs lost during the latest recession. In light of the sharp drop in the rate of productivity growth in 2011 to 0.4%, the slowness of the employment rebound would be surprising but for the 2007- 2009 recession's association with a financial crisis. The experiences of other countries suggest it takes longer for economies to fully recover from such recessions compared with recessions unrelated to financial crises.

Some within the public-policy community also believe that an increase in offshoring of jobs historically performed in the United States may be an additional factor sapping the strength of job growth. This perspective arguably contributed to Congress's support for a Buy America provision in the ARRA to increase demand for goods manufactured in the United States. Although not expressly intended to dampen offshoring, a tax provision in the HIRE Act encourages firms to maintain and expand their U.S. employment as well. However, the widespread nature of worker displacement during the recession and the fact that the jobs of workers in the especially hard hit construction industry do not possess characteristics making them vulnerable to offshoring suggests that offshoring has had a smaller effect than macroeconomic conditions on the pace of recovery.[8]

INDUSTRY CHARACTERISTICS OF JOB LOSS AND GAIN

Saying that offshoring may have slowed the pace of U.S. job growth is different from saying that certain industries will not return to their shares of employment at the recession's outset. Some suggest that the Great Recession, like the 2001 recession, was accompanied by a substantial reallocation of labor across sectors as certain industries permanently downsized employment due to globalization and technological among other innovations. As a result, some of the workers displaced during the 2007-2009 recession may endure unusually long spells of unemployment while they search for new jobs in faster-growing industries. Most economists agree, however, that the majority of displacement during the latest recession is cyclical rather than structural in origin.[9]

Manufacturing and Construction

As shown in *Table 1*, the two cyclically sensitive industries that accounted for nearly one of every two jobs lost during the latest recession have had markedly different experiences during the recovery.

Construction firms cut payrolls by almost 1.5 million jobs, and manufacturers by 2.0 million jobs, out of a total of 7.5 million nonfarm jobs lost between December 2007 and June 2009. (See column 4.)

Manufacturing has been recovering much faster than construction. Manufacturers added 217,000 jobs (a 1.9% increase) during the recovery to date, whereas construction lost 484,000 jobs (an 8.1% decrease). (See columns 6 and 7.)

The bursting of the housing bubble led those who worked for residential builders and for specialty trade contractors in residential construction to be the hardest-hit groups within the construction industry.

Employment in residential building construction fell by 263,000 jobs (29.4%) during the recession and by an additional 64,000 jobs (10.1%) during the recovery thus far, according to BLS establishment survey data. Similarly, employment at specialty trade contractors in residential construction fell by 565,000 jobs (26.1%) during the recession and by an additional 131,000 jobs (8.2%) during the recovery.

Some of the states with the weakest housing markets have experienced comparatively large cutbacks in employment of the industry's mostly blue-collar work force. Employment declines in the construction industry (i.e., residential and nonresidential building construction, heavy and civil engineering construction, and specialty trades contractors) in Nevada, Arizona, Florida, and California have been especially steep according to BLS establishment survey data.

Within manufacturing, the problems at General Motors, Chrysler, and motor vehicle parts suppliers were so grave during the recession that the Bush and Obama Administrations chose to provide them with financial assistance.[10] The industry's employment has subsequently increased.

After employment at motor vehicle and parts manufacturers fell by 335,000 jobs (34.9%) between December 2007 and June 2009, it then rose by 153,000 jobs (24.5%) through September 2012 according to BLS establishment survey data. Temporary programs enacted by Congress to increase demand for vehicles (e.g., "cash for clunkers," P.L. 111-32, enacted in June 2009) likely led automakers and their parts suppliers to subsequently recall from layoff their predominantly blue-collar workforce to rebuild depleted inventories.[11] Nonetheless, motor vehicle and parts manufacturers employed 182,000 fewer workers in September 2012 than at the recession's start.[12]

Nonetheless, manufacturing would need to gain 1.8 million jobs to return to its employment level at the recession's outset. Construction, for its part, would need to gain 1.9 million jobs. (See column 8.)

Table 1. Employment Change During the 2007-2009 Recession and the Ensuing Recovery, by Industry (numbers in thousands)

						Employment Change			
	Number of Jobs			During the Recession, Dec. 2007-June 2009		During the Recovery, June 2009-Sept. 2012		Since the Recession's Start, Dec. 2007-Sept. 2012	
	(1)	(2)	(3)	(4)	(5)	(6)	(7)	(8)	(9)
Industry	Dec. 2007	June 2009	Sept. 2012[a]	Number	Percentage	Number	Percentage	Number	Percentage
All nonfarm industries	137,982	130,503	133,500	-7,479	-5.4	2,997	2.3	-4,482	-3.2
All private nonfarm industries	115,606	107,933	111,499	-7,673	-6.6	3,566	3.3	-4,107	-3.6
Goods-producing sector	21,937	18,417	18,304	-3,520	-16.0	-113	-0.6	-3,633	-16.6
Mining and logging	740	685	839	-55	-7.4	154	22.5	99	13.4
Construction	7,490	6,007	5,523	-1,483	-19.8	-484	-8.1	-1,967	-26.3
Manufacturing	13,743	11,725	11,942	-2,018	-14.7	217	1.9	-1,801	-13.1
Private service-providing sector	93,633	89,516	93,195	-4,117	-4.4	3,679	4.1	-438	-0.5
Wholesale trade	6,038	5,577	5,644	-461	-7.6	67	1.2	-394	-6.5
Retail trade	15,571	14,527	14,768	-1,060	-6.7	241	1.7	-803	-5.2
Transportation and warehousing	4,548	4,228	4,408	-320	-7.0	180	4.3	-140	-3.1
Utilities	557	560	565	3	0.5	5	0.9	8	1.4
Information	3,024	2,794	2,632	-230	-7.6	-162	-5.8	-392	-13.0
Financial activities	8,224	7,749	7,758	-475	-5.8	9	0.1	-466	-5.7
Professional and business services	18,051	16,445	17,956	-1,606	-9.0	1,511	9.2	-95	-0.5
Education and health services	18,554	19,179	20,408	625	3.4	1,229	6.4	1,854	10.0
Leisure and hospitality	13,550	13,084	13,670	-466	-3.4	586	4.5	120	0.9
Other services	5,516	5,373	5,358	-143	-2.6	-15	-0.3	-158	-2.9
Government	22,376	22,570	22,001	194	0.9	-569	-2.5	-375	-1.7

Source: Calculated by CRS from U.S. Bureau of Labor Statistics' establishment survey data.

Notes: The establishment survey is asked of a sample of nonfarm employers and covers wage and salary workers on their payrolls.

[a] Data for September 2012 are preliminary. Initial monthly estimates are revised twice in the immediately succeeding months to incorporate additional information that was not available at the time of their original publication.

Table 2. Employment Change During the 2007-2009 Recession and the Ensuing Recovery, by Gender, Age, Race, Ethnicity, and Educational Attainment (numbers in thousands)

				Employment Change					
	Number of Employed Persons			During the Recession, Dec. 2007-June 2009		During the Recovery, 2009-Sept. 2012		Since the Recession's Start, Dec. 2007-Sept. 2012	
	(1)	(2)	(3)	(4)	(5)	(6)	(7)	(8)	(9)
Characteristic	Dec. 2007	June 2009	Sept. 2012	#	%	#	%	#	%
Gender									
Men	78,307	73,692	75,752	-4,615	-5.9	2,060	2.8	-2,555	-3.3
Women	67,967	66,312	67,222	-1,653	-2.4	910	1.4	-743	-1.1
Age									
16-19	5,853	4,952	4,425	-901	-15.4	-527	-10.6	-1,431	-24.4
20-24	13,747	12,753	13,482	-988	-7.2	729	5.7	-259	-1.9
25-34	31,616	30,017	30,768	-1,602	-5.1	751	2.5	-851	-2.7
35-44	34,085	31,693	30,663	-2,383	-7.0	-1,030	-3.2	-3,413	-10.0
45-54	34,760	33,554	32,947	-1,216	-3.5	-607	-1.8	-1,823	-5.2
55 and older	26,243	27,105	30,639	865	3.3	3,534	13.0	4,399	16.8
Race or ethnicity									
White	120,003	115,109	114,992	-4,872	-4.1	-117	-0.1	-4,989	-4.2
Black	15,999	15,053	15,881	-940	-5.9	828	5.5	-112	-0.7
Hispanic	20,473	19,631	22,050	-839	-4.1	2,419	12.3	1,580	7.7
Educational attainment									
Less than high school	11,319	10,403	9,932	-926	-8.1	-471	-4.5	-1,397	-12.3
High school or equivalent	36,820	34,697	33,455	-2,179	-5.9	-1,242	-3.6	-3,421	-9.3
Some college/AA	34,992	33,848	35,191	-1,121	-3.2	1,343	4.0	222	0.6
Bachelor's or advanced degree	43,597	43,344	46,503	-231	-0.5	3,159	7.3	2,928	6.7

Source: Created by CRS from U.S. Bureau of Labor Statistics' data from the Current Population Survey.

Notes: The survey of households provides data for all workers (including the self-employed, private household workers, and unpaid family workers) in all sectors of the economy (i.e., farm and nonfarm) aged 16 and older, except for educational attainment data which relate to workers aged 25 and older.

Manufacturing-dependent states tend to be especially vulnerable to recessions, a time during which consumers and businesses usually postpone buying costly long-lasting products in particular (e.g., household appliances, cars, farm and construction machinery). Manufacturing industries also are sensitive to weakened global demand and impaired access to credit. More than 1 in 10 employees in Indiana, Michigan, Mississippi, Ohio, and Wisconsin worked for durable goods manufacturers in 2006, the last full year before the onset of the recession.[13] Three of the five states—Michigan, Indiana, and Ohio—recorded among the largest percentage decreases in nonfarm employment during the recession.[14]

Private-Service Sector Industries

A third industry group that incurred many of the recession's job losses is professional and business services. (See *Table 1.)* More than one-fifth of all jobs lost during the recession were at firms that provide professional and business services (e.g., accounting, computer, other professional-technical services, and administrative support services). Temporary help agencies accounted for one-half of the 1.6 million decrease in employment at professional and business services providers between December 2007 and June 2009.[15] Employment rebounded by 1.4 million jobs at professional and business services providers thus far into the recovery. This was due in large part to a 780,000 job gain at temporary help agencies. When companies are unsure of a recovery's robustness they typically prefer to temporarily hire employees from the help industry rather than commit themselves to hiring permanent employees.

Retail trade is another industry group in which many of the recession's job losses occurred. The decrease in employment at such firms as automobile dealers, clothing and accessories stores, department stores, furniture and home furnishings stores, and building material and garden supply stores accounted for 14% of all jobs lost between December 2007 and June 2009. Retail employment fell precipitously during the recession (by 1.0 million or 6.7%), as shown in columns 4 and 5 in *Table 1.* Since the start of the recovery, retailers have added 241,000 jobs (a 1.7% increase), as shown in columns 6 and 7. Retail employment would have to expand by about 800,000 jobs (5.2%) to return to its cyclical peak. (See the last two columns in the table.)

Although the recession was precipitated by a financial crisis and housing market collapse, the industries that compose the financial activities industry group have been recovering at different rates.

- Almost one of every five job losses in financial activities during the recession occurred among real estate agents and other employees of the real estate industry.[16] Between December 2007 and June 2009, employment declined by 81,000 (5.4%). Housing conditions continued to be a drag on the economy during the recovery, and real estate employment fell further through early 2011. By September 2012, it had eked out a small gain (13,000 jobs or 0.9%) compared with the industry's employment at the recovery's start. Nonetheless, real estate employment at 39 months into the recovery was 68,000 (4.6%) below its level in December 2007.

- Almost one of every six job losses in financial activities during the recession occurred in the depository credit intermediation industry (e.g., commercial banks and savings institutions). Between December 2007 and June 2009, employment declined by 73,000 (4.0%). The industry cut additional jobs during the recovery, but in September 2012, bank employment was only 1,000 jobs (0.06%) below its level in June 2009. Nonetheless, employment in the deposit credit intermediation industry at 39 months into the recovery was 74,000 (4.1%) below its level at the recession's outset.
- Almost one of every 10 job losses in financial activities during the recession occurred at securities brokers, securities and commodity contracts brokers, and exchanges and other investment firms. Between December 2007 and June 2009, employment declined by 51,000 (6.0%). In September 2012, employment at securities brokers et al was only 5,000 jobs (0.06%) below its level in June 2009. Nonetheless, employment in this segment of financial activities at 39 months into the recovery was 56,000 (6.5%) below its level at the recession's outset.

Government

Government is the only industry group that gained jobs during the recession but has lost jobs during the recovery thus far. The increase in government employment during the recession occurred at the federal, state, and local levels.

The pattern of federal employment during the recovery has in part been affected by the Census Bureau hiring workers chiefly in the first half of 2010 to assist the agency while conducting the decennial population count. This source of job growth was eliminated once the temporary workers were let go.[17] Federal employment has trended downward thereafter, falling to somewhat over 2.8 million. The Budget Control Act of 2011 (P.L. 112-25) is estimated to lead to further declines in federal employment if sequestration comes to pass as scheduled in early January 2013.[18]

The decrease in public-sector employment since the recovery began has occurred mainly in state and especially in local government. State government employment at 39 months into the recovery was 105,000 (2.0%) below its level in June 2009. Local government joss loss was even greater since June 2009, at 463,000 (3.2%). Congress was motivated by the budget problems of state and local governments to include assistance for them in the American Recovery and Reinvestment Act (P.L. 111-5) enacted in February 2009, and in the Education Jobs and Medicaid Funding bill (P.L. 111-226) enacted in August 2010. President Obama's American Jobs Act (H.R. 12 and S. 1549) includes additional assistance, as does the Teachers and First Responders Back to Work Act (S. 1723) and the Fix America's Schools Today Act (H.R. 2948/S. 1597).

Individual Characteristics of Job Loss and Gain

This section analyzes the changes in employment by individual characteristics shown in *Table 2*. The employment trends of women and men over the course of a business cycle differ in part due to their employment distributions by industry. During the Great Recession, women lost jobs to a lesser degree than men (2.4% and 5.9%, respectively, as shown in column 5) in part because men account for the majority (over 7 out of 10 employees) in the recession-wracked construction and manufacturing industries.[19] But, women gained relatively fewer jobs than men during the recovery (1.4% and 2.8%, respectively, as shown in column 7). In this instance, the greater presence of women in the occupations that populate local governments in particular (e.g., teachers) likely worked against them.[20] As noted earlier, employment in local government greatly decreased during the recovery.

The oldest and youngest workers have had very different employment experiences in the past several years. As shown in columns 4 through 7 of *Table 2*, employment of persons aged 55 and older increased during the recession and the recovery. The seniority that usually comes with age appears to have worked to their advantage. In contrast, the employer practice of "last hired, first fired" likely operated to the disadvantage of the youngest workers. Employment decreased more precipitously among 16- to 19-year-olds than any other age group. Almost one in four teenagers employed at the start of the recession did not have jobs in September 2012, as shown in the last column of the table.

A larger share of black compared with white workers lost jobs during the recession, but their situation has reversed during the recovery. As shown in column 5 of *Table 2*, employment of black workers fell by 5.9% whereas employment of white workers fell by 4.1% between December 2007 and June 2009. Since then, the employment of black workers has rebounded more strongly than that of white workers. (See columns 6 and 7.)

Hispanics, who can be of any race, have experienced comparatively strong job growth during the recovery (12.3%) after their employment fell by 4.1% during the recession. (See columns 7 and 5, respectively, in *Table 2.)* In September 2012, the employment of Hispanics substantially exceeded its level at the recession's start, as shown in the table's last column. Some might regard this as surprising because, according to BLS data from the Current Population Survey, one in four workers in the construction industry were of Hispanic origin in 2006 (the last full year before the recession's onset). However, Hispanics also comprised over one in five workers in the accommodation and food services industry in that year. The industry is part of the leisure and hospitality group which, as of March 2012, had recouped all of the jobs it lost during the recession.

The lower a worker's educational attainment, the worse they typically fared between December 2007 and September 2012. As shown in the last column of Table 2, employment over the 57- month period decreased by 12.3% among workers without a high school diploma and by 8.1% among those with a high school diploma. In contrast, employment increased by 0.6% among workers with some college or an associate's degree and by 6.7% among workers with a bachelor's or advanced diploma. (See columns 6 through 9.)

End Notes

[1] For information of the legislation, see CRS Report R41578, Unemployment: Issues in the 112th Congress, by Jane G. Gravelle, Thomas L. Hungerford, and Linda Levine.

[2] CRS Report R40798, Unemployment and Employment Trends Before and After the End of Recessions, by Linda Levine.

[3] For additional information, see CRS Report R41332, Economic Recovery: Sustaining U.S. Economic Growth in a Post-Crisis Economy, by Craig K. Elwell.

[4] The unemployment rate is affected by the number of unemployed workers (the numerator) and the number of persons in the labor force (the denominator). The number of persons in the labor force is, in turn, partly related to the size of the working-age population.

[5] U.S. Bureau of Labor Statistics (BLS) derives the number of employed and unemployed persons and calculates the unemployment rate from the Current Population Survey (also known as the household survey), which is conducted monthly by the Census Bureau. The Census Bureau asks a member of the approximately 66,000 households surveyed about the labor force status of each household member aged 16 and older in the civilian noninstitutional population. BLS derives payroll employment (i.e., the number of wage and salary workers) from the Current Employment Statistics survey (also known as the establishment survey), which queries 141,000 nonfarm businesses and government agencies. The Employment Situation that BLS releases each month presents data from both surveys. The survey of employers is widely regarded as providing a better indicator of employment than the household survey. Only in the final section of this report are employment data from the household survey used because it, unlike the establishment survey, provides statistics on various demographic characteristics of workers.

[6] The Economic Growth and Tax Relief Reconciliation Act of 2001 (P.L. 107-16) and the Job Growth and Tax Relief Reconciliation Act of 2003 (P.L. 108-27) were passed to speed the recovery from the 2001 recession by amending the Internal Revenue Code. For information on the stimulus approaches included in legislation to mitigate the effects of the 2007-2009 recession (e.g., income tax relief, infrastructure spending, assistance to state and local governments), see CRS Report R41578, Unemployment: Issues in the 112th Congress, by Jane G. Gravelle, Thomas L. Hungerford, and Linda Levine.

[7] U.S. Bureau of Labor Statistics, Productivity and Costs series.

[8] For additional information, see CRS Report RL32292, Offshoring (or Offshore Outsourcing) and Job Loss Among U.S. Workers, by Linda Levine.

[9] For more information, see CRS Report R41785, The Increase in Unemployment Since 2007: Is It Cyclical or Structural?, by Linda Levine.

[10] For more information, see CRS Report R40003, U.S. Motor Vehicle Industry: Federal Financial Assistance and Restructuring, coordinated by Bill Canis.

[11] For more information, see CRS Report R40654, Accelerated Vehicle Retirement for Fuel Economy: "Cash for Clunkers," by Brent D. Yacobucci and Bill Canis.

[12] Calculated by CRS from BLS establishment survey data.

[13] Calculated by CRS from BLS establishment survey data.

[14] The four states previously mentioned as having experienced very large decreases in construction jobs because of conditions in their housing markets recorded large percentage decreases in total nonfarm employment as well.

[15] Calculated by CRS from BLS establishment survey data.

[16] Calculated by CRS from BLS establishment survey data.

[17] In the Employment Situation—August 2010, BLS noted that the number of temporary workers hired for Census 2010 peaked in May 2010 at 564,000. By August, that number had fallen to 82,000.

[18] See, for example, CRS Report R42763, Sequestration: A Review of Estimates of Potential Job Losses, by Linda Levine.

[19] According to data from the BLS establishment survey, women comprised just 28.7% of employment across all manufacturing industries and just 20.4% of employment in the residential building construction industry in 2006, the last full year before the latest recession began.

[20] According to data from the BLS establishment survey, women comprised 59.3% of employment in local government overall and 68.3% of employment in local government's education function in 2006, the last full year before the latest recession began.

In: Recovery after Recession: Select Research and Analyses ISBN: 978-1-62417-777-4
Editors: Drew Symmes and Amanda Zulpo

Chapter 3

WHAT ACCOUNTS FOR THE SLOW GROWTH OF THE ECONOMY AFTER THE RECESSION?*

Congressional Budget Office

Inflation-Adjusted Gross Domestic Product After Recessions

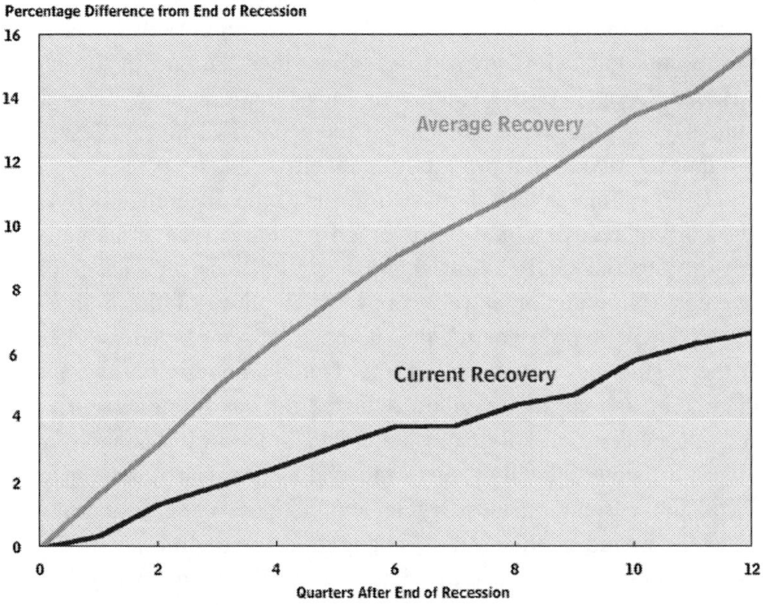

NOTE

Some figures use white vertical bars to indicate periods of recession. (A recession extends from the peak of a business cycle to its trough.)

* Mark Lasky and Charles Whalen prepared this study which was released by the Congressional Budget Office on November 2012.

SUMMARY AND INTRODUCTION

The U.S. economy has grown slowly since the deep recession in 2008 and 2009, which was triggered by a sharp drop in house prices and a subsequent financial crisis. During the three years following the recession (that is, the third quarter of 2009 through the second quarter of 2012), the economy's output grew at less than half the rate exhibited, on average, during other recoveries in the United States since the end of World War II.[1] All told, between the end of the recession and the second quarter of 2012, the cumulative rate of growth of real (inflation-adjusted) gross domestic product (GDP) was nearly 9 percentage points below the average for previous recoveries. Researchers continue to grapple with understanding the roles that steep declines in house prices and financial crises play in slowing the growth of output.[2]

In the current recovery, both potential GDP, a measure of the underlying productive capacity of the economy, and the ratio of real GDP to potential GDP have grown unusually slowly. Because potential GDP is an estimate of the amount of real GDP that corresponds to a high rate of use of labor and capital resources, it is not typically affected very much by the up-and-down cycles of the economy; in contrast, because the ratio of real GDP to potential GDP depends on the degree of the economy's use of resources, it captures cyclical variations in real GDP around its potential level. In the first 12 quarters after the last recession, both potential GDP and the ratio of real GDP to potential GDP grew at less than half the rate that occurred, on average, in the aftermath of other recessions since World War II (see Figure 1). Disaggregating the unusually slow growth in output since the end of the last recession, the Congressional Budget Office's (CBO's) analysis shows that that pace is mostly owing to slow growth in the underlying productive capacity of the economy and to a lesser extent, to slow growth in real output relative to that productive capacity.

Specifically, CBO estimates that about two-thirds of the difference between the growth in real GDP in the current recovery and the average for other recoveries can be attributed to sluggish growth in potential GDP.[3] That sluggish growth reflects weaker performance than occurred on average following other recessions by all three of the major determinants of potential GDP: potential employment (the number of employed workers, adjusted for variations over the business cycle); potential total factor productivity (average real output per unit of combined labor and capital services, adjusted for variations over the business cycle); and the productive services available from the capital stock in the economy. Although some of the sluggishness of potential GDP since the end of the last recession can be traced to unusual factors in the current business cycle, much of it is the result of longterm trends unrelated to the cycle, including the nation's changing demographics.

The remaining one-third of the unusual slowness in the growth of real GDP can be explained by the slow pace of growth in the ratio of real GDP to potential GDP— which in CBO's assessment, is attributable to a shortfall in the overall demand for goods and services in the economy. To identify the causes of that shortfall in demand, CBO analyzed the contribution of each main component of demand. Compared with past recoveries, this recovery has seen especially slow growth in four of those components:

- Purchases of goods and services by state and local governments,
- Purchases of goods and services by the federal government,

- Residential investment (consisting primarily of the construction of new homes, home improvements, and brokers' commissions), and
- Consumer spending.

Among those four components, purchases by state and local governments account for the largest portion of the unusual weakness. In contrast, two other components of demand—namely, investment by businesses and net exports—grew faster relative to potential GDP in the first 12 quarters of the current recovery than was the case, on average, in past recoveries.

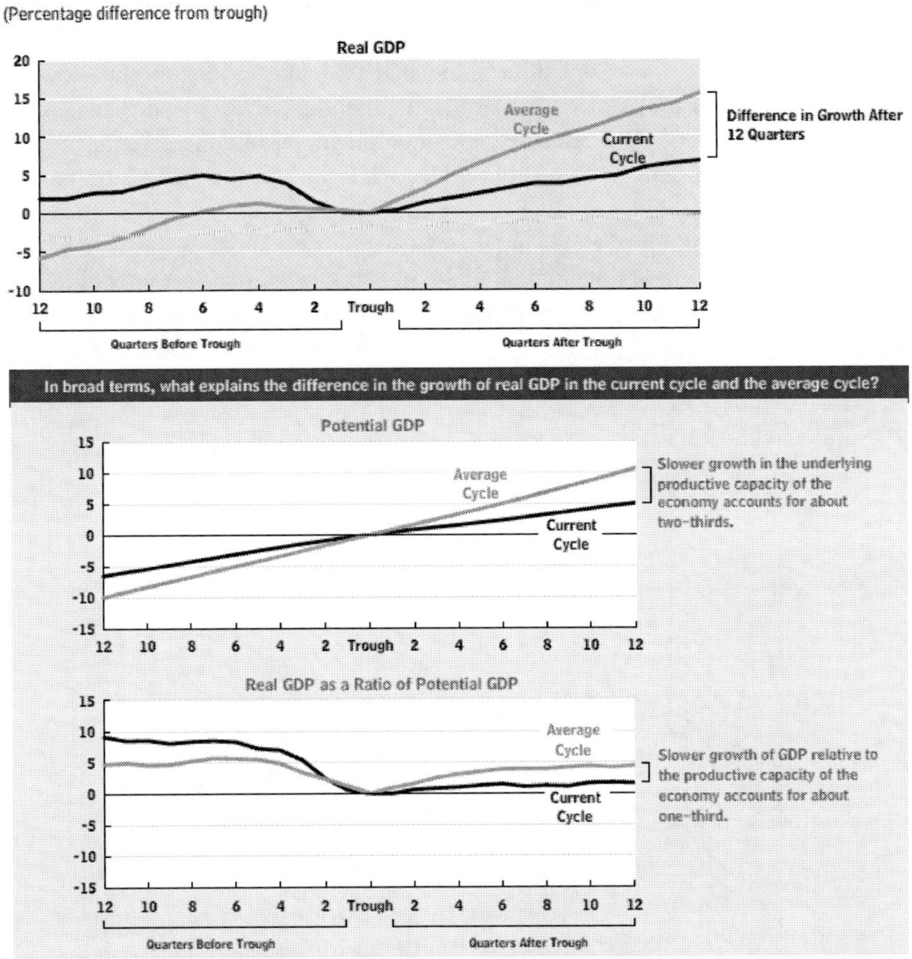

Sources: Congressional Budget Office; Department of Commerce, Bureau of Economic Analysis.

Notes: Real gross domestic product (GDP) is the total amount of goods and services produced in the United States, adjusted to remove the effects of inflation. Potential GDP is CBO's estimate of the level of GDP that corresponds to a high rate of use of labor and capital, adjusted to remove the effects of inflation.

The average cycle, or the pattern of economic growth before and after a trough, is the average for cycles since 1945 that were not followed by another recession within 12 quarters.

Figure 1. Gross Domestic Product Before and After Recessions.

A key underlying reason why the overall demand for goods and services by governments, businesses, and households has increased more slowly than usual in this recovery—and thus why real GDP has increased more slowly relative to potential GDP—has been the limitations faced by the Federal Reserve in providing support to the economy. Most important, because the interest rate that the Federal Reserve generally uses to conduct monetary policy (the federal funds rate) was already low at the start of the recovery, the central bank could not lower it much further even as the gap between real GDP and potential GDP failed to close quickly.

Moreover, the economy has been less responsive than usual to low interest rates because of the oversupply of homes, the desire of households to reduce their indebtedness, and credit restraints imposed by lenders, among other reasons.

Much of the distress and dislocation associated with the recession and slow recovery stems from the shortfall of real GDP relative to potential GDP. In particular, during the recession and the early part of the recovery, the unemployment rate increased by 5 percentage points as real GDP fell relative to potential GDP, while during the rest of the recovery, the unemployment rate has declined somewhat as real GDP has stabilized (and slightly edged up) relative to potential GDP. In CBO's judgment, the portion of slow growth in real GDP stemming from slow growth in potential GDP did not substantially affect unemployment.[4]

Therefore, the bulk of CBO's examination in this report focuses on the cyclical factors that help account for the sluggishness of the growth in real GDP relative to potential GDP, such as weak revenues for state and local governments and overbuilding during the housing boom.

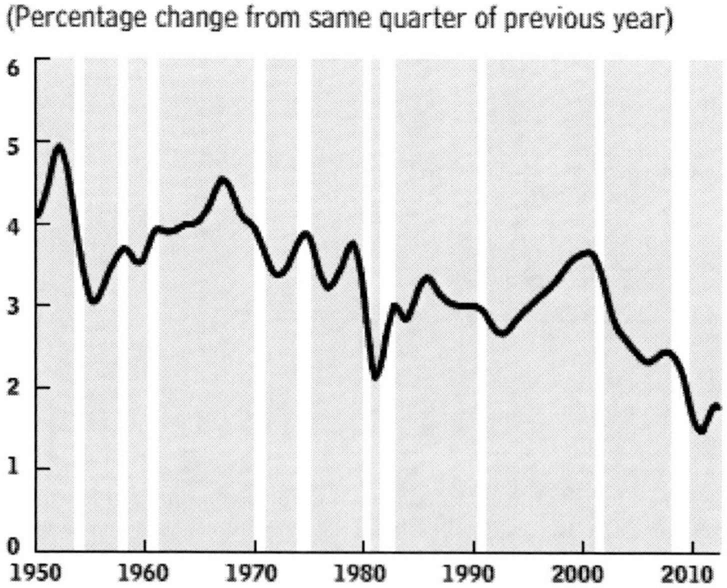

Source: Congressional Budget Office.

Notes: Potential gross domestic product (GDP) is CBO's estimate of the level of GDP that corresponds to a high rate of use of labor and capital, adjusted to remove the effects of inflation.

Data are quarterly and are plotted through the second quarter of 2012.

Figure 2. Potential GDP.

POTENTIAL GDP

According to CBO's analysis, the unusually slow growth of output over the 12 quarters following the last recession in large part reflects slower growth in potential output than has occurred on average following other recessions.

In CBO's assessment, the growth of potential GDP has been trending downward since the late 1960s (see Figure 2). That slowdown initially reflected a reduction in the growth of total factor productivity and then, beginning in the mid-1970s, a reduction in the growth of potential employment.[7] Since the end of the last recession, the relatively slow growth of potential GDP has reflected slower growth of all three of its major determinants than occurred, on average, following other recessions.

By CBO's estimates, the slower growth of potential employment, as compared with the average during previous recoveries, directly accounts for more than a third of the slowed pace of growth of potential GDP since the end of the last recession. Potential employment grew by 2.3 percent between the second quarter of 2009 and the second quarter of 2012, CBO estimates. That figure is less than half the 5.0 percent average increase during previous post–World War II recoveries, although it is close to the growth following the mild recession in 2001.

That slower growth of potential employment primarily reflects three developments. The most important is that, since about 1980, demographic trends have slowed the growth of the population that is working age and, therefore, the growth of the potential labor force (the labor force that exists at a labor force participation rate adjusted for the effects of fluctuations in aggregate demand). In several earlier recoveries, the baby boomers were entering the labor force; now, they are beginning to retire. Another important development is an end to the long-standing increase in women's participation in the labor force, which had boosted the growth of the labor force in recoveries before 2000. Finally, the number of people who would be unemployed if output was at its potential level has risen in the current recovery. An unusually large number of people have had their skills and connection to the workforce erode because they have been out of work for a long time. Some of those people will probably never work again, and it will take more time than usual for the rest to find suitable jobs.

Slower growth of potential total factor productivity, as compared with the average for previous post–World War II recoveries, directly accounts for about one-fifth of the slowed pace of growth of potential GDP since the end of the most recent recession.

According to CBO's estimates, in the nonfarm business sector, which produces roughly three-quarters of the nation's output, potential total factor productivity grew by 3.6 percent in the three years following the end of the last recession, compared with 4.6 percent, on average, during past recoveries.[8]

Although the growth in potential total factor productivity after the last recession has been stronger than it was, on average, after recessions during the 1970s and 1980s, it has been below the average rate after recessions during the 1950s and 1960s. In CBO's estimation, the financial crisis and recession reduced the growth of potential total factor productivity in the nonfarm business sector by about 0.2 percentage points during the 12 quarters after the end of the recession.

Slower growth of capital services accounts for more than a third of the slowness in the growth of potential GDP during the recovery. By CBO's estimates, capital services in the nonfarm business sector grew by 6.4 percent in the first 12 quarters of the current recovery, compared with an average of 11.7 percent in past recoveries.

That reduction reflects a much lower amount of net investment (investment minus depreciation) relative to the existing capital stock in this recovery.

That smaller amount of net investment can be attributed, in turn, to several forces. One is the nature and severity of the recession. The ratio of net business investment to GDP fell to unusually low levels during the recession because of weak demand for goods and services and a high cost of capital, and even though that ratio rose rapidly after the recession, it is still low by historical standards. Moreover, the ongoing housing slump has sharply curtailed growth of the stock of housing capital.

A second force restraining investment has been the slower growth of potential employment, which means that smaller increases in the stock of structures, equipment, and software are needed to equip the workforce with the same amount of capital per worker.

A third force has been the slower growth of total factor productivity, which reduces growth of the productivity of capital and thereby tends to reduce real investment per worker.

The effects of the recession and slow recovery on potential output will persist over the coming decade. According to CBO's estimates, the recession and weak recovery will reduce the level of potential GDP in 2022 by about 11/2 percent. That effect arises roughly equally from all three determinants of potential GDP.[9]

The Cyclical Variation of GDP Around Potential GDP

The unusually slow growth of real GDP since the end of the last recession also reflects slow growth in the ratio of real GDP to potential GDP—the cyclical variation in real GDP around its potential value. Of the major components of GDP, four have exhibited especially weak growth relative to that in past recoveries:

- Purchases of goods and services by state and local governments,
- Purchases of goods and services by the federal government,
- Residential investment, and
- Consumer spending.

Purchases by state and local governments account for the largest portion of the unusual weakness in growth; each of those other components accounts for a modestly smaller amount of the remaining slowness (see Table 1). In contrast, investment by businesses and net exports grew faster relative to potential GDP in the first 12 quarters of the current recovery than in past recoveries.

Particular factors associated with the nature and circumstances of the recession help to explain why the growth of those four components of output (measured as the contribution to the growth of real GDP as a ratio of potential GDP) was so slow.

Falling house prices depressed the growth of property tax revenues, which combined with falling revenues from income and sales taxes to restrain state and local governments' purchases. Federal purchases climbed immediately following the recession, peaking after five quarters, but began falling after that point because of reductions in purchases for national defense. Residential investment was weak because of a glut of vacant homes, created by overbuilding during the housing boom before the recession and the slow formation of new households thereafter. Weakness in the housing market slowed the recovery of consumer spending by retarding a recovery in house prices and, therefore, the value of households' wealth. Also slowing the growth of consumer spending were the unusually large decline in the share of national income that constitutes returns on labor (in other words, income derived from employment, as opposed to being returns on the ownership of capital) and reduced confidence about future economic activity.

Table 1. Contributions to the Cyclical Variation in Real GDP, 12 Quarters Following Recessions

Component	Current Recovery	Average Recovery	Difference	Major Factors Contributing to the Difference
State and Local Governments' Purchases	-11/4	-1/4	-1	Slow growth in tax revenues and federal grants
Federal Government's Purchases	-1/2	1/4	-3/4	A decline in defense purchases
Residential Investment	0	3/4	-3/4	Overbuilding during the housing boom; weak household formation
Consumer Spending	1	13/4	-3/4	Loss of wealth; a bigger decline in the share of national income going to labor; weak confidence
Business Investment[a]	23/4	21/2	1/4	Rebound from unusually weak investment during the recession
Net Exports	-1/2	-1	1/2	Slow growth in the United States; strong growth in emerging markets
Total	11/2	41/4	-23/4	

Sources: Congressional Budget Office; Department of Commerce, Bureau of Economic Analysis.

Notes: Real gross domestic product (GDP) is the total amount of goods and services produced in the United States, adjusted to remove the effects of inflation. Potential GDP is CBO's estimate of the level of GDP that corresponds to a high rate of use of labor and capital, adjusted to remove the effects of inflation.

The average recovery is the average after recessions since 1945 that were not followed by another recession within 12 quarters. Numbers are rounded to the nearest one-quarter of a percentage point and, hence, do not add up to totals.

[a] Includes investment in nonresidential structures, equipment, software, and inventories.

Ranking factors by their importance in slowing the growth of output is difficult. One reason is that the factors had indirect effects on the economy and have affected one another. For example, factors slowing consumer spending indirectly contributed to slower growth in business investment, which slowed hiring and in turn consumer spending. Another reason is that the role of various factors changed as the recovery progressed. For example, according to surveys of bank loan officers, most lenders began easing standards and terms for commercial and industrial loans in mid-2010, so the availability and cost of credit probably became less of a restraining factor than they were at the start of the recovery.10 As another example, some temporary factors contributed to slow growth for a few quarters; those factors include increases in prices for energy and food, which reduced consumers' purchasing power, and disruptions in the global supply chain caused by the earthquake and nuclear accident in Japan in 2011. Consequently, the ranking of the importance of the factors depends on the period of interest.

Government Purchases

Relative to the average for past recoveries, purchases by federal, state, and local governments were more restrained in the 12 quarters after the end of the last recession (see Figure 3 on page 10). Government purchases, which contribute directly to GDP, are outlays for goods and services, including compensation of government employees and investment in structures, equipment, and software.[11] In contrast, other government spending (such as transfer payments to people) and taxes affect GDP indirectly through their influence on other components of output, such as consumer spending. During and after the recession, federal policymakers enacted a variety of tax and spending measures that aimed to reduce the severity of the recession and aid the recovery (see Box 1). The positive impact of those fiscal policy actions on the level of output was larger late in the recession and early in the recovery than it was later in the recovery.

Purchases by State and Local Governments

Over the first 12 quarters following the last recession, weak growth in purchases by state and local governments slowed the growth of the ratio of real GDP to potential GDP by about 1 percentage point more than the average for previous recoveries (see Table 1 and Figure 3 on page 10). That weak growth in purchases stemmed equally from three sources.

Reductions in employment (of teachers and other personnel) account for a third of that weakness through lower payrolls; 12 quarters after the recession, growth in the number of workers employed by state and local governments was 12 percentage points lower than during the average recovery (see Figure 4 on page 11). Weakness in state and local governments' purchases of goods and services from other sectors and a relatively slow pace of construction by those governments also each account for about a third of the overall weakness. Most of the weakness in state and local governments' purchases apart from their spending on construction can be traced to a below-average rebound in tax revenues and the need to balance general-fund budgets, but additional pressure came from below-average growth in federal grants.[12]

The American Recovery and Reinvestment Act of 2009 (ARRA) authorized an increase in federal grants to states and localities through 2011; those grants helped support state and local purchases for a while, including in the final months of the recession, by raising the amount of assistance to states and localities above what it would have been otherwise. However, the winding down, beginning in 2011, of payments from that increase in federal grants was most likely a drag on the rate of growth of state and local governments' purchases last year and in the first half of this year.

In contrast, state and local governments' construction spending was probably held back primarily by general budgetary pressures and by tight credit markets early in the recovery, because federal grants for capital projects in the current recovery have been in line with those during previous recoveries since 1959 (the first year for which such data are available).

Purchases by the Federal Government

Over the first 12 quarters following the recession, weak growth in purchases by the federal government slowed the growth of the ratio of real GDP to potential GDP by about three-quarters of a percentage point compared with the average for previous recoveries (see Table 1 and Figure 3 on page 10). Over the first half of that period, those purchases contributed more to economic growth (measured by growth of real GDP relative to potential GDP) than they did on average over the same period following other postwar recessions. Since the start of 2011, however, purchases by the federal government have provided less support, primarily as a result of weaker spending on national defense.

As in the analysis of other sectors of the economy, the possibility of indirect effects complicates estimating federal purchases' contribution to the growth of output since the trough of the recession. When an economy is operating near (or above) its potential level, higher government spending can shift resources away from production in other sectors to government-funded projects. That indirect crowding-out effect means that increases in government spending may be offset by declines in purchases and investment elsewhere in the economy. However, by CBO's estimates, that offset has been mod est since the recession ended because of an economic environment in which unemployment has been high, a large amount of capital resources has gone unused, and interest rates have remained extraordinarily low.[13]

Box 1. The Effects of Recent Fiscal Policy Actions on the Economy

Federal lawmakers enacted a variety of tax and spending measures aimed at reducing the severity of the recession and spur the recovery. Some of those measures increased federal purchases, particularly in the first six quarters following the recession, when total federal purchases added more to the growth of real (inflation-adjusted) gross domestic product (GDP) than they had on average in previous recoveries. Other measures provided a substantial indirect boost to the economy during the recession and recovery. Those measures included increasing transfers to people (such as unemployment benefits), lowering taxes, and providing support to the financial system. The key fiscal policy actions were these:

- Direct fiscal stimulus came from the Economic Stimulus Act of 2008, which was enacted in February 2008, and the much larger American Recovery and Reinvestment Act of 2009 (ARRA), which was enacted in February 2009. The Economic Stimulus Act provided tax rebates to low- and middle-income taxpayers, tax incentives to stimulate business investment, and an increase in the limits imposed on mortgages eligible for purchase by Fannie Mae and Freddie Mac. ARRA authorized purchases of goods and services by the federal government, transfers to state and local governments (for spending on infrastructure and other purposes), payments to individuals, and temporary tax reductions for individuals and businesses (such as the Making Work Pay tax credit and favorable tax treatment of business investment). The Congressional Budget Office (CBO) estimates that ARRA raised real GDP by between 0.7 percent and 4.1 percent in 2010 and by smaller amounts in 2009 and more recently.[1]

- Other laws that were intended to have stimulative effects were ones that extended unemployment insurance benefits (which ARRA did as well); cut the payroll tax paid by employees in 2011 (which was later extended through 2012); provided credits for first-time home buyers (which were extended once by ARRA and again by the Worker, Home-ownership, and Business Assistance Act of 2009); and created the Car Allowance Rebate System (commonly referred to as "Cash for Clunkers").
- The Troubled Asset Relief Program (TARP) bolstered financial markets and institutions, largely by providing equity capital to banks and other financial firms.[2]

In addition, fiscal stimulus without the need for new legislation came from the effect of the federal government's so-called automatic stabilizers. Those stabilizers arise from the response of the federal tax system and social safety-net programs, such as the Supplemental Nutrition Assistance Program (formerly called the Food Stamp program), regular unemployment insurance benefits, and Medicaid. The stabilizers automatically dampen swings in economic activity, by decreasing tax payments to the government and increasing benefit payments to households when economic activity slows and by having the opposite effect when economic activity picks up. For 2009 through 2011, federal fiscal support from the automatic stabilizers equaled about 21/4 percent to 23/4 percent of potential GDP, CBO estimates.[3]

In CBO's assessment, because the economy has been operating significantly below its potential level during the past few years, the boost to economic activity caused by fiscal policy actions was not significantly offset by a shift of resources away from production elsewhere in the economy—which is to say that little crowding out of production occurred. However, when the economy is again operating close to its potential level, the increase in government borrowing that has resulted from the recent fiscal stimulus will tend to reduce the amount of funds available for private investment.

Therefore, policies that increase demand when the economy is weak often involve a trade-off between boosting economic output in the short run and reducing output in the long run, unless future policy changes are made to offset the additional accumulation of government debt.[4]

[1] See Congressional Budget Office, Estimated Impact of the American Recovery and Reinvestment Act on Employment and Economic Output from April 2012 Through June 2012 (August 2012). In estimating the effects of each provision of ARRA, CBO chose, on a judgmental basis, low and high estimates to encompass most economists' views about the effects of that type of provision. For a more detailed discussion of CBO's approach to analyzing short-term fiscal policy, see Felix Reichling and Charles Whalen, Assessing the Short-Term Effects on Output of Changes in Federal Fiscal Policies, Congressional Budget Office Working Paper 2012-08 (May 2012).

[2] The Emergency Economic Stabilization Act of 2008 authorized the Secretary of the Treasury—through the TARP—to purchase or insure troubled financial assets, up to a limit of $700 billion in assets outstanding at any one time. Authority to make new purchases expired in October 2010. See Congressional Budget Office, Report on the Troubled Asset Relief Program—October 2012 (October 2012).

[3]. Similar but smaller automatic changes occur in state and local governments' revenues and spending. However, automatic changes at the state and local levels are blunted by budgetary decisions made to comply with rules for maintaining balanced budgets. Those decisions include

cutting state and local spending and increasing tax rates and various fees.

[4]. For further discussion of such trade-offs, see the statement of Douglas W. Elmendorf, Director, Congressional Budget Office, before the Senate Committee on the Budget, Policies for Increasing Economic Growth and Employment in 2012 and 2013 (November 15, 2011), pp. 17–22.

RESIDENTIAL INVESTMENT

Residential investment typically plays an important positive role in economic recoveries. In the current business cycle, however, it has not contributed to the recovery, reducing the growth of real output relative to potential output by about three-quarters of a percentage point relative to the average in previous recoveries (see Table 1 on page 6 and Figure 3).

According to CBO's analysis, the main reason why residential investment has grown more slowly in the current recovery than in past recoveries has been the extraordinarily large number of vacant housing units (see Figure 5).

Even in normal times, the number of vacant housing units is substantial, reflecting the often lengthy process of home sellers finding suitable and interested home buyers, as well as the large number of second homes and seasonal units.

But during the past few years, the number of vacant units has far exceeded what is typical, reducing the incentive for building new homes. In addition, the excess has slowed construction by diminishing the boost usually provided by low interest rates.

Excess vacant units account for about two-thirds of the slower pace of growth of residential investment during the current recovery relative to past recoveries, according to CBO's estimates, with the remaining one-third attributable to other factors.

Excess Vacant Units

A major cause of excess vacancies was overbuilding during the housing boom, accounting for about half of the total impact of excess vacancies on real GDP in the first 12 quarters of the current recovery compared with past recoveries.

Builders constructed an average of nearly 1.9 million housing units every year from 2002 to the peak of the bubble in 2006, significantly more than the average of less than 1.5 million per year during the previous two decades (as measured by what are termed housing starts). Because vacancies tend to affect homebuilding slowly, the adverse impact of that overbuilding on residential investment continued to grow during the recession and into the recovery. In addition, homebuilding during the recovery was probably slowed by builders' fear that future foreclosures would further increase the number of vacant units.

The remaining source of excess vacancies was weak household formation during and after the recession. Much of that phenomenon—of people's unwillingness or inability to set up new households—can be traced to people's low expectations for home prices to appreciate; the high unemployment rate also played a role. But in the past year, household formation has been weaker than can be explained by those factors. Other contributing factors may include uncertainty about future gains in income and access to credit that remains constrained compared with what it was prior to the financial crisis.

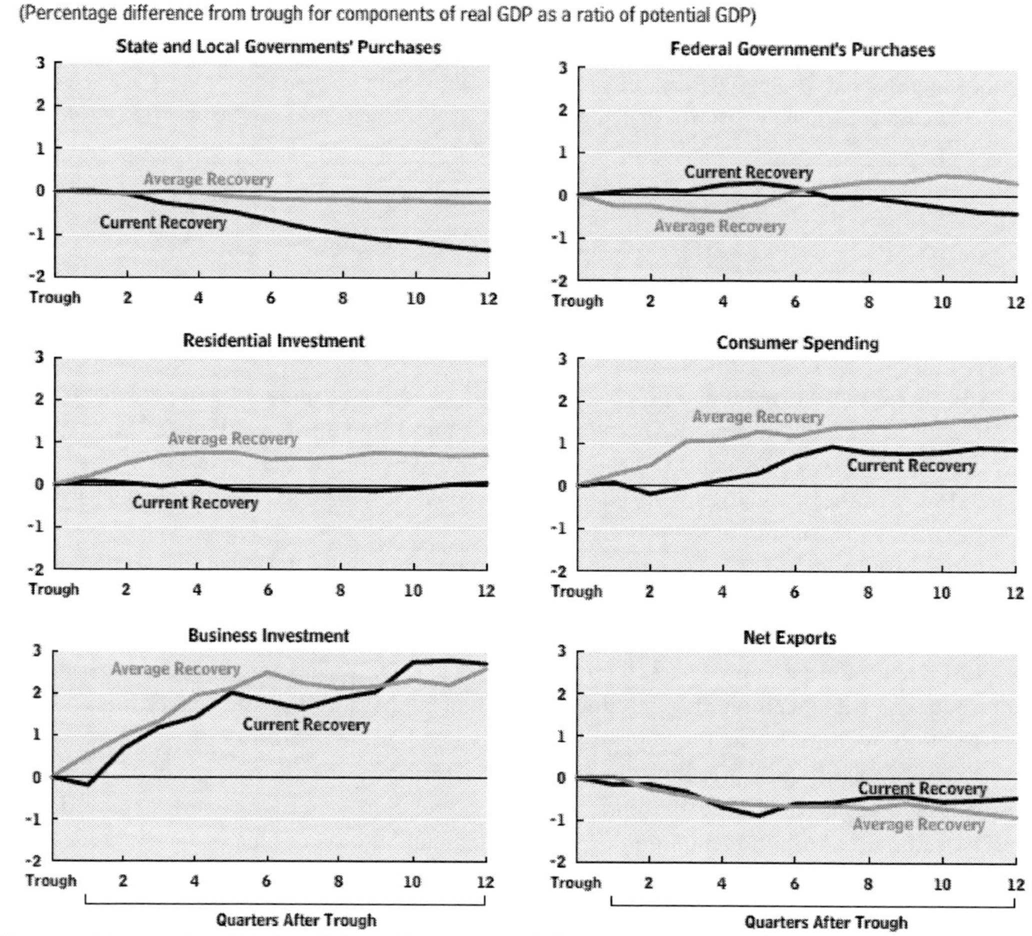

Sources: Congressional Budget Office; Department of Commerce, Bureau of Economic Analysis.

Notes: Real gross domestic product (GDP) is the total amount of goods and services produced in the United States, adjusted to remove the effects of inflation. Potential GDP is CBO's estimate of the level of GDP that corresponds to a high rate of use of labor and capital, adjusted to remove the effects of inflation.

The average recovery is the average after recessions since 1945 that were not followed by another recession within 12 quarters.

Figure 3. Contributions to the Cyclical Variation in Real GDP Following Recessions.

Vacancies have affected housing construction in several ways. First is the direct effect: The greater the number of vacant units, the more difficult it is for builders to sell new homes and thus the less incentive they have to build homes. Leading into many past recessions, high mortgage rates and tight lending conditions reduced construction more than they curtailed household formation, resulting in fewer vacant units at the troughs. However, before and during the most recent recession, the number of excess vacant units shot up. Although excess vacancies have diminished since the recession ended, their adverse impact continued to grow until the second half of 2011 and remained nearly the same in early 2012.

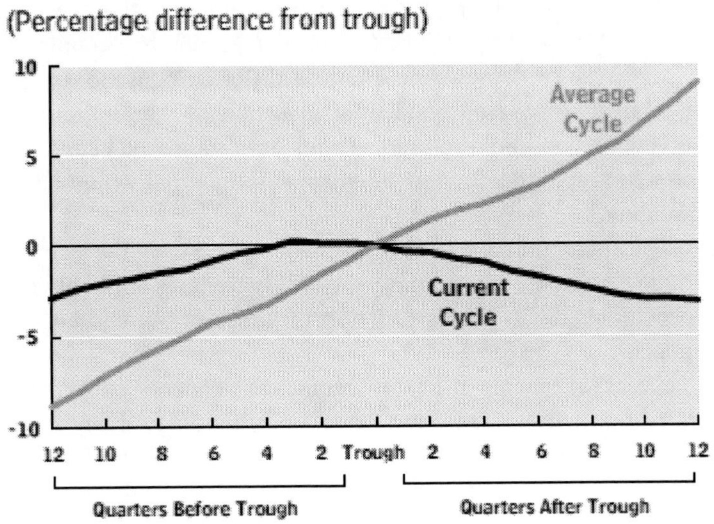

Sources: Congressional Budget Office, Department of Labor, Bureau of Labor Statistics.

Note: The average cycle, or the pattern of economic growth before and after a trough, is the average for cycles since 1945 that were not followed by another recession within 12 quarters.

Figure 4. State and Local Government Employment.

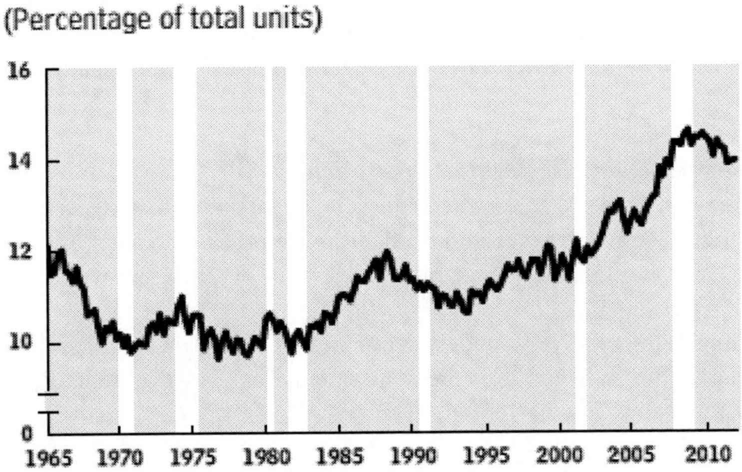

Sources: Congressional Budget Office; Department of Commerce, Census Bureau.

Notes: Housing units comprise occupied units and vacant units, including units intended for year-round use and seasonal use.

Data are quarterly and are plotted through the second quarter of 2012.

Figure 5. Vacant Housing Units.

Second, not only do excess vacant units directly reduce the incentive to build new homes, but they also dampen the positive impact that improvements in economic factors, such as lower mortgage rates, have on homebuilding. When a new household is formed as a result of improved economic conditions—for example, because lower mortgage rates or a stronger outlook for house prices makes a home look like a better investment—that household can buy either a vacant home or a new home. (The other option, buying an occupied home, just shifts the choice of buying a vacant or new home onto a different household and is therefore not meaningful in an analysis of overall residential investment.) The more vacant homes there are, the more likely that a household formed as a result of improved economic conditions will purchase a vacant home rather than a new home, absorbing what would have been a positive impact on homebuilding.

Third, excess vacancies have probably influenced some of the economic factors that normally affect home buying. For example, excess vacancies probably lowered potential homebuyers' expectations about the appreciation of house prices and hence the demand for homes as investments.

In addition, excess vacancies probably worsened lenders' expectations about house prices, which probably, in turn, was one reason (in addition to many others) why lenders tightened standards for mortgages more than for most other types of credit. Between mid-2006 and mid-2010, the net percentage of respondents to the Federal Reserve's Senior Loan Officer Opinion Survey who said that they tightened standards for mortgage loans was closely correlated with the change in excess vacant housing units during the preceding two and one-half years.[14]

Fourth, the high vacancy rate for owner-occupied homes, which tend to be single-family homes, has probably shifted the mix of construction toward lower-value rental units. Roughly one-half as much labor, capital, and materials is required to build a multifamily unit (each unit within a larger building) as a single-family unit. Consequently, for a given number of housing starts, a decrease in the share constituted by single-family units resulting from disproportionately high vacancy rates for owner-occupied homes leads to lower residential investment.[15]

Other Factors Affecting Residential Investment

Since the last recession, several economic factors that usually drive housing starts—changes in mortgage rates, expectations about house prices, the level of house prices relative to the trend, and the unemployment rate—have been weaker, on average, than in the three previous recoveries.[16]

For example, the relatively modest decline in mortgage rates, given that those rates were already remarkably low when the recession ended, has provided a smaller boost to housing starts than is typical.

Consumer Spending

Unusually modest growth in spending by consumers has slowed the growth of real GDP by roughly as much as spending by the federal government and residential investment have, but by less than spending by state and local governments has.

In the first 12 quarters after the end of the recent recession, consumer spending made just a little over half of the contribution (nearly 1 percentage point) to the growth of the ratio of real GDP to potential GDP that it did, on average, in other recoveries since World War II (see Table 1 on page 6 and Figure 3 on page 10).

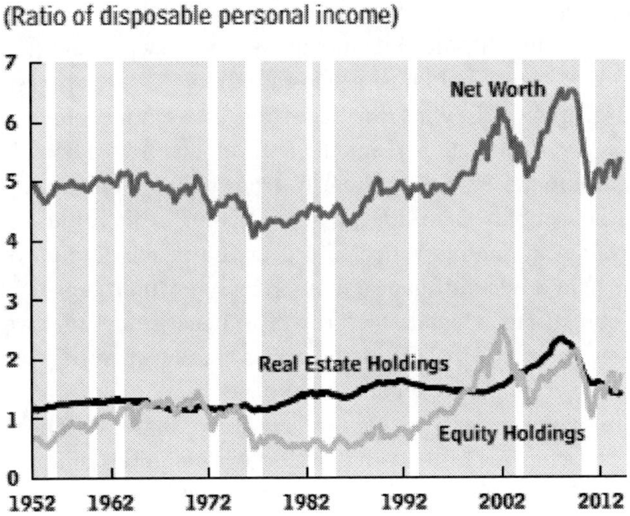

Sources: Congressional Budget Office; Department of Commerce, Bureau of Economic Analysis; Federal Reserve.

Notes: Household net worth comprises total assets minus total liabilities on households' balance sheets as reported in the Federal Reserve's flow-of-funds accounts.

Disposable personal income is the after-tax income of individuals.

Equity holdings of the household sector are the total market value of corporate stocks held either directly or indirectly (in mutual funds and pension plans, for example).

Household real estate holdings are the total owner-occupied real estate owned by households.

Data are quarterly and are plotted through the second quarter of 2012.

Figure 6. Household Net Worth and Selected Components.

Three main factors, to which CBO assigns roughly equal importance, explain that weak spending: relatively modest improvement in the value of households' wealth (primarily reflecting continued weakness in the value of real estate assets) following an unusually large drop during the recession; a large decline in, and continued low level of, the share of the nation's income going to labor; and weak confidence and perhaps heightened uncertainty. Other factors also have affected the pattern of consumer spending during the recovery. For example, tighter lending standards have made borrowing and mortgage refinancing more difficult for some households. In addition, the efforts of some households to pay down debt and resist taking on new debt may have surpassed households' typical reactions to changes in wealth and income. At the same time, significant temporary changes in fiscal policy, such as the cut in payroll taxes that began in January 2011, have bolstered consumer spending (see Box 1 on page 8).

Wealth

An important reason for the weakness in consumer spending is that households' wealth (assets minus liabilities) fell by an unprecedented amount after the housing bubble burst and has grown unusually slowly since then. To rebuild their wealth following those losses, households pulled back on their spending.[17]

The wealth (or net worth) of households fell by more than $16 trillion, or 24 percent, from the third quarter of 2007 to the first quarter of 2009. At the beginning of that period, total wealth was 6.4 times greater than total disposable personal income; by the end of the period, wealth had fallen to 4.8 times income, mainly because of declines in house prices and in the value of corporate equity holdings (see Figure 6).

In the first 12 quarters following the recession, households' total wealth increased by roughly $10 trillion, or about 20 percent, to a level that was about $5 trillion below its previous peak. That rebound resulted primarily from gains in the value of corporate stocks and a reduction in households' liabilities. The reduction in liabilities, a process sometimes referred to as deleveraging, mainly reflected a decrease in the amount owed on home mortgages, as borrowers paid down mortgages, took on less new mortgage debt, and in some cases defaulted on their obligations. Despite the growth in households' real wealth during the first 12 quarters following the recession, its increase was smaller than its average increase in past recoveries, slowing the growth of real consumer spending.

CBO's estimate of the impact of the slow recovery of wealth on consumer spending is based on the view that changes in the value of corporate equities and real estate have similar effects on households' spending, a view that lies roughly in the middle of the views of economists. At one end, some economists suggest that, in the aggregate, households respond more to changes in wealth held in real estate, possibly because real estate wealth is more widely held than corporate equities and because households can use real estate wealth as collateral for borrowing.[18]

At the other end, some economists believe that the weakness in house prices may have had little effect on consumer spending: Lower house prices mean that the cost of housing is lower, so homeowners may not view the reduced value of their houses as a net loss. And the expectation of lower housing costs for future generations could actually boost some households' spending now.[19] Some researchers also have concluded that changes in real estate prices (and hence wealth) and in consumer spending are both determined largely by a third factor, such as expected growth of income. Under that theory, changes in real estate wealth have no direct effect on spending.[20]

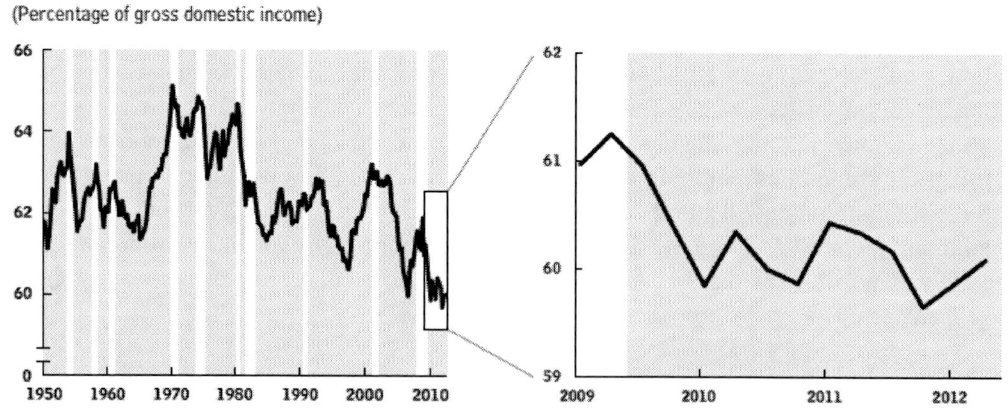

Sources: Congressional Budget Office; Department of Commerce, Bureau of Economic Analysis.

Notes: Labor income is defined as labor compensation plus 65 percent of proprietors' income. Gross domestic income is the sum of all income earned in the production of gross domestic product. Data are quarterly and are plotted through the second quarter of 2012.

Figure 7. Labor Income.

Labor Income

Another important reason for the slow revival of consumer spending is that labor income as a share of gross domestic income (GDI, which reflects the income earned in the production of GDP) has fallen by a larger amount than in the typical recovery.[21] Over the first 12 quarters of the average recovery, the labor share of GDI fell by about 0.3 percentage points. However, in the first 12 quarters of the current recovery, it fell by 1.2 percentage points (see Figure 7). That difference means that a smaller proportion of the growth in value of the economy's output was distributed in the form of wages, salaries, benefits, and proprietors' income during the current recovery than in past recoveries. Instead, capital income in the form of domestic corporate profits, another major component of GDI, rose more rapidly than usual.[22]

Among the components of labor income, the growth of real (inflation-adjusted) compensation (wages, salaries, and benefits) of employees in the first 12 quarters following the recession was considerably weaker than the average in past recoveries. A significant part of that weakness reflects the soft labor market, which has held down the growth of wages and employment. Increases in energy prices for consumers also played a role in slowing the growth of real compensation. During the recession, those prices fell sharply, but in the following 12 quarters, the price index for consumer energy goods grew much faster than all consumer prices, on average. If energy prices had risen as much as the prices of other goods and services, then, all else being equal, households' real compensation would have risen at an average annual rate of about 1.5 percent over the 12 quarters, rather than at an average annual rate of 1.0 percent. In the typical recovery between 1949 and 2000, energy prices rose more slowly than all consumer prices in the first 12 quarters, on average. Smaller increases in energy prices would have contributed to households' purchasing power and thereby led to a stronger recovery in consumer spending.

Confidence and Uncertainty

Consumers also have restrained their spending because of an unusually high degree of concern about their financial prospects. Since the end of the recession, consumer confidence has been lower than during most other recoveries. Indeed, throughout 2010 and 2011, only about 10 percent of consumers expected to see real gains in their income in the year ahead, matching a level of pessimism last seen in 1980.[23] In addition, persistent weakness in the labor market may well have exacerbated uncertainty and dampened spending for even those households not currently facing unemployment. It is difficult to distinguish the effect of confidence on spending from the effects of households' reduced wealth and the decline in the returns on labor as a share of GDI, but consumer confidence has often appeared lower in the current recovery than can be readily explained by those factors.

Although most of the weakness in consumer confidence probably reflects the weak labor market and poor prospects for future growth of household income, some of the weakness in consumer confidence during the recovery could reflect uncertainty about public policy. For example, although a number of the temporary tax provisions enacted or extended during the recovery provided direct stimulus to the economy, they may also have added to that uncertainty. Moreover, the future course of U.S. fiscal policy remains particularly uncertain: How policy-makers will deal with the continuing weak economy, the significant amount of fiscal tightening scheduled to occur next year, and the surge in federal debt is currently unclear. Many households also face uncertainty about how they will be affected by implementation of recently enacted federal laws, especially legislation involving financial markets (the Dodd-Frank Wall Street Reform and Consumer Protection Act) and health care (the Affordable Care Act).[24] The degree to which uncertainty about public policy has restrained decisions to spend, however, is difficult to determine.[25]

Other Factors

Changes in wealth, labor income, and confidence explain much of the unusual weakness in consumer spending. But other factors also contributed, particularly early in the recovery, including stricter standards and terms for borrowing by consumers and efforts by households to deleverage that went beyond their typical reactions to changes in wealth and income.

Standards and Terms for Borrowing. At least a small portion of the slow recovery in consumer spending can be attributed to the tightness in standards and terms for borrowing. Responding to unexpectedly large losses (on mortgages and other consumer and commercial loans) and to the prospect of additional losses in the future, banks made credit less available during the recession and even into the recovery by raising their lending standards and tightening their terms—requiring larger down payments, shorter loan maturities, and higher credit scores—for both mortgage and consumer borrowing. Standards and terms for consumer loans began to ease in mid-2010, but standards for home mortgages remained particularly strict through the second quarter of 2012, especially compared with the unusually lax standards and terms that were in force before the recession.[26]

Mortgage standards affect not just people purchasing a home but also homeowners looking to refinance. Households might refinance to take advantage of lower interest rates and, if they increase the size of their mortgage, to borrow against their home equity to finance other spending.

During the recovery, tighter standards made refinancing more difficult. In addition, households who had a mortgage that was larger than their home's value (in other words, who were "underwater") faced considerable difficulties in refinancing in order to lower their interest rate and had no home equity to borrow against.[27]

Deleveraging. A portion of the slow recovery in consumer spending can also be attributed to households' reducing their debt by more than the amount suggested by recent changes in asset prices and income and by spending and borrowing patterns in recent decades.[28]

Households' debt, defined here as the sum of home mortgage debt plus consumer credit, rose especially rapidly in dollar terms and as a percentage of disposable (after-tax) personal income in the decade leading up to the recession. Since the beginning of the recession, households' debt has fallen both in dollar terms and as a share of income, even though interest rates on many consumer loans and home mortgages have been much lower than they were before the recession.

As discussed above, tightness in credit markets has probably constrained borrowing by households. Some of the decline in households' debt has also been attributable to defaults, particularly on home mortgages.[29]

Separately from those factors, some households may have been trying to get their debt level back to a historical relationship with their income and level of assets.[30] In fact, weak demand for consumer loans and home mortgages during the recovery is consistent with that possibility.[31]

If households are targeting historical levels of debt to income or assets, that sort of deleveraging could continue to hold down spending for some time.

Investment by Businesses

Over the 12 quarters after the recession, real business investment grew somewhat more rapidly than in past recoveries, adding about 1/4 percentage point more to growth in the ratio of real GDP to potential GDP than in the average cycle (see Table 1 on page 6 and Figure 3 on page 10). That performance mainly reflects how far nominal business investment had fallen relative to potential GDP during the recession, which means that even brisk growth in investment during the recovery has left the level of net business investment (investment minus depreciation) fairly low relative to potential GDP.

Business investment was probably held back during the recovery by unusually subdued business confidence and stricter standards and terms for borrowing; indeed, during the first nine quarters of the recovery, the ratio of real business investment to potential GDP grew more slowly than in the average cycle.

Business Confidence

The recent recession was uncommon in a number of ways, including the magnitude of the decline in GDP, the role of the financial crisis, and the fact that the Federal Reserve lowered short-term interest rates nearly to zero.

Consequently, businesses probably had unusually high uncertainty about the sustainability of the upturn, especially early in the recovery, and thus unusually high uncertainty about future demand for their goods and services.

A lack of business confidence could also reflect expectations of changes in government policies or uncertainty about future policies. For example, concerns and questions about each of the following could have affected business confidence: the overall levels of federal taxes and spending that will occur in coming years; the future impact of the significant changes in the health insurance system and in the regulation of the financial system enacted in the past few years; and environmental and other regulations that will be imposed or removed over time. The magnitude of the effects of such factors on business investment is difficult to determine, however.

Stricter Standards and Terms for Borrowing

Difficulties in obtaining financing also have probably restrained business investment to some extent. Banks continued to tighten standards and terms on commercial real estate loans during 2009 and 2010 and eased them very little in 2011. In addition, the decline in home prices, along with stricter credit standards for mortgages than the ones in place before the financial crisis, probably put home equity loans out of reach for many owners of small businesses, who, under other circumstances, tend to borrow against that equity for business purposes.

Nevertheless, stricter standards and terms have probably not played a large role in slowing business investment. Many large and stable corporations have faced few impediments to borrowing and, in fact, have been taking advantage of historically low interest rates to refinance large amounts of debt.[32] In addition, since the recession, only a small percentage of respondents to surveys of small businesses have identified credit as their most important problem; rather, they have been much more concerned about poor sales.[33]

Net Exports

Real net exports, measured as a contribution to the ratio of real GDP to potential GDP, fell somewhat less in the first 12 quarters following the most recent recession than in past recoveries, contributing about 1/2 percentage point more to the growth of output than in the average recovery (see Table 1 on page 6 and Figure 3 on page 10). Both real imports and real exports increased by more than they did in past recoveries; however, the growth in real exports outpaced the growth in real imports. Slower growth of demand in this country for all types of goods and services restrained the growth of imports, while exports were helped by strong growth in emerging markets during the first seven quarters of the recovery.

Since the end of the last recession, net exports could have been even stronger had the Federal Reserve been able to further reduce short-term interest rates. (For a discussion of limitations faced by the Federal Reserve in stimulating economic activity in this recovery, see Box 2.)

Lower U.S. interest rates would have reduced the return on U.S. assets relative to foreign assets, weakening the demand for U.S. assets and thus the value of the dollar. A lower value of the dollar would have boosted the competitiveness of U.S. exports in foreign markets and of domestic production against imports. That improved competitiveness would have increased real net exports.

Box 2. Monetary Policy and the Slow Growth of Output

An important reason for the slow growth of the U.S. economy relative to its potential during this economic recovery is that the Federal Reserve's ability to lower interest rates to stimulate economic activity has run into the limit that interest rates cannot be lower than zero. Moreover, the economy has been less responsive to a decline in interest rates in this recovery.

Monetary policy has often spurred economic recoveries. The Federal Reserve effectively sets the federal funds rate (the interest rate that financial institutions charge each other for overnight loans of their monetary reserves), which influences the demand for goods and services.

The Federal Reserve usually can boost demand by reducing the federal funds rate, which typically lowers other interest rates, increases the prices of assets such as corporate equities, and lowers the exchange rate.

However, the Federal Reserve has been constrained in combating the recent recession. During that recession and early in the subsequent recovery, the historical relationships between the federal funds rate, economic activity, and the rate of inflation generally suggested that the federal funds rate would be less than zero.[1] Because setting interest rates below zero is not possible, the Federal Reserve could only reduce the federal funds rate to near zero, where it has been since late 2008 (see the figure).

As a result, the Federal Reserve has used nontraditional policies, including large-scale purchases of securities issued by the Treasury and government-sponsored enterprises, to push down longer-term interest rates on both Treasury borrowing and private-sector borrowing, such as mortgages. Those nontraditional policies noticeably reduced longer-term interest rates, but they have not been powerful enough to spur strong economic growth.[2]

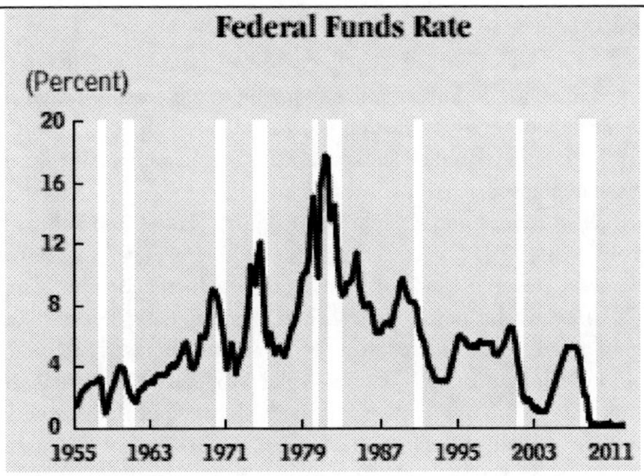

Sources: Congressional Budget Office; Federal Reserve.

Notes: The federal funds rate is the interest rate that financial institutions charge each other for overnight loans of their monetary reserves. The Federal Reserve uses the federal funds rate to conduct monetary policy.

Data are quarterly and are plotted through the second quarter of 2012.

Even if the Federal Reserve had been able to engineer a larger reduction in longer-term interest rates, the economy might still have grown relatively slowly because households and businesses have been less sensitive to, or less able to take advantage of, changes in interest rates than they normally would have been. For example, the excess of vacant homes lowered the response of housing construction to low mortgage interest rates. Moreover, many homeowners have been unable to refinance mortgage loans in order to take advantage of historically low mortgage rates because lenders have generally kept their standards and terms for mortgage loans tight. In addition, to the extent that households are trying to reduce their debt or face constraints on borrowing, they may respond less to lower interest rates on credit for buying consumer goods and services.

The Federal Reserve's ability to spur economic activity also has been hampered by the stress on U.S. financial markets caused by financial problems in Europe. For example, some U.S. banks have tightened standards on loans to nonfinancial firms that have operations in the United States and significant exposure to European economies.[3]

1. Analysts often gauge the Federal Reserve's preferred level of the federal funds rate using models that capture the rate's past responses to inflation and unemployment. Such models are widely termed Taylor-rule models (named for their originator, economist John B. Taylor). Most Taylor-rule specifications indicate that, if it had been possible, the Federal Reserve's target federal funds rate would have been well below zero during the recession and would have remained below zero in 2010.

2. See Joseph Gagnon and others, Large-Scale Asset Purchases by the Federal Reserve: Did They Work? Federal Reserve Bank of New York Staff Report 441 (March 2010), www.newyorkfed.org/research/staff_reports/sr441.html; and James D. Hamilton and Jing Cynthia Wu, "The Effectiveness of Alternative Monetary Policy Tools in a Zero Lower Bound Environment," Journal of Money, Credit, and Banking, vol. 44, no. 1, supplement (February 2012), pp. 3–46.

3. See, for example, Board of Governors of the Federal Reserve System, The July 2012 Senior Loan Officer Opinion Survey on Bank Lending Practices (August 6, 2012), www.federalreserve.gov/boarddocs/snloansurvey.

End Notes

[1] In this analysis, a recovery is the period of economic expansion that begins just after the trough of a recession. The analysis excludes two periods of recovery from post–World War II recessions—those following the recessions of August 1957 to April 1958 and January to July 1980—because, in each case, new recessions began before 12 quarters of recovery had elapsed.

[2] See, for example, Carmen M. Reinhart and Kenneth S. Rogoff, "The Aftermath of Financial Crises," American Economic Review, vol. 99, no. 2 (May 2009), pp. 466–472; Carmen M. Reinhart and Vincent R. Reinhart, "After the Fall," in Federal Reserve Bank of Kansas City, Macroeconomic Challenges: The Decade Ahead (proceedings of the 2010 economic policy symposium, Kansas City: Federal Reserve Bank of Kansas City, 2011); Luc Laeven and Fabian Valencia, Resolution of Banking Crises: The Good, the Bad, and the Ugly, IMF Working Paper 10/146 (Washington, D.C.: International Monetary Fund, June 2010), www.imf.org/external/pubs/cat/longres.cfm?sk=23971.0; Greg Howard, Robert Martin, and Beth Anne Wilson, Are Recoveries from Banking and Financial Crises Really So Different? International Finance Discussion Paper 1037 (Washington, D.C.: Board of Governors of the Federal Reserve System, November 2011), www.federalreserve.gov/pubs/ifdp/2011/1037/default.htm; and Michael D. Bordo and Joseph G. Haubrich, Deep Recessions, Fast Recoveries, and Financial Crises: Evidence from the American Record, Working Paper 12-14 (Cleveland: Federal Reserve Bank of Cleveland, June 2012), www.clevelandfed. org/research/research_publication.cfm?id=35.

[3] A decline in potential GDP reduces real GDP through several channels. For example, if people decide to leave the labor force, which reduces potential GDP, their expected future income decreases, leading them to consume less. Also, lower total factor productivity, which also reduces potential GDP, lowers wages and capital income, leading to less consumer spending and business investment. A lower capital stock, another drag on potential GDP, also lowers wages and capital income.

[4] An alternative perspective on the increase in the unemployment rate since before the recession is offered in Casey B. Mulligan, The Expanding Social Safety Net, Working Paper 17654 (Cambridge, Mass.: National Bureau of Economic Research, December 2011), www.nber.org/ papers/w17654. Mulligan writes that various changes in federal policies since 2007—such as extensions of unemployment insurance—increased the effective tax rate on labor income. As a result, he argues, those policies were primarily responsible for the sharp increase in the unemployment rate during the recession and have slowed the recovery in the labor market since then. See also Casey B. Mulligan, The Redistribution Recession: How Labor Market Distortions Contracted the Economy (New York: Oxford University Press, 2012). For an opposing view, see Jesse Rothstein, "The Labor Market Four Years into the Crisis: Assessing Structural Explanations," Industrial and Labor Relations Review, vol. 65, no. 3 (March 2012).

[5] Consistent with CBO's analysis, economists James H. Stock and Mark W. Watson argue that a decline in the trend component of GDP accounts for much of the slowness in GDP growth in the current recovery compared with growth in recoveries before 1984. See James H. Stock and Mark W. Watson, Disentangling the Channels of the 2007–2009 Recession, Working Paper 18094 (Cambridge, Mass.: National Bureau of Economic Research, May 2012), www.nber.org/papers/w18094.

[6] Potential output also depends on the average number of hours worked per worker and shifts in the number of workers among sectors of the economy with different levels of productivity. But changes in those factors matter only a little in explaining the unusual slowness in the growth of potential output in this recovery. In addition, potential output depends on the quality of the labor force (including the education and training that workers have received). CBO does not estimate labor quality but includes its impact in the agency's estimate of the growth of total factor productivity. For additional information on potential GDP, see Congressional Budget Office, CBO's Method for Estimating Potential Output: An Update (August 2001).

[7] See Congressional Budget Office, An Update to the Budget and Economic Outlook: Fiscal Years 2012 to 2022 (August 2012), p. 39, and CBO's Labor Force Projections Through 2021 (March 2011).

[8] The growth of potential total factor productivity in sectors other than nonfarm business also has contributed less to the growth of potential GDP in recent years than in the past, according to CBO's analysis.

[9] For a discussion of the impact of the recession on potential output, see Congressional Budget Office, An Update to the Budget and Economic Outlook: Fiscal Years 2012 to 2022, Box 2-2, pp. 40–41.

[10] See Board of Governors of the Federal Reserve System, The July 2012 Senior Loan Officer Opinion Survey on Bank Lending Practices (August 6, 2012), www.federalreserve.gov/ boarddocs/ snloansurvey.

[11] In the national income and product accounts, maintained by the Department of Commerce's Bureau of Economic Analysis, government purchases are called government consumption expenditures and gross investment.

[12] For a discussion of the budgetary pressures faced by local governments, see Congressional Budget Office, Fiscal Stress Faced by Local Governments (December 2010). Those budgetary pressures have arisen both from developments during the recession and recovery and from trends in state and local governments' spending and revenues prior to the recession.

[13] For a discussion of how CBO estimates the effects of the government's fiscal policies on the economy, see Congressional Budget Office, The Economic Impact of the President's 2013 Budget (April 2012), pp. 2–3 and 13–18.

[14] For evidence of tightened standards, see, for example, Board of Governors of the Federal Reserve System, The July 2010 Senior Loan Officer Opinion Survey on Bank Lending Practices (August 16, 2010).

[15] Housing starts refer to the number of units started, not to the number of buildings started. For example, beginning construction on a 100-unit apartment building counts as 100 starts.

[16] The housing market has changed considerably since the late 1970s, so it is difficult to compare the influence of those factors in the current recovery with their effect in all of the recoveries since World War II.

[17] For a discussion of how CBO estimates the effects of changes in housing wealth on consumer spending, see Congressional Budget Office, Housing Wealth and Consumer Spending (January 2007).

[18] See, for example, Karl Case, John Quigley, and Robert Shiller, "Comparing Wealth Effects: The Stock Market Versus the Housing Market," Advances in Macroeconomics, vol. 5, no. 1 (2005), pp. 1–32.

[19] See Jonathan Skinner, "Housing Wealth and Aggregate Saving," Regional Science and Urban Economics, vol. 19, no. 2 (May 1989), pp. 305–324.

[20] See Orazio P. Attanasio and others, "Booms and Busts: Consumption, House Prices and Expectations," Economica, vol. 76, no. 301 (2009), pp. 20–50.

[21] CBO defines labor income as the sum of employees' compensation and 65 percent of proprietors' income.

[22] The effect of the fall in the labor share of GDI on households' aggregate spending was only partially offset by the effect of the increase in wealth resulting from higher capital income, because the owners of that wealth, who tend to be higher-income households, tend to have lower propensities to spend out of changes in their resources.

[23] See Thompson Reuters/University of Michigan, "Political Deadlock Hurts Consumer Spending" (press release, December 22, 2011), http:// thomsonreuters.com/news_ideas/ press_releases/ ?itemId=531852, and "Stagnant Incomes Growing Concern" (press release, May 27, 2011), http://thomsonreuters.com/content/press_ room/financial/2011_05_27_ stagnant_incomes _growing_concern.

[24] For further discussion of the possible effects of such legislation on the economy, see the statement of Douglas W. Elmendorf, Director, Congressional Budget Office, before the Senate Committee on the Budget, Policies for Increasing Economic Growth and Employment in 2012 and 2013 (November 15, 2011), pp. 44–52.

[25] One recent paper finds that uncertainty about economic policy (at least uncertainty of the sort generated by widely publicized events such as last year's debate over raising the U.S. debt ceiling) may have had large economic effects. However, interpreting the economic correlations presented in that research requires strong assumptions about how indicators of economic performance and uncertainty are interrelated. See Scott R. Baker, Nicholas Bloom, and Steven Davis, "Measuring Economic Policy Uncertainty" (working paper, Stanford University and the University of Chicago, June 4, 2012), www.policyuncertainty. com/papers.html. For additional analyses, see Mark E. Schweitzer and Scott Shane, "Economic Policy Uncertainty and Small Business Expansion," Economic Commentary, Federal Reserve Bank of Cleveland (November 29, 2011), www.clevelandfed.org/research/ commentary/ 2011/2011-24.pdf; and Lawrence Mishel, Regulatory Uncertainty: A Phony Explanation for Our Jobs Problem, Briefing Paper 330 (Washington, D.C.: Economic Policy Institute, September 27, 2011), www.epi.org/publication/regulatory -uncertainty-phony-explanation.

[26] See Board of Governors of the Federal Reserve System, The July 2012 Senior Loan Officer Opinion Survey on Bank Lending Practices.

[27] At the end of the second quarter of 2012, more than one-fifth of mortgage borrowers were underwater. See CoreLogic, Negative Equity Report (September 12, 2012). For a discussion of policy options, see Mitchell Remy, Deborah Lucas, and Damien Moore, An Evaluation of Large-Scale Mortgage Refinancing Programs, Congressional Budget Office Working Paper 2011-04 (September 2011).

[28] See, for example, Atif Mian, Kamalesh Rao, and Amir Sufi, "Household Balances Sheets, Consumption, and the Economic Slump" (working paper, June 2012), http://ssrn.com/ abstract=1961211.

[29] The effect of mortgage defaults on the recovery is uncertain. Although defaults create losses for investors and hinder households' ability to borrow in the future, defaults also can reduce the portion of households' income going to housing costs, which, all else being equal, boosts consumer spending.

[30] See Karen Dynan, "Is a Household Debt Overhang Holding Back Consumption?" Brookings Papers on Economic Activity (Spring 2012), www.brookings.edu/about/projects/bpea/past-editions.

[31] See, for example, Board of Governors of the Federal Reserve System, The July 2012 Senior Loan Officer Opinion Survey on Bank Lending Practices.

[32] Yields on corporate bonds have fallen to a greater extent during the current recovery than during any past postwar recovery. The resulting lower cost of funding new capital has contributed to the recovery in investment. However, if the Federal Reserve had been able to lower short-term rates further, bond yields would also have fallen further, giving more of a boost to investment.

[33] See William C. Dunkelberg and Holly Wade, NFIB Small Business Economic Trends (Nashville, Tenn.: National Federation of Independent Business Research Foundation, various monthly editions), www.nfib.com/research-foundation/small-business -economic-trends-sbet-archive.

In: Recovery after Recession: Select Research and Analyses ISBN: 978-1-62417-777-4
Editors: Drew Symmes and Amanda Zulpo

Chapter 4

POLICIES FOR INCREASING ECONOMIC GROWTH AND EMPLOYMENT IN 2012 AND 2013. STATEMENT OF DOUGLAS W. ELMENDORF, DIRECTOR, CONGRESSIONAL BUDGET OFFICE. HEARING ON "ECONOMIC EFFECTS OF FISCAL POLICY CHOICES"*

Chairman Conrad, Senator Sessions, and Members of the Committee, thank you for inviting me to testify on the outlook for the economy and policy options for boosting economic output and employment during the next few years.

SUMMARY

The U.S. economy has struggled to recover from the deep recession that began in December 2007 and ended in June 2009. Although total output started to expand again more than two years ago, the pace of the recovery in output and employment has been slow compared with the average recovery since World War II, and the economy remains in a severe slump. The Congressional Budget Office (CBO) expects that, under current law, economic growth will continue to be slow and real (inflation-adjusted) gross domestic product (GDP) will stay well below the economy's potential—a level that corresponds to a high rate of use of labor and capital—for several years. As a result, a large portion of the economic and human costs of the recession and slow recovery remains ahead. Those costs fall disproportionately on people who lose their jobs, who are displaced from their homes, or who own businesses that fail.

The slow recovery of output and employment largely reflects the nature of the recession. The collapse of house prices and the financial crisis—conditions unlike anything this country has seen since the Great Depression—pushed the economy into a deep recession. In the aftermath of such a crisis, it takes time for households to rebuild their wealth and pay down

* This is an edited, reformatted and augmented version of testimony given on November 15, 2011 before the Senate Budget Committee.

their debts, for financial institutions to restore their capital bases and the supply of credit, and for businesses to regain the confidence necessary to invest in new facilities and equipment.

CBO expects real GDP to grow in the vicinity of 11/2 percent this calendar year (as measured by the change between the fourth quarter of 2010 and the fourth quarter of 2011) and around 21/2 percent next year. With modest growth in output, CBO expects employment to expand very slowly during the rest of this year and next year, leaving the unemployment rate close to 9 percent through the end of 2012. Weakness in the demand for goods and services is the principal restraint on hiring, but structural impediments in the labor market—such as a mismatch between the requirements of existing job openings and the characteristics of job seekers (including their skills and geographic location)—appear to be restraining hiring as well.

So that CBO's projections can serve as a benchmark for assessing the impact of legislative proposals, the agency's economic forecast reflects the provisions of current law. Under current law, the expiration of tax cuts and constraints imposed by the recently enacted Budget Control Act of 2011 (Public Law 112-25)—along with automatic changes in the budget as the economy grows (namely, higher tax revenues and lower spending for some income support programs)—will cause federal fiscal policy to significantly restrain economic growth in 2012 and 2013.

Concerns that the economic recovery will continue to be slow and protracted have prompted the consideration of fiscal policy actions to spur economic growth and increase employment during the next few years. Three key criteria for evaluating such actions are:

- Timing—providing help when it is needed;
- Cost-effectiveness—generating a large amount of additional output and employment per dollar cost to the federal budget; and
- Consistency with long-term fiscal objectives—not worsening the long-run budget outlook.

Other considerations include who would be helped the most by the policy; what would be the value to society of any additional goods and services produced; and how uncertain would the outcomes be.[1]

This testimony assesses the potential impact of a variety of temporary fiscal policy actions that might be considered to promote economic growth and increase employment in the near term. CBO estimates that the policies analyzed here would raise real GDP in 2012 and 2013 by an amount ranging from as little as 10 cents per dollar of budgetary cost to as much as $1.90 per dollar of budgetary cost; the impact of the policies on employment would range from a marginal increase to an increase of as much as 19 years of full-time-equivalent (FTE) employment per million dollars of budgetary cost over that two-year span (see Figure 1). Thus, changes in fiscal policy, if appropriately designed, would promote economic growth and increase employment during the next few years.

Comparing the estimated effects of different policy actions shows the following:

- Policies that would have the largest effects on output and employment per dollar of budgetary cost in 2012 and 2013 are ones that would reduce the marginal cost to businesses of adding employees or that would be targeted toward people who would be most likely to spend the additional income. Such policies include reducing employers' payroll taxes (especially if limited to firms that increase their payroll), increasing aid to the unemployed, and providing additional refundable tax credits in 2012 for lower- and middle-income households.

- Policies that would primarily affect businesses' cash flow but would have little impact on their marginal incentives to hire or invest would have only small effects. Such policies include reducing business income taxes and reducing tax rates on repatriated foreign earnings.

Despite the near-term economic benefits that would arise from reductions in taxes and increases in government spending, such actions would add to the already large projected budget deficits, either immediately or over time.

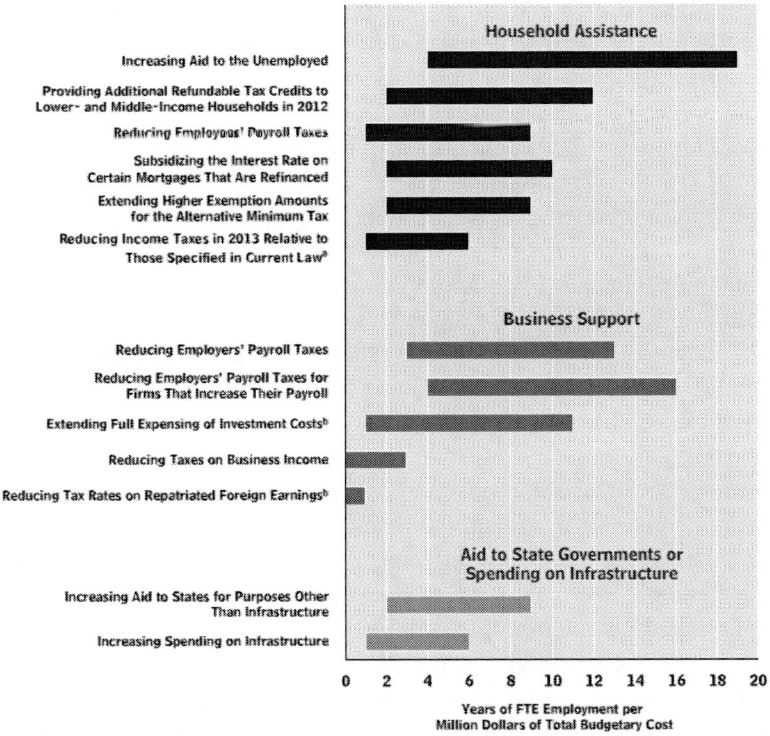

Source: Congressional Budget Office.

Notes: The ranges of estimates were chosen, on a judgmental basis, to encompass most economists' views.

Estimates represent years of full-time-equivalent employment (FTE-years) with a given policy minus FTE-years without the policy. (An FTE-year is 40 hours of employment per week for one year.) Estimates are per million dollars of total budgetary cost, which is the amount of tax revenues or outlays over the full duration of a policy's effects, except as specified in note b below.

All years are calendar years. Unless otherwise specified, increased spending authority is assumed to be available as of January 2012, and tax options are assumed to be in effect only for 2012.

[a] Includes the effects of extending higher exemption amounts for the alternative minimum tax in 2012.

[b] For this option, total budgetary cost is calculated as a discounted present value rather than as the sum of changes in tax revenues over the full duration of the policy's effects.

Figure 1. Ranges of Cumulative Effects of Policy Options on Employment in 2012 and 2013.

Unless offsetting actions were taken to reverse the accumulation of additional government debt, the nation's capital stock, its future output, and people's future incomes would tend to be lower than they otherwise would have been. If policymakers wanted to boost the economy in the near term while seeking to achieve long-term fiscal sustainability, a combination of policies would be required: changes in taxes and spending that would widen the deficit now but reduce it later in the decade. Such an approach would work best if the future policy changes were sufficiently specific and widely supported so that households, businesses, state and local governments, and participants in financial markets believed that the future fiscal restraint would truly take effect.

Lawmakers could also influence economic growth and employment during the next few years by changing policies that do not involve, or whose scope extends well beyond, taxation and government spending.

For example, legislation could modify existing or proposed regulations, significantly alter the government's role in a particular sector of the economy, or change trade relationships with other countries. Other types of policy changes that do not require legislation, such as those related to monetary policy or those that can be implemented by federal agencies under current law, could also affect economic activity, but they are outside the scope of this testimony.

The near-term economic impact of changing a regulation or other policy apart from fiscal policy would depend importantly on how doing so affected businesses' investment and hiring decisions. In addition, changes in policies that increased or decreased households' purchasing power or wealth would influence how much they spend.

Moreover, changes to regulations and other policies could affect expectations about future income or make businesses and households more or less uncertain about future government policies and economic conditions, which would affect economic growth and employment in the near term.

This testimony discusses some potential changes in regulatory policies and other policies related to energy and the environment, the financial and health care sectors, and international trade. But estimating the near-term effects on overall economic activity of such policy changes is exceedingly difficult, and few analytic tools are available for that purpose. Accordingly, CBO did not attempt to quantify the effects of those potential changes with any precision. Some changes in policies that CBO considered would probably raise output and employment during the next few years; other changes would probably lower output and employment; and some changes would have effects on economic activity whose sign is difficult to determine.

However, in CBO's judgment, the economic effects of the specific changes in regulatory policies or other policies apart from fiscal policies that are discussed in this testimony probably would be too small or would occur too slowly to significantly alter overall output or employment in the next two years. (The policy changes examined here are illustrative rather than exhaustive; many others, which might have larger or smaller economic effects, are possible.) This testimony does not speak to other critical considerations in evaluating such policy changes, including the long-term effects on the economy, on people's health, and on the environment.

THE ECONOMIC OUTLOOK

The U.S. economy has struggled to recover from the deep recession that, according to the National Bureau of Economic Research, began in December 2007 and ended in June 2009. Although total output started to expand again more than two years ago, the pace of the recovery in output and employment has been quite slow, and the economy remains in a severe slump. Real GDP in the third quarter of 2011 was about 5 percent below CBO's estimate of its potential—a level that corresponds to a high rate of use of labor and capital. By contrast, 21/4 years after the end of previous recessions since 1948 (except after the brief 1980 recession), real GDP was between 3.2 percent below and 3.8 percent above its potential. CBO expects that, under current law, economic growth will continue to be slow and real GDP will stay well below the economy's potential for several years (see Figure 2).

The Slow Recovery

Real GDP rose by 5.6 percent from the second quarter of 2009 through the third quarter of 2011, roughly retracing its 5.1 percent decline during the recession but falling well short of the average of 12.2 percent growth during the same span (the first nine quarters) in previous recoveries since the end of World War II (see Figure 3, top panel). The slow pace of the recovery is particularly unusual given the severity of the recession. It contrasts sharply with the vigorous recoveries that followed the deep recessions that began in 1973 and 1981; for example, after falling by 3.2 percent during the 1973–1975 recession, real GDP grew by almost 12 percent during the first nine quarters of the subsequent recovery. The modest growth of output can be traced in large part to a weak rebound in consumer spending and continued low levels of homebuilding. Consumer spending has increased more slowly in this recovery than it did, on average, following previous postwar recessions, even though it declined more than usual during the most recent recession. Real investment in residential structures (such as houses and apartment buildings) plunged from 2006 through mid-2009 and has edged down further since the end of the recession; in contrast, increases in such investment have played a key role in most past recoveries. Gains in employment during the recovery have also been much weaker than might have been expected given the sharp drop in employment during the recession and the experience of previous recoveries. After falling by 7.5 million during the recession, employment increased by only about 1 million jobs (or 0.8 percent), on net, between June 2009 and October 2011. By contrast, employment rose by an average of 6.7 percent during the same span in past recoveries (see Figure 3, bottom panel). Moreover, the growth of employment has slowed markedly during the past several months compared with its pace earlier in the year. The total number of jobs increased at an average monthly rate of about 180,000 in the first four months of this year, more than double the average pace in 2010 (see Figure 4); but from May through October, the number of jobs increased at an average monthly rate of only about 90,000.

Consequently, the unemployment rate has fallen by only a small amount. It climbed to 10.1 percent of the labor force in October 2009, approaching the 10.8 percent reached in November and December 1982 (which was the highest rate since 1948, when comparable data first became available), and is still at 9.0 percent (see Figure 5).

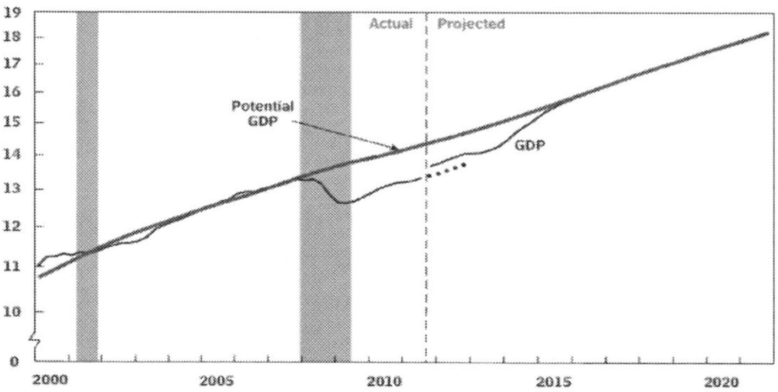

Sources: Congressional Budget Office; Department of Commerce, Bureau of Economic Analysis.

Notes: Real gross domestic product (GDP) is the output of the economy adjusted to remove the effects of inflation. Potential GDP is CBO's estimate of the output that the economy would produce with a high rate of use of its labor and capital resources.

Data are quarterly. Actual data for GDP, which are plotted through the third quarter of 2011, incorporate the July 2011 revisions of the national income and product accounts. The projections of GDP indicated by the solid line are taken from Congressional Budget Office, *The Budget and Economic Outlook: An Update* (August 2011). They are plotted through the fourth quarter of 2021 and are based on data issued before the revisions. The projections of GDP indicated by the dotted line incorporate the effects of the revisions and events since early July, when the previous forecast was completed; they are plotted through the fourth quarter of 2012.

Shaded vertical bars indicate periods of recession.

Figure 2. Real Gross Domestic Product, (Trillions of 2005 dollars, logarithmic scale).

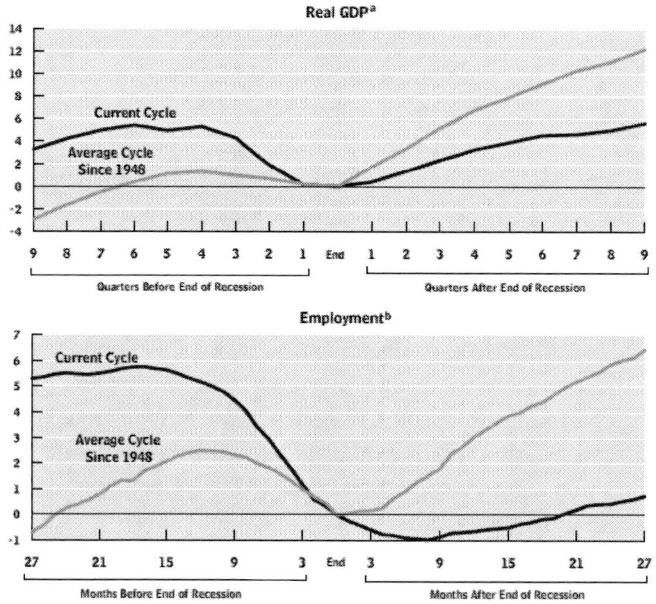

Sources: Congressional Budget Office; Department of Commerce, Bureau of Economic Analysis; Department of Labor, Bureau of Labor Statistics.

Note: The average cycle since 1948 excludes the 1980 cycle (because the subsequent quarters included another recession) and the current cycle.

[a] Real gross domestic product (GDP) is the output of the economy adjusted to remove the effects of inflation.

[b] Employment comprises all nonfarm payroll employees. The data exclude temporary census workers in 1990, 2000, and 2010.

Figure 3. Recovery in Real Gross Domestic Product and Employment, (Percentage difference from value at end of recession).

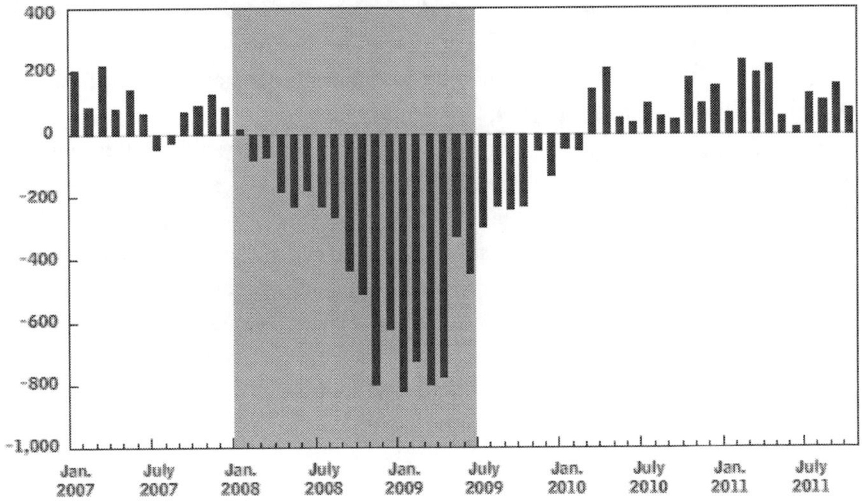

Sources: Congressional Budget Office; Department of Labor, Bureau of Labor Statistics. Notes: Data are monthly and are plotted through October 2011. They exclude temporary jobs associated with the 2010 census.

The shaded vertical bar indicates a period of recession.

Figure 4. Net Job Growth per Month, (Thousands of jobs).

The unemployment rate would have been even higher during the past few years had the size of the labor force not fallen as much as it did. The decline in the labor force is partly owing to a marked rise in the number of unemployed workers who report dropping out of the labor force because they were discouraged about their job prospects. If those discouraged workers were counted as being in the labor force and unemployed, the unemployment rate in October would have been 9.6 percent rather than the actual 9.0 percent; in November 2007, before the recession, counting discouraged workers would have added only about 0.2 percentage points to the reported 4.7 percent unemployment rate.

The weakness of the recovery largely reflects the nature of the recession. An extraordinary surge in house prices and favorable borrowing conditions encouraged an unprecedented run-up in household debt and high levels of home construction and consumer spending relative to income by the mid-2000s. The subsequent plunge in house prices and the financial crisis—conditions unlike anything this country has seen since the Great Depression—pushed the economy into a deep recession. Despite the strong international evidence that recoveries following financial booms and busts tend to be very protracted, the importance of the various factors involved is unclear. For the United States today, the following factors appear to be playing some role:

- The large drop in household wealth before and during the recession and a desire by households to reduce their indebtedness, which is causing them to increase their saving and reduce their spending;
- Difficulty for some households and businesses in obtaining credit because lenders have imposed standards and terms for loans that are generally stricter than those in the years immediately before the recession and, in some instances, stricter even than

those seen in prior years—leading potential borrowers to reduce their consumption and investment;

- A large glut of vacant homes, which has pushed the construction of new homes to the lowest levels since at least 1959;
- Uncertainty and worries about future economic activity and government policies in the United States and about the stability of the European financial system, leading households to spend less and businesses to undertake less investment and hiring;
- The very low level of the interest rate the Federal Reserve usually adjusts to implement monetary policy (the federal funds rate) and a reduced responsiveness of the economy to a decline in interest rates (because of the oversupply of vacant homes and the desire of households to lower their debt)—resulting in less ability for monetary policy to support economic growth; and
- A decreased share of national income going to the compensation of workers, which reduces consumer spending overall.

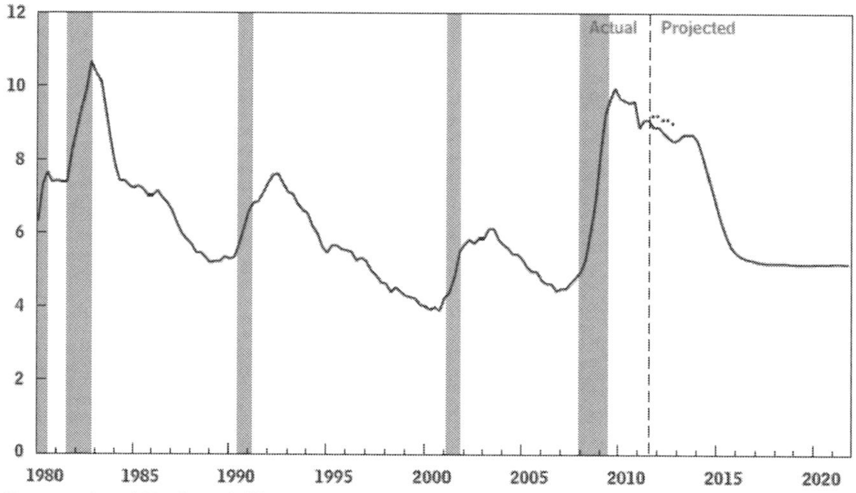

Sources: Congressional Budget Office; Department of Labor, Bureau of Labor Statistics.

Notes: The unemployment rate is a measure of the number of jobless people who are available for work and are actively seeking jobs, expressed as a percentage of the labor force.

Data are quarterly. Actual data are plotted through the third quarter of 2011. The projections indicated by the solid line are taken from Congressional Budget Office, *The Budget and Economic Outlook: An Update* (August 2011) and are plotted through the fourth quarter of 2021. The projections indicated by the dotted line incorporate the effects of events since early July, when the previous forecast was completed; they are plotted through the fourth quarter of 2012.

Shaded vertical bars indicate periods of recession.

Figure 5. Unemployment Rate, (Percent).

The Economic Outlook for 2011 and 2012

CBO expects the pace of economic recovery to remain modest for the next few years if current laws governing taxes and spending remain in effect. Growth slowed and inflation increased in the first half of 2011, in part because of developments that have proved temporary, including jumps in energy and food prices and disruptions to the global supply chain caused by the earthquake and nuclear accident in Japan. As the effects of those developments faded, the U.S. economy rebounded a little, supported by continued strength in business investment, small increases in consumer spending, and expansions in net exports (exports minus imports) and residential investment. Nevertheless, the pace of growth will probably be restrained for several more years by the lingering effects of the financial crisis and the recession and by the path of federal fiscal policy under current law.

Economic Growth and the Labor Market

CBO published its most recent economic forecast in August.[2] The agency initially completed that forecast in early July, and it updated its projections in August to reflect the policy changes enacted in the Budget Control Act of 2011 but no other developments. The news since CBO completed that work suggests that economic growth for the remainder of this year and next is likely to be weaker than the agency anticipated in that forecast—with growth in the vicinity of 11/2 percent this calendar year (as measured by the change between the fourth quarter of 2010 and the fourth quarter of 2011) and around 21/2 percent next year. Other forecasters have also modified their expectations. For example, between early July and early November, the *Blue Chip* consensus forecast (compiled from about 50 forecasts by private-sector economists) for real growth of GDP in 2011 was marked down from 2.6 percent to 1.6 percent. For 2012, the *Blue Chip* forecast was lowered from 3.0 percent to 2.3 percent.

CBO's projections reflect the agency's expectations of modest increases in spending by consumers, continued strong growth in investment by businesses, gains in net exports, and the beginning of a recovery in home construction. CBO expects consumer spending to improve in the near term as the temporary factors such as higher energy prices and supply disruptions fade further, as credit conditions improve more; and as households' net worth slowly increases. Strong growth in business investment will continue, CBO expects, as businesses expand capacity to meet increases in demand for their products. According to the agency's projections, residential construction will also increase in the near term. Still, with an unusually large number of vacant homes, CBO anticipates that it will take several years for the construction of new housing units to return to levels consistent with the growth of the population and the demand for replacement units.

The period since early July that has led many forecasters to lower their projections for near-term growth has included weakness in the financial markets, downward revisions to historical data on GDP, and diminished prospects for world economic growth. Stock prices, as measured by the value of the Standard & Poor's 500 index, fell by about 6 percent between early July and early November, returning to their level of early in the year. The annual revisions to the national income and product accounts and more recent data issued by the Commerce Department show that the economy was weaker from 2008 through mid-2011 than was previously thought. Furthermore, growth slowed in major foreign economies in mid-2011, and the near-term outlook for growth abroad has softened in light of the sovereign debt crisis in Europe.

With modest growth in U.S. output, CBO expects employment to expand very slowly during the rest of this year and next year. Weakness in the demand for goods and services is the principal constraint on hiring, but structural impediments in the labor market—such as a mismatch between the requirements of existing job openings and the characteristics of job seekers (including their skills and geographic location)— appear to be hindering hiring as well. As a result, the unemployment rate is likely to be around 9.0 percent through the fourth quarter of next year. (In CBO's August forecast, the unemployment rate fell to 8.5 percent by the fourth quarter of 2012.) Between early July and early November, the *Blue Chip* consensus similarly raised its forecast for the unemployment rate in the fourth quarter of 2012—from 8.1 percent to 8.9 percent.

Inflation and Interest Rates

Inflation increased markedly in the first half of 2011, spurred largely by a sharp rise in oil prices, but CBO projects that it will diminish in the second half of the year and be low in 2012. The increase in oil prices since late 2010 has been partly reversed, and trading in financial markets points to fairly steady prices for oil and other commodities in the next few years. In addition, the large amount of unused or underemployed resources in the economy will continue to hold down the growth of wages and prices.

CBO projects that the price index for personal consumption expenditures (PCE) will increase by about 21/2 percent this year and by about 11/2 percent next year (as mea-

sured by the change from the fourth quarter of the previous year). The "core" version of the PCE price index, which excludes prices for food and energy, is projected to rise by about 13/4 percent in 2011 and by about 11/2 percent in 2012. The consumer price index for all urban consumers and its core version are expected to increase more rapidly than their PCE counterparts, especially in 2011. CBO currently expects inflation in 2011, as measured by both the PCE price index and the consumer price index, to be higher than the agency forecast in August because gasoline prices have remained high and inflation in housing rents has been higher than projected; expected higher inflation in rents accounts for the upward revision to CBO's outlook for inflation in 2012.

With modest inflation and slow economic growth, interest rates are likely to remain quite low through 2013. The interest rate on 3-month Treasury bills is likely to remain barely above zero, and as indicated by the financial markets, the rate on 10-year Treasury notes will probably remain less than 31/2 percent.

The Output Gap and Its Costs

Economic growth at the rates CBO anticipates will leave a very large and persistent gap between actual output and the agency's estimate of potential output; that is, a large amount of labor and capital resources will be unused for some time. In CBO's August baseline projections, the output gap is about 5 percent of potential GDP at the end of 2011 and does not close fully until the second half of the 2011–2021 projection period.[3]

As a result, a large portion of the economic and human costs of the recession and slow recovery remains ahead. In mid-2011, according to CBO's estimates, the economy was only about halfway through the cumulative shortfall in output relative to its potential level that will result from the recession and the weak recovery. Between late 2007 and mid-2011, the cumulative difference between GDP and estimated potential GDP amounted to roughly $21/2 trillion; by the time the nation's output rises back to its potential level, the cumulative shortfall is expected to equal about $5 trillion.

Not only are the costs associated with the output gap immense, but they are also borne unevenly. Those costs fall disproportionately on people who lose their jobs, who are displaced from their homes, or who own businesses that fail. In the first quarter of 2011, for example, the recession and weak recovery led to a shortfall of about 10 million jobs relative to the number that would have existed had the recession not occurred and had job growth matched the average rate in the previous business cycle. The unemployment rate has now exceeded 8.5 percent for 32 months, the longest such period since 1947, and the number of workers who are employed part time but want full-time work has averaged almost 9 million since early 2009, about double the number before the recession. Moreover, many of those who are unemployed have been out of work for a long time. In October, 42 percent of workers who were unemployed had been out of work for more than 26 weeks and about 30 percent for a year or more—rates of long-term unemployment that are unprecedented in the period following World War II. In addition, although the number of unemployed workers per job opening has fallen significantly since the end of the recession, it still remains much higher than at its peak following the 2001 recession, when the rebound in employment was also unusually slow. Even among workers who find new jobs, experience suggests that many will end up with lower earnings, not only in the short term but for many years to come.[4]

The underutilization of capital and labor resources also affects the federal budget. If the economy was operating at its potential, the projected federal deficit in fiscal year 2012 would be about a third lower, or roughly $630 billion (4.0 percent of GDP) instead of the $973 billion (6.2 percent of GDP) projected in CBO's most recent baseline.[5] If the economy was operating at its potential, people's incomes and federal revenues would be higher, while federal outlays for certain income support programs would be lower.

The Impact of Fiscal Policy

Under current law, federal fiscal policy has provided decreasing support for economic activity this year and will significantly restrain economic growth in 2012 and 2013.[6] One reason for that pattern is that the stimulative impact of the American Recovery and Reinvestment Act (ARRA, P.L. 111-5) is winding down. CBO estimates that relative to what would have happened without that law, ARRA raised real GDP by between 0.7 percent and 4.1 percent in 2010 but is raising GDP by a smaller amount in 2011 and will do so by even less in 2012.[7] ARRA's boost to employment is also diminishing. CBO estimates that the law raised employment (relative to what it would have been otherwise) by between 0.7 million and 3.3 million jobs in 2010, but the law's impact on employment will be progressively smaller in 2011 and 2012.

Economic support provided by federal fiscal policy is also decreasing because the effect of the government's so-called automatic fiscal stabilizers is declining as the economy continues to grow (albeit slowly). Those stabilizers are the automatic responses of revenues and outlays to cyclical movements in real GDP and unemployment. For example, when GDP falls relative to potential GDP during a recession, the reduction in income causes tax revenues to decrease automatically. In addition, some outlays— such as those for unemployment insurance and federal nutrition programs—increase because unemployment rises and more people experience reductions in income, qualifying them to enter existing programs. Those automatic responses provide fiscal support when economic activity slows and provide fiscal restraint when economic activity picks up.[8] Federal fiscal support from the automatic stabilizers equaled roughly 21/2 percent of potential GDP in 2010, CBO estimates, but is likely to be smaller in 2011 and 2012.

In addition, economic support from fiscal policy will diminish as provisions of the Tax Relief, Unemployment Insurance Reauthorization, and Job Creation Act of 2010 (P.L. 111-312, referred to here as the 2010 tax act) expire as scheduled over the next two years and as the Budget Control Act is implemented. In particular:

- The 2010 tax act temporarily extended numerous tax cuts that were slated to expire at the end of 2010 and included new provisions that are also scheduled to expire within the next two years. For example, it continued through December 2012 various tax reductions enacted in the Economic Growth and Tax Relief Reconciliation Act of 2001 (EGTRRA) and the Jobs and Growth Tax Relief Reconciliation Act of 2003 (JGTRRA), and it extended through December 2011 provisions limiting the reach of the alternative minimum tax (AMT).[9] It also reduced the employee's share of the Social Security payroll tax in 2011, provided temporary tax incentives for business investment, and extended certain additional unemployment insurance benefits through January 3, 2012.
- The Budget Control Act set caps on discretionary appropriations that will reduce discretionary spending in real terms over time. It also created a Congressional Joint Select Committee on Deficit Reduction, whose stated goal is to propose further policy changes that would save at least $1.5 trillion over 10 years. If, by January 15, 2012, legislation originating from that committee and projected to achieve at least $1.2 trillion in deficit reduction over the next 10 years is not enacted, automatic procedures established by the new law will reduce spending between fiscal years 2013 and 2021 by the difference between $1.2 trillion and any savings that are achieved by enacting proposals from the committee. That spending reduction (with an allowance for interest savings subtracted) would be distributed evenly among those fiscal years.

CBO estimates that the fiscal restraint stemming from the expiration of provisions in the 2010 tax act and from enactment of the Budget Control Act—including $1.2 trillion in deficit reduction from legislation originating from the deficit reduction committee or from automatic spending cuts—will decrease real GDP in 2013 by between about 11/2 percent and about 31/2 percent compared with what it would have been otherwise.[10] However, CBO also estimates that the reduction in deficits resulting from those policies will boost output later in the decade.

Future fiscal policy is likely to differ from that embodied in current law in at least some respects, and those differences could have a significant impact on the economy. For example, the Congress might enact legislation from the deficit reduction committee that includes a different composition of policy changes or different timing for them than CBO has assumed in its baseline budget projections, or the Congress might alter fiscal policy in other ways. To illustrate how some widely anticipated changes to current law would affect the economy, CBO has examined an alternative path for fiscal policy that includes these assumptions: Most of the provisions of individual income taxes and estate and gift taxes now scheduled to expire in December 2012 are extended through 2021; limits to the reach of the AMT that are set to expire at the end of 2011 are also continued through 2021; and Medicare's payment rates for physicians are maintained at their 2011 levels. (Those possible changes to current law would be a continuation of current policies that have previously been extended; they do not represent a prediction or recommendation about future policies.) Under that set of policies, budget deficits would be significantly larger than those in CBO's baseline budget projections, and federal debt held by the public would accumulate much more rapidly.

Under those alternative assumptions, real GDP would be higher in the first few years of the projection period than it is in CBO's economic forecast. For example, CBO estimates that real GDP in 2013 would be between 0.6 percent and 2.3 percent greater than projected under current law. Faster GDP growth would result in a lower unemployment rate in 2013 by between 0.3 percentage points and 1.1 percentage points; it would also result in somewhat higher interest rates that year—the rate on 10-year Treasury notes would be 20 to 30 basis points higher.[11] In later years, however, real GDP would fall below the level in CBO's baseline projections by ever larger amounts over time. The lower marginal tax rates under those alternative assumptions would increase people's incentives to work and save, but the larger budget deficits would reduce ("crowd out") private investment in productive uses of capital. By the end of 2021, as the effect of larger budget deficits outweighed that of lower tax rates, real GDP would be between 0.3 percent and 1.9 percent smaller than it would be under current law, CBO estimates.[12] In years beyond 2021, the impact of the alternative assumptions in reducing real GDP relative to the amounts under current law would increase.

Uncertainty in the Economic Outlook

Economic forecasts are always subject to a considerable degree of uncertainty, but the current uncertainty surrounding the economic outlook is especially great because the present business cycle has been unusual in a variety of ways. CBO constructs its economic forecasts to be in the middle of the distribution of possible future outcomes for the economy under an assumption that current law remains unchanged. Many developments could cause economic outcomes to differ substantially, in one direction or the other, from those CBO has projected. Key areas of uncertainty in the economic outlook include the following factors:

- The degree to which households want to increase their savings and further reduce their debt burdens,
- The ways in which lenders adjust their standards and terms for borrowing,
- The pace at which firms hire and invest,
- The timing and magnitude of a recovery in the housing market,
- The evolution of people's and businesses' confidence about the path of the economy,
- Changes in stock prices and long-term interest rates,
- The resolution of concerns that some European governments may default on their debts, and
- The path of U.S. fiscal policy.

Different outcomes for those factors could combine to have quite divergent effects: from boosting the growth of the U.S. economy significantly to causing a new recession, or producing some result in between.

Selected Fiscal Policy Options for Increasing Economic Growth and Employment in 2012 and 2013

The weakness of the economic recovery to date and the high levels of unemployment projected by most forecasters for the next few years have spurred ongoing discussions among analysts and policymakers about what steps the federal government might take to boost growth and employment. Some possible actions involve changes in tax or spending policies; others involve changes in regulatory policies or other policies.

To aid the Congress in the assessment of policy alternatives, CBO has estimated the effects of a variety of changes in tax and spending policies on output and employment over the next two years. The policy options that CBO analyzed would affect the economy in three different ways:

- Primarily by boosting households' disposable income,
- Primarily by providing support to businesses, and
- By increasing aid to state governments or government spending on infrastructure.

CBO estimated that the policy options it considered would range in their potential effect on GDP in 2012 and 2013 from raising it by as little as 10 cents per dollar of budgetary cost to increasing it by as much as $1.90 per dollar of budgetary cost. The largest feasible magnitude of the total budgetary cost varies among the policies, but all of the options considered are sufficiently scalable such that they could involve at least $10 billion of spending increases or tax cuts in 2012 and 2013. Some fiscal policies that would have little effect on the budget in 2012 and 2013 could nonetheless significantly affect output and employment in those years. For example, large changes to tax or spending policies that were enacted today and were scheduled to take effect in 2014 could affect the behavior of households and firms right away. However, this analysis does not include any fiscal policy options of that sort.

Considerations in Designing Fiscal Policy

Some policymakers and analysts have advocated near-term reductions in taxes or increases in federal spending to boost output and employment in the next few years. At the same time, many are concerned about the prospect of a further rise in federal debt. There is no inherent contradiction, however, between using fiscal policy to support the economy today, while unemployment is high and many factories and offices are underused, and imposing fiscal restraint some years from now, when output and employment will probably be close to their potential.[13]

Even without any additional policy action, market forces will ultimately bring output and employment back to their potential. Before that occurs, however, many workers will remain or will become unemployed, and much capacity of facilities and equipment will be unused. Those unemployed workers and unused capital resources represent a waste of the economy's ability to produce goods and services, and the production that is lost cannot be made up later. Increased private and public spending during this period would employ those resources and raise the economy's production. After the economy has returned to its potential, the constraint on output will be the economy's capacity to produce goods and services, which depends on the stock of productive capital, the quantity and quality of labor, and the efficiency with which those resources are combined. Over that longer term, the more that households, businesses, and governments save, the more that can be invested in productive capital, which is why economists tend to emphasize the long-term benefits of saving relative to spending.

The current challenge for policymakers is that the reductions in taxes and increases in federal spending that would boost demand for goods and services in the short term would also increase government debt, which in turn would reduce the capital stock in the long term. Moreover, if people believed that policy changes that increased near-term deficits presaged larger deficits in the future and thus that the federal budget outlook had become even bleaker, the economy could be hurt in the near term by a faltering of business and consumer confidence and an increase in interest rates. Therefore, if policymakers wanted to use fiscal policy to provide a short-term economic boost without hindering the economy later, a combination of policies would be required: changes in taxes and spending that would widen the deficit now but reduce it later in the decade.

In evaluating fiscal policy that is intended to boost demand in the short term, three important considerations are whether the policy change is *timely*—providing help when it is needed; *cost-effective*—generating a large amount of additional output and employment per dollar cost to the federal budget; and *consistent with long-run fiscal objectives*—not worsening the long-run budget outlook.[14] Other considerations include the distribution of benefits among different people, the social value of additional goods and services that would be produced, and uncertainty about a policy's effectiveness.

Timing

Fiscal policies differ greatly in how quickly they would affect the demand for goods and services, and some measures might take effect too slowly in two respects. First, they might miss the period of greatest need in terms of both unemployment and unused capacity. Second, they might persist while the amount of unemployment and excess capacity dropped into a range where the risk of pushing up inflation could be more significant.

Current law implies significant fiscal restraint in 2012 and 2013. Because of that restraint and the other factors slowing the recovery, CBO projects that the unemployment rate will remain close to 9 percent through the end of 2012; at that level, it will be about 3 percentage points above the agency's estimate of the rate that could be reached without raising the rate of inflation.[15] Additional policy actions that had their greatest impact during the next few years would affect the economy when its output will probably be well below its potential, the risk of greater weakness remains elevated, and the risk of excessive inflation is low. If widely anticipated changes to current law, such as an extension of tax cuts that are scheduled to expire under current law, were enacted, economic growth would be notably stronger in 2013, according to CBO's projections. However, even under those alternative policies, the economy would still be considerably below potential over the next few years.

Certain decreases in taxes or increases in federal spending could be implemented fairly quickly, and households, businesses, and other levels of government might respond with changes in their own spending fairly quickly as well. However, other changes in taxes or government spending might affect the economy only with considerable lags. For example, larger increases in funding for government activities tend to be spent more slowly than smaller increases, and many public infrastructure projects—which require extensive planning and coordination among different levels of government— take some time to implement.

Cost-Effectiveness

Possible reductions in taxes or increases in federal spending differ in the extent to which they would boost spending by households, businesses, and governments per dollar of budgetary cost. Cost-effectiveness can be assessed by the cumulative dollar effect on output and employment per dollar of budgetary cost.

Households

Tax cuts and government transfers to individuals increase households' disposable income. The cost-effectiveness of such policies depends on the fraction of the additional income that is spent on purchasing goods and services. Measures targeting households facing financial problems, such as those that have low income or unemployed members, tend to have larger impacts on spending and thus are more cost-effective. By contrast, measures that are less well targeted, such as across-the-board reductions in income tax rates or broad tax rebates, provide large parts of their relief to people who are less constrained financially. Such people are likely to save much of a tax reduction, especially if it is temporary. In that case, the policy would be less cost-effective in boosting output and employment in the short run.

Businesses

Some policies seek to encourage business spending by providing incentives for new investment, such as allowing firms to "expense" their investment costs for tax purposes—that is, to deduct the cost of an investment in the year it is made. Those policies increase firms' after-tax return on investment by reducing the present value of taxes, and they increase firms' cash flow for the year in which the new investment is made. The success of such incentives in encouraging spending probably depends on the economic conditions when the incentives are in effect: A reduction in the cost of capital is likely to have less effect on a business's decision to buy new machinery if demand for the business's output is so low that the machinery would get little use. Several studies suggest that the impact of being able to expense investment costs in the early 2000s, when demand was weak, was modest.[16]

Other fiscal policies encourage hiring by temporarily or permanently reducing the cost of labor. The cost-effectiveness of those policies depends on firms' responses to the benefits received: whether they pass the benefits on to customers in the form of lower prices, to employees in the form of higher wages, or implicitly to shareholders by retaining them as profits—and how much they increase hiring and hours worked during a period when labor is temporarily less expensive.

Government

The federal government can boost demand by increasing its own purchases of goods and services or by providing funds to state and local governments. Purchases by the federal government tend to be cost-effective in terms of the number of jobs generated per dollar of budgetary cost because they involve direct purchases from firms or the hiring of workers. Federal grants to state and local governments can increase total demand by inducing those governments to keep their taxes lower, or their transfer payments and purchases of goods and services higher, than they would otherwise. However, if greater federal aid simply leads state and local governments to borrow less, with no effect on their taxes or spending, then it does not increase demand in the short run.[17]

In the current economic environment, additional federal aid to state and local governments would probably reduce the size of tax increases and spending cuts enacted by those jurisdictions to balance their budgets. The amount of state and local budget cutting has been very large in recent years, despite the additional federal aid provided through ARRA and other legislation, and would probably have been even larger without such additional aid. For example, employment by state and local governments has fallen by nearly 650,000 since its peak in August 2008. Heading into fiscal year 2012 (which began in July for most states), 38 states faced projected budget shortfalls; of those, 21 states faced imbalances of 10 percent or more of their general fund spending. Although states made changes to their policies to eliminate those near-term gaps, a number of states are already projecting shortfalls for the next few years.[18]

Consistency with Long-Run Fiscal Objectives

In large part because of the weak economy and actions the government has taken in response, the budget deficit has been larger relative to GDP during the past three years than in any other years since 1945. As a result, debt held by the public at the end of fiscal year 2011 was 68 percent of GDP—the highest since 1950 and up from 40 percent at the end of 2008. Under current law, deficits are projected to drop markedly as a share of GDP over the next few years. However, current law provides for substantial changes to tax and spending policies in coming years. If those changes did not occur and current policies were continued instead, much larger deficits and much greater debt would result.[19]

If taxes were cut permanently or government spending was increased permanently, and no other changes were made to fiscal policy, the economy would suffer in the medium term and long term as the federal debt mounted. Indeed, if people believed that policy changes that increased near-term deficits would also widen budget deficits in subsequent years, the economy could be hurt in the near term by a weakening of business and consumer confidence and an increase in interest rates. Moreover, even if tax cuts or spending increases were temporary, the additional debt accumulated during that temporary period would weigh on the budget and the economy over time.

Therefore, if policymakers wanted to achieve both a short-term economic boost and longer-term fiscal sustainability, a combination of policies would be required: changes in taxes and spending that would widen the deficit now but reduce it later in the decade. Such an approach would work best if the future policy changes were sufficiently specific and widely supported so that households, businesses, state and local governments, and participants in financial markets believed that the future fiscal restraint would truly take effect.

Other Considerations

Other considerations also are relevant for decisions about fiscal policies to promote economic growth and employment in the near term—for example, who would be helped the most by the new policies. Different sorts of spending increases and tax reductions would provide direct benefits to different people and firms. Such distributional considerations are not analyzed in this testimony.

Another consideration involves the types of additional goods and services that society would produce and from which it would realize benefits. Some analysts have argued that countercyclical fiscal policy should be evaluated on the basis of how well it recreates the composition of total spending that would be achieved in the absence of other constraints on policy.[20] Other observers have offered their own analyses and judgments about what sorts of additional goods and services would be most valuable for society. The key point is that fiscal policies can be judged not only on their contribution to growth and job creation in the near term but also on the extent to which they accomplish other goals.

A third consideration involves the combination of policies that might be chosen. Most economists agree that fiscal policies can boost demand during economic downturns and help smooth business cycles. However, some economists are skeptical about the efficacy of such policies and the magnitude of their effects. One benefit of a diversified portfolio of policies is that the overall effect on the economy would be less uncertain than with a single policy. Moreover, the benefits of such a portfolio of policies might spread more widely among different groups in the population and thus accomplish a larger variety of goals.

CBO's Analytical Approach

CBO assessed the potential of selected fiscal policy options for promoting economic growth and increasing employment.[21] The policy options would work somewhat differently depending on whether they sought to support spending by households, businesses, or governments:

- Policy options aimed at assisting households would spur demand for goods and services to varying degrees and thereby boost production to varying degrees. Because businesses' decisions on investing and hiring depend on the demand for their products, greater demand and production would lead to more investment and hiring. The size of those effects would depend largely on which households paid less in taxes or received more in benefits.
- Policy options that supported businesses would operate somewhat differently. Certain policies would reduce labor costs or the cost of investment, which would spur hiring and investment and in turn increase production and household income. The rise in income would support consumer demand and increase production by other firms.
- Additional government spending for goods and services would also boost output and employment, both directly (through the government-funded activity) and indirectly (through increases in consumer demand for goods and services resulting from the higher income of the households and firms that directly benefited from the government activity).

For this analysis, fiscal policy options were assumed to be temporary by design— that is, to be in effect for specific time periods or for specific dollar amounts. However, some options that would extend policies currently in place might be viewed as permanent by the beneficiaries. Alternatively, policies could also be designed to be permanent.

The analysis of each fiscal policy option presented in this testimony focuses on how it would affect output and employment. For each option, CBO used evidence from empirical studies and econometric models to estimate the impact on:

- Output—the cumulative effects on GDP per dollar of total budgetary cost (measured in terms of additional government spending or reduction in taxes), and
- Employment—the cumulative effects on years of full-time-equivalent employment (FTE-years) per million dollars of total budgetary cost.

Those effects were estimated for 2012 and for 2012 and 2013 together. The approach adopted to measure the effects of policies is similar to the method that CBO has used to assess the effects of ARRA.[22]

Estimated impacts on output include the direct and indirect effects of a dollar's worth of a given policy. Direct effects consist of immediate effects on economic activity. For example, government purchases of goods and services directly elicit economic activity and thereby have a direct dollar-for-dollar impact on output. Indirect effects may enhance or offset the direct effects. For example, if the economy has idle resources, as it does now, government funding for projects can lead to the hiring of otherwise unemployed workers. The additional spending by those workers, who now would have more income, would constitute a positive indirect effect. In contrast, a substantial increase in government spending financed by borrowing tends to drive up interest rates, which discourages spending on investment and on durable goods by raising the cost of borrowed funds. Those indirect crowding-out effects would offset some of the direct effects. Low and high estimates of the effects on output for a given policy were chosen, on a judgmental basis, to encompass most economists' views about the effects of that type of policy.

Fiscal policies may also affect spending by altering uncertainty or confidence about future economic conditions or government policies. For example, many firms appear to be uncertain today about future demand for their products, and that uncertainty seems to be leading them to be cautious about increasing their investment and hiring. Fiscal policy actions that boosted demand might help dissipate that uncertainty and increase employment.[23] However, some fiscal policy actions might exacerbate uncertainty about future government policies—for example, if firms' managers wondered whether a temporary policy might later be extended or what other changes in fiscal policy might be made later. Because quantifying reactions of this sort to changes in fiscal policy would be extremely difficult, the analysis in this testimony does not incorporate such reactions.

The monetary policy of the Federal Reserve has an important influence on the economic effects of changes in taxes and government spending. On the basis of the economic conditions that CBO projects and the stated intentions of the Federal Reserve, in this analysis CBO assumed that, through 2013, the Federal Reserve would not reduce the amount of support to economic activity it was providing through its own policies (such as decisions about setting the federal funds rate and using other tools) to offset any additional output and employment generated by fiscal policy. In contrast, under more normal economic conditions, CBO estimates, changes in interest rates would offset roughly two-thirds of the cumulative short-term impact on GDP of changes in fiscal policy.

To assess a policy's impact on employment, CBO used a series of steps to translate the estimated effects on output into estimated effects on FTE-years. First, CBO calculated the impact on the output gap—the percentage difference between actual output and potential output. Next, CBO calculated the magnitude and timing of effects of changes in the output gap on productivity, hours per worker, and the unemployment rate using the historical relationships between those measures. Changes in the output gap affect unemployment gradually over several quarters. Initially, part of a rise in output shows up as higher productivity and hours per worker rather than as reduced unemployment. CBO also took account of the effect on the size of the labor force of changes in employment, because discouraged workers and people who have chosen to pursue activities such as schooling rather than work tend to return to the labor force when unemployment declines and the economic environment improves.

Measuring the impact on employment per million dollars of budgetary cost in FTE-years (each being 40 hours of employment per week for one year) incorporated the effects of policies on hours worked in addition to their impact on the number of people who would be employed. Projected increases in the average number of people employed during a year do not include shifts from part-time to full-time work or overtime and are generally somewhat smaller than increases in FTE-years.

CBO's estimates imply that, for most policy options, one year of FTE employment is created for roughly every $110,000 in additional GDP. Therefore, if a policy increases cumulative GDP by one dollar per dollar of budgetary cost, one year of FTE employment is created for roughly $110,000 in budgetary cost. Policy options with smaller effects on GDP require more budgetary resources to generate a given amount of employment, and those with larger effects on GDP require less budgetary resources.[24]

In this analysis, CBO considered each policy in isolation. Certain combinations of policies could have larger effects per dollar of budgetary cost than those reported here. For example, undertaking a policy with a relatively large effect on output per dollar of budgetary cost and cutting back by an equal amount on an existing policy with a smaller effect on output per dollar of budgetary cost would increase output and employment in the short run at no net budgetary cost.

The effects on output and employment estimated in this analysis differ from those estimated in CBO's January 2010 analysis for several reasons:[25]

- First, as a result of its ongoing review of relevant research, CBO has reduced the lower end of its range of estimates of the short-term effects of changes in fiscal policy on output and employment, while leaving the upper end of the range unchanged.
- Second, for the earlier analysis, CBO assumed that policies beginning in 2010 would take effect in March of that year; for this analysis, CBO assumed that policies beginning in 2012 would take effect in January. The earlier implementation tends to increase the estimated economic effects in the first year.
- Third, at the time of the January 2010 analysis, CBO projected that the Federal Reserve would begin to tighten monetary policy by the fourth quarter of 2011 and therefore would be more likely to tighten further by that point in response to the changes in fiscal policy. Because of the ongoing weakness of the economy, CBO now projects that the Federal Reserve will not begin to tighten monetary policy until the first quarter of 2014. Because the Federal Reserve is assumed to not respond to

fiscal policy changes for a longer period, the estimated economic effects of such policy changes are greater.[26]

- Finally, specific changes were made in the analysis of certain options. Those changes are noted in the presentation of results for those options.

Fiscal Policy Options for Assisting Households

Policies that would temporarily increase the after-tax income of people who are relatively well off would probably have little effect on their spending because they are able to consume out of their current income or assets. However, policies that increased the resources of families with lower income, few assets, and poor credit would probably have a larger impact on their spending. Because of the extent of job losses and declines in asset prices in this economic downturn, more families probably have those attributes now than was the case in the immediate aftermath of many previous recessions. CBO analyzed the following fiscal policy options that would affect the economy primarily by assisting households:

- Increasing aid to the unemployed,
- Providing additional refundable tax credits to lower- and middle-income households in 2012,
- Reducing employees' payroll taxes,
- Subsidizing the interest rate on certain mortgages that are refinanced,
- Extending higher exemption amounts for the alternative minimum tax, and
- Reducing income taxes in 2013 relative to those specified in current law.

Increasing Aid to the Unemployed

Under current law, some people who exhaust their unemployment benefits are eligible to begin receiving additional weeks of benefits through emergency unemployment compensation (EUC) through January 3, 2012. (Benefits will begin to phase out after that date, with no EUC being paid after May 2012.) EUC currently provides up to 53 weeks of additional benefits (depending on the unemployment rate in one's state) after regular state benefits (which generally last up to 26 weeks) have been exhausted. The policy option analyzed by CBO would provide further assistance to the unemployed by extending the date by which individuals can start to receive EUC by a year—to January 3, 2013; under this option, no added benefits would be paid after May 2013. Extending additional unemployment benefits would directly help those who would otherwise exhaust their unemployment benefits during calendar year 2012. Households receiving unemployment benefits tend to spend the additional benefits quickly, making this option both timely and cost-effective in spurring demand for goods and services, and thereby economic activity and employment. In addition to increasing aggregate demand, extending additional unemployment benefits would also influence the labor market in other ways. Extending those benefits would encourage some people to continue to seek employment in order to collect benefits rather than dropping out of the labor force, but it would also reduce the intensity of some workers' efforts to search for a new job because the higher benefits would lessen the hardship of being unemployed. Both of those effects of the benefit extensions would tend to increase the unemployment rate. However, many jobs that were not sought by workers receiving unemployment insurance would go instead to individuals who were not eligible for such benefits (such as new entrants to the labor force) and might otherwise be unemployed themselves, so the net impact on the unemployment rate from some workers' reduced efforts to find a job would be slight. In addition, other effects of extending unemployment benefits would boost employment. For example, some of the unemployed who would otherwise have dropped out of the labor force and instead continue job hunting in order to collect benefits would find jobs. In addition, because unemployment insurance can facilitate mobility to new occupations by providing a safety net if job transitions do not work out, it may also lead to better matches between workers and jobs. In CBO's assessment, the various effects of extending additional unemployment benefits *apart from* the effects on the overall demand for goods and services would, on balance, increase the measured unemployment rate (primarily by keeping workers in the labor force) but have little effect on the number of people employed. Accordingly, CBO's estimates of the impact of this policy option on output and employment include only the effects of boosting demand for goods and services. CBO estimates that this policy option would raise output cumulatively in 2012 and 2013 by $0.40 to $1.90 per dollar of total budgetary cost (see Table 1). CBO also estimates that the policies would add 4 to 19 cumulative years of FTE employment in 2012 and 2013 per million dollars of total budgetary cost.

Providing Additional Refundable Tax Credits for Lower- and Middle-Income Households in 2012

Some tax credits are refundable—that is, the government makes cash payments to people for whom the credit exceeds their income tax liability. The Economic Stimulus Act of 2008 included a particular type of refundable tax credit, one that was prepaid via checks mailed to households. ARRA also contained several provisions regarding refundable tax credits, including the Making Work Pay credit. CBO analyzed a policy similar to the credit in the Economic Stimulus Act that would result in payments to households during the last three quarters of 2012.[27] Refundable credits are often phased out when income is above some amount and thus are effectively limited to lower- and middle- income households. Moreover, credits that are refundable provide a larger income boost to those households than do comparable credits that are not refundable, because lower-income households are more likely not to owe income tax. Therefore, providing additional refundable credits would increase after-tax income for households that are more likely than average to be restricted in their consumption by their current income and hence would spend a greater share of the funds received. As a result, providing such credits would increase output and employment by more per dollar of budgetary cost than would cutting taxes for a broader set of taxpayers whose consumption is less likely to be restrained by their current income. CBO estimates that providing additional refundable tax credits would raise output cumulatively in 2012 and 2013 by $0.20 to $1.20 per dollar of total budgetary cost. CBO also estimates that the policy would add 2 to 12 cumulative years of FTE employment in 2012 and 2013 per million dollars of total budgetary cost.

Reducing Employees' Payroll Taxes

Social Security, which consists of Old-Age, Survivors, and Disability Insurance (OASDI), is financed by payroll taxes. Under current law, in 2012 and subsequent years, both employers and employees will pay 6.2 percent of the employees' annual earnings in Social Security payroll taxes up to a ceiling ($110,100 in 2012). For 2011, that rate was temporarily reduced to 4.2 percent for employees. This option would extend that tax reduction through the end of 2012. A temporary reduction in employees' portion of the payroll tax would not immediately affect employers' costs. Instead, it would increase workers' disposable income. The increase in take-home pay would spur additional spending by the households receiving the higher income, and that higher spending would, in turn, increase production and employment. Those effects would be spread over time, however, and CBO expects that the majority of the temporary increase in take-home pay would be saved rather than spent.

Table 1. Estimated Effects of Fiscal Policy Options on Output and Employment

	Cumulative Effects on GDP[a] (Dollars per dollar of total budgetary cost)		Cumulative Effects on Employment[b] (Years of FTE employment per million dollars of total budgetary cost)	
	2012	2012–2013	2012	2012–2013
	Household Assistance			
Increasing Aid to the Unemployed	0.4 to 1.5	0.4 to 1.9	3 to 11	4 to 19
Providing Additional Refundable Tax Credits to Lower- and Middle-Income Households in 2012	0.2 to 1.0	0.2 to 1.2	2 to 8	2 to 12
Reducing Employees' Payroll Taxes	0.1 to 0.6	0.1 to 0.9	1 to 5	1 to 9
Subsidizing the Interest Rate on Certain Mortgages That Are Refinanced	0.1 to 0.5	0.2 to 1.1	1 to 3	2 to 10
Extending Higher Exemption Amounts for the Alternative Minimum Tax	*	0.2 to 1.1	**	2 to 9
Reducing Income Taxes in 2013 Relative to Those Specified in Current Law[c]	*	0.1 to 0.6	**	1 to 6
	Business Support			
Reducing Employers' Payroll Taxes	0.2 to 0.8	0.2 to 1.3	2 to 6	3 to 13
Reducing Employers' Payroll Taxes for Firms That Increase Their Payroll	0.2 to 0.8	0.2 to 1.3	3 to 8	4 to 16
Extending Full Expensing of Investment Costs[d]	0.1 to 0.7	0.1 to 1.1	1 to 5	1 to 11
Reducing Taxes on Business Income	* to 0.2	* to 0.3	** to 1	** to 3
Reducing Tax Rates on Repatriated Foreign Earnings[d]	* to 0.1	* to 0.2	** to 1	** to 1
	Aid to State Governments or Spending on Infrastructure			
Increasing Aid to States for Purposes Other Than Infrastructure	0.1 to 0.5	0.2 to 1.0	1 to 4	2 to 9
Increasing Spending on Infrastructure	0.1 to 0.2	0.1 to 0.7	0 to 1	1 to 6

Source: Congressional Budget Office.

Notes: The ranges of estimates were chosen, on a judgmental basis, encompass most economists' views. Total budgetary cost is the amount of tax revenues or outlays over the full duration of a policy's effects, except as specified in note d below. All years are calendar years. Unless otherwise specified, increased spending authority is assumed to be available as of January 2012, and tax options are assumed to be in effect only for 2012.

GDP= gross domestic product; FTE = full-time-equivalent; * = between zero and 0.05; ** = between zero and 0.5.

[a] Estimated as GDP with a given policy minus GDP without the policy.

[b] Estimated as years of FTE employment (FTE-years) with a given policy minus FTE-years without the policy. (An FTE-year is 40 hours of employment per week for one year.)

[c] Includes the effects of extending higher exemption amounts for the alternative minimum tax in 2012.

[d] For this option, total budgetary cost is calculated as a discounted present value rather than as the sum of changes in tax revenues over the full duration of the policy's effects.

CBO estimates that reducing employees' payroll taxes would raise output cumulatively in 2012 and 2013 by $0.10 to $0.90 per dollar of total budgetary cost. CBO also estimates that the policy would add one to nine cumulative years of FTE employment in 2012 and 2013 per million dollars of total budgetary cost.

Subsidizing the Interest Rate on Certain Mortgages That Are Refinanced

Numerous policy changes have been proposed to provide additional government support to the mortgage and housing markets and thereby boost overall output and employment. Some of those policy changes could be implemented by the Federal Reserve, Fannie Mae, Freddie Mac, or federal agencies under current law, while other proposed changes could require legislative action.

One area of concern among analysts is that, although mortgage rates have fallen to historically low levels, the volume of mortgage refinancing remains low for a number of reasons. One is that many homeowners owe more on their existing mortgages than their homes are worth, so a refinanced mortgage with the same principal balance would not meet the loan-to-value standard required by Fannie Mae and Freddie Mac for guaranteeing new mortgages. Another is that lenders are reluctant to refinance mortgages because of the liabilities associated with closing new loans (generally called representations and warranties), limits on their ability to process large numbers of applications in a cost-effective manner, and difficulties arising from borrowers' second liens and mortgage insurance.

There have been a number of proposals for federal programs to provide refinancing opportunities to more mortgage borrowers. In 2009, the Administration created the Home Affordable Refinance Program (HARP) with that objective, and in October 2011, it announced an expansion of the program.[28] HARP allows borrowers with an existing mortgage guaranteed by Fannie Mae or Freddie Mac to refinance their mortgage with a streamlined underwriting process and relaxed eligibility criteria compared with standard mortgage refinancing terms. Policymakers could increase the impact of HARP by subsidizing the mortgage interest rate that participants pay. Such a subsidy would boost participation in the program and lower monthly mortgage payments for all borrowers who participate. CBO analyzed a policy that would provide a 0.25 percentage-point interest rate subsidy for the refinancing of loans during 2012 under the terms that are expected to apply under the newly expanded HARP.

That policy would lead more people to refinance their mortgages at lower interest rates. Those households would benefit from lower monthly mortgage payments, freeing up additional income for other purchases. The lenders and investors who hold those mortgages (directly or through mortgage-backed securities) would see those assets drop in value and would decrease their spending in response. However, that reduction in spending would be less than the increase in spending by borrowers for three reasons: Some of the holders of mortgages are institutions that are part of, or under the control of, the federal government (such as the Treasury Department, the Federal Reserve, Fannie Mae, and Freddie Mac); some of the holders are foreign citizens or institutions; and the private-sector holders in the United States generally would reduce their current spending by only a small share of the loss in their wealth. In addition, the reduction in mortgage payments for people who refinance would reduce the probability of their defaulting on their payments in the future, which would benefit both borrowers and lenders.[29]

The budgetary cost of this policy would include the subsidy itself as well as the effects of the decline in the value of mortgage-backed securities held by the Treasury, the Federal Reserve, and government-sponsored enterprises such as Fannie Mae.[30] However, that cost would be partly offset by the resulting decrease in the number of loan defaults, which would reduce the cost to the government of making good on loan guarantees. CBO estimates that this policy would affect about 250 mortgages per million dollars of budgetary cost.

CBO estimates that adding this interest rate subsidy to HARP would raise output cumulatively in 2012 and 2013 by $0.20 to $1.10 per dollar of total budgetary cost.[31] CBO also estimates that the policy would add 2 to 10 cumulative years of FTE employment in 2012 and 2013 per million dollars of total budgetary cost.

Extending Higher Exemption Amounts for the Alternative Minimum Tax

The AMT was originally intended to impose taxes on high-income individuals who used tax preferences to greatly reduce or eliminate their liability under the regular income tax. For most of its existence, the AMT has played a minor role in the tax system, accounting for less than 2 percent of revenues from the individual income tax and affecting fewer than 1 percent of taxpayers in any year before 2000. However, unlike the regular income tax, the AMT is not indexed for inflation. As a result, the AMT will affect significantly larger numbers of taxpayers over time under current law, and lawmakers have acted repeatedly since 2001 to slow the expansion of the AMT and prevent it from affecting more taxpayers outside of higher-income groups. At the expiration of each of those "patches," the exemptions have been scheduled to revert to their prior-law levels, so the prospective year-to-year change in tax revenues from maintaining current law regarding the AMT has become larger each year. The current AMT patch expires at the end of December 2011. Hence, in 2012, under current law, the AMT will affect about 18 percent of taxpayers (up from less than 3 percent in 2009), who will pay, on average, $3,900 more in taxes than they would under the regular income tax system; nearly every married taxpayer filing jointly with income between $100,000 and $500,000 will owe some alternative tax. The option considered here would reduce taxes by extending the AMT patch for one year, through the end of 2012.

Although this policy would extend the AMT patch for only one year, CBO has concluded that most affected households would probably regard an extension of the AMT patch (relative to the current-law expiration of the existing patch) as permanent because it has routinely been extended in the past. Therefore, an extension of the patch would be viewed by many households as having a lasting impact on their disposable income and would have a correspondingly greater impact on consumption than would a change that was viewed as temporary.[32]

Still, the impact of this option on consumption would probably be smaller than that of a tax cut that applied more broadly because the AMT largely affects people in the upper part of the income distribution, who, in comparison with others, would spend less of the income retained. In addition, although an extension of an AMT patch would affect people's tax liability in 2012, most of its impact on consumption would probably occur in 2013. The effect would be delayed both because many taxpayers are allowed to pay their 2012 AMT liability in 2013 and because the increase in liability in 2012 under current law would probably not be recognized immediately. In particular, taxpayers who have not previously paid the AMT may not know that they are becoming liable, and those previously liable for the AMT probably expect that another extension will be enacted; for both of those groups, the increased AMT liability under current law would not affect their consumption much until 2013, so changing the law would also not have much effect on their consumption until 2013.

CBO estimates that a one-year AMT patch would raise output cumulatively in 2012 and 2013 by $0.20 to $1.10 per dollar of total budgetary cost. CBO also estimates that the policy would add two to nine years of cumulative FTE employment in 2012 and 2013 per million dollars of total budgetary cost.

Reducing Income Taxes in 2013 Relative to Those Specified in Current Law

Various provisions originally enacted in the Economic Growth and Tax Relief Reconciliation Act of 2001 and the Jobs and Growth Tax Relief Reconciliation Act of 2003, and then extended by the Tax Relief, Unemployment Insurance Reauthorization, and Job Creation Act of 2010 (the 2010 tax act), will expire at the end of 2012, raising tax liabilities for most people. Policymakers could defer those increases as well as extend the higher exemption amounts for the AMT. Accordingly, CBO analyzed a policy that would extend for one year (through 2013) the tax reductions in the 2010 tax act related to EGTRRA and JGTRRA and would increase the exemption amounts for the AMT in both 2012 and 2013.

CBO has concluded that most households view the provisions of EGTRRA and JGTRRA as permanent. Therefore, in this analysis, CBO projects that households would respond to the extension of the EGTRRA and JGTRRA provisions as though those changes would have a lasting effect on their disposable income (just as they would view an extension of the AMT patch).[33] As compared with the effect of a one-year AMT patch, a greater share of the tax reduction from this option would benefit households who are farther down the income scale and therefore would probably spend a larger fraction of an increase in after-tax income. Still, only a small fraction of the tax cut in this option would be received by those whose consumption is restricted by their current disposable income.

Deferring the scheduled increases in tax rates in 2013 would help some businesses as well as households. In particular, it would keep lower tax rates in place in that year for businesses that do not pay the corporate income tax (that is, businesses such as sole proprietorships, partnerships, S corporations, and limited liability companies). However, increasing the after-tax income of businesses typically does not create much incentive for them to hire more workers in order to produce more, because production depends principally on their ability to sell their products.

CBO estimates that a two-year AMT patch and one-year deferral of the tax increases that are scheduled to result from expiration of the 2010 tax act provisions related to EGTRRA and JGTRRA would raise output in 2012 and 2013 by $0.10 to $0.60 per dollar of total budgetary cost. CBO also estimates that the policy would add one to six years of cumulative FTE employment in 2012 and 2013 per million dollars of total budgetary cost.

The effects of this policy per dollar of budgetary cost in 2012 and 2013 are smaller than the effects of just extending the AMT patch primarily because a greater portion of the effects of the AMT on revenues would occur earlier in 2013; thus, more of the effects on output and employment from extending the AMT patch would occur by the end of 2013. Much of the economic impact of this policy, by contrast, would not be felt until 2014.

One variant on this option would be to defer for one year most of the tax increases associated with the expiration of the 2010 tax act but allow the rate increases for the top brackets to go into effect. That option would be more cost-effective in boosting output and employment in the short run because the higher-income households that would probably spend a smaller fraction of any increase in their after-tax income would receive a smaller share of the reduction in taxes (relative to current law). However, the difference relative to the option analyzed here would be small, because excluding the top brackets from the tax cut would still not lead to a large portion of the tax reduction going to the low-income households who would be likely to spend a large share of additional income.

Fiscal Policy Options Providing Support to Businesses

CBO analyzed the following fiscal policy options that would affect the economy primarily by providing support to businesses:

- Reducing employers' payroll taxes,
- Reducing employers' payroll taxes for firms that increase their payroll,
- Extending full expensing of investment costs,
- Reducing taxes on business income, and
- Reducing tax rates on repatriated foreign earnings.

Reducing Employers' Payroll Taxes

Under current law, in 2012 and subsequent years, both employers and employees will pay 6.2 percent of the employees' annual earnings in Social Security payroll taxes up to a ceiling ($110,100 in 2012).[34] CBO analyzed an option that would reduce employers' payroll taxes for 2012, while leaving employees' tax rate at 6.2 percent.

Firms would probably respond to this temporary reduction in their portion of the payroll tax through a combination of four channels. First, some firms would respond to lower employment costs by reducing the prices they charge in order to sell more goods or services. Those higher sales would in turn spur production, which would then increase hours worked and hiring.

Second, some firms would pass the tax savings on to employees in the form of higher wages or other forms of compensation, which in turn would encourage more spending by those employees. However, wages tend to be inflexible in the short run because of negotiation and administrative costs, so that response is not likely to be very large.

Third, some firms would retain the tax savings as profits. Higher profits would raise companies' stock prices, and the resulting higher household wealth would encourage more consumption, although shareholders would probably spend only a small portion of their gains. Higher profits would also improve cash flow, enabling firms facing borrowing constraints to buy new equipment.

Fourth, some firms would use slightly more labor during a period when it was temporarily less expensive. Some firms would use additional labor to enhance the quality of products and services in ways not reflected in GDP. Some would use additional labor to increase maintenance of existing equipment (such as preventive maintenance for motor vehicles), which would make equipment last longer and delay the need to invest in replacements. Depending on the type of products they made, some firms would also increase their use of labor that was temporarily less expensive while the policy was in effect and reduce their use of labor later. And some firms would hire a little sooner to cover anticipated increases in their labor needs. Under this option, however, most of the money forgone by the government would go to reduce taxes that firms pay for existing workers, so—per dollar of forgone revenues—the added incentive from lower labor costs to increase employment and hours worked would be small.

CBO estimates that reducing employers' payroll taxes would raise output cumulatively in 2012 and 2013 by $0.20 to $1.30 per dollar of total budgetary cost (see Table 1 on page 28). CBO also estimates that the policy would add 3 to 13 cumulative years of FTE employment in 2012 and 2013 per million dollars of total budgetary cost.

In comparison with the effects of reducing employees' payroll taxes, the effects of reducing employers' payroll taxes would be somewhat larger per dollar of forgone revenues. Reducing employers' payroll taxes for one year has an economic effect related to that of a temporary cut in sales taxes because a temporary reduction in prices (the first channel described above) would encourage purchases while the reduction was in effect. The effects on output and employment through that channel are estimated to be somewhat larger than the corresponding effects of increases in take-home pay from reducing employees' payroll taxes.

Reducing Employers' Payroll Taxes for Firms That Increase Their Payroll

The Hiring Incentives to Restore Employment Act of 2010 (HIRE, P.L. 111-147) reduced employers' payroll tax liabilities, but eligibility was limited to firms that hired people who had recently been unemployed.[35] CBO analyzed a related policy that would give employers a one-year nonrefundable credit against their payroll tax liability for incremental increases in their payroll—resulting either from hiring new workers or from increasing the hours worked by the firm's current workforce—during 2012.

Because the credit would be nonrefundable, the credit amount would not exceed the firm's payroll tax liability. Such a credit would be based on the payroll in each calendar quarter so that firms could receive the credit quickly. To prevent firms from firing existing employees and hiring new ones in order to obtain the credit, the amount of the credit would be based on the difference between the wage base in the current quarter and the wage base four quarters earlier. In addition, the eligible wage base would be capped at an annual amount for each employee. Wage bases can be calculated quarterly for most employers from information already reported to the Internal Revenue Service (under the Federal Insurance Contributions Act and the Federal Unemployment Tax Act), thus reducing the administrative costs of this option.

Providing tax credits for increases in payrolls would increase both output and employment. The effect on output would come through the same four channels as the effect on output of reducing employers' payroll taxes. CBO estimates that this option and the preceding one would have approximately the same economic impact per dollar of budgetary cost through the first three channels discussed above. Through the fourth channel, however, this option would provide a substantially larger increase in employment and hours worked than the previous option because this policy would provide tax benefits linked to payroll *growth*; fewer budget dollars would be used to cut taxes for workers who would have been employed anyway, so the incentive to increase payroll per dollar of forgone revenues would be greater. However, linking the availability of the credit to payroll growth would provide no incentive to maintain employment at firms that have been shrinking and thus less incentive to maintain employment overall in industries and regions where the economy remains the weakest.[36]

CBO estimates that reducing payroll taxes for firms that increase their payroll would raise output cumulatively in 2012 and 2013 by $0.20 to $1.30 per dollar of total budgetary cost. CBO also estimates that the policy would add 4 to 16 cumulative years of FTE employment in 2012 and 2013 per million dollars of total budgetary cost.

This policy would generate greater effects on employment per dollar of GDP than the other policies in support of businesses that are analyzed here because it would provide direct incentives for employers to increase employment in addition to its indirect effects on employment through its effects on output.

The choice of what cap (if any) to impose on the eligible wage base would affect the types of employment the policy fostered. A low cap would especially encourage the hiring of low-wage and part-time workers. For example, if the credit was calculated using the Federal Unemployment Tax Act wage base (which includes earnings only up to $7,000 annually for each employee), firms might have an incentive to hire, say, three part-time employees with annual wages of $20,000 each instead of one full-time employee with an annual wage of $60,000, because the former would increase payroll by $21,000 for the purpose of the credit, compared with an increase of only $7,000 for the latter.

Another design choice is whether the tax credit would be broad based or would apply only to a subset of firms. For example, if the main objective was to assist small businesses in hiring, the credit could be made available just for firms with a total number of employees, or total revenues, below some specified threshold. However, because small firms have more volatile employment dynamics (exhibiting high rates of creating and losing jobs and of entering and leaving the market), the average duration and the economic benefits of each subsidized job would probably be less than those under a broad-based program. In addition, because of that volatility, a greater fraction of the tax credits would be paid in response to payroll growth that would have occurred even without the policy.

The effects of this type of tax credit would also depend on other design choices.[37] To reduce efforts by firms to maximize their credit in ways inconsistent with the intent of the policy, growth that occurred through acquiring an existing business might be deemed not to count as a net increase in employment; however, such restrictions would make the policy more difficult to administer. If the credit was applied against businesses' income tax liability instead of their payroll tax liability and was nonrefundable, the policy would have a smaller effect: Employers that did not owe any income taxes—including firms with net operating losses, tax-exempt organizations, and state and local governments—would not be eligible for the credit. Firms with net operating losses could be allowed to apply the credit to tax liabilities in a subsequent year; still, among firms with net operating losses, the effect on hiring would be smaller because the credit would not be received immediately even if their payroll increased in 2012. Finally, the credit could be limited to certain categories of employees.

Extending Full Expensing of Investment Costs

The 2010 tax act allowed businesses to fully expense (deduct immediately from taxable income) the cost of their investment in qualifying property (mainly equipment) made in late 2010 and all of 2011; that provision expanded the partial expensing (sometimes called bonus depreciation) of 50 percent that was in effect from 2008 through most of 2010. The 2010 tax act also provided partial expensing of 50 percent for 2012. CBO analyzed a policy that would provide further incentives to invest by extending full expensing for one more year, through 2012.

Partial expensing or full expensing of investment costs allows firms to realize the tax benefits of depreciation deductions more quickly, which provides a greater incentive for investment because a dollar of tax benefit this year is more valuable than a dollar of tax benefit in a future year. Initial reductions in revenues are nearly fully offset by later increases. Therefore, CBO estimated the policy's effects per dollar of the present value of the revenue effects of the policy (discounted at businesses' cost of debt and equity) instead of per dollar of total budgetary cost.

The effect of the incentive is probably smaller when the economy is weak than when it is strong: Firms are less likely to increase investment when they have idle capacity and when they are less confident about the future demand for their products and services. In addition, when the economy slows, more firms incur losses and pay no income tax; some of those firms therefore get less benefit from immediate tax deductions, although firms that paid taxes in previous years may be able to reclaim some of those taxes. To the extent that temporarily reducing the after-tax price of investment accelerates the purchase of capital goods into the period when the tax incentive is available, that increased investment may be partially offset by a subsequent decrease when the incentive expires. In addition, the policy would probably have the greatest effect on investment just before it expired at the end of 2012 (as firms accelerated equipment purchases from 2013), so much of the indirect effect on output and employment would spill over into 2013.

CBO estimates that allowing full or partial expensing of investment costs would raise output cumulatively in 2012 and 2013 by $0.10 to $1.10 per dollar of the present value of budgetary cost. CBO also estimates that the policy would add 1 to 11 cumulative years of FTE employment in 2012 and 2013 per million dollars of net budgetary cost.

Reducing Business Income Taxes

Businesses—whether organized as C corporations, S corporations, partnerships, or sole proprietorships—are liable for income taxes that apply to their net income.[38] Income tax rates for businesses vary by organizational form and amount of income; a simple way to effectively reduce all of those tax rates by the same proportion is to allow all types of businesses to deduct a percentage of their net income in calculating their tax liability. CBO analyzed a policy that would allow such a percentage deduction in 2012.

The impact of this policy on output and employment would come primarily through its effect on the income and wealth of business owners and stockholders, who generally have higher-than-average income and would therefore tend to spend a fairly small share of temporary additions to their income and wealth. The proposal would also reduce the cost of capital for businesses because a larger share of pretax returns would be available to compensate investors after taxes were paid; however, that reduction would be only temporary under this policy, so it would probably have little effect on investment. In addition, the proposal could reduce prices slightly, because it would reduce the cost of labor compensation that is taken in the form of business income. (For example, a portion of the business income of sole proprietors represents compensation for their labor.) However, that effect would probably be most pronounced in industries that are generally composed of partnerships and sole proprietorships, and it is likely to be quite small in the aggregate.

CBO estimates that a one-year reduction in taxes on business income would raise output cumulatively in 2012 and 2013 by something between a negligible amount and $0.30 per dollar of total budgetary cost. CBO also estimates that the policy would add up to three cumulative years of FTE employment per million dollars of total budgetary cost.

A similar tax reduction targeted at small businesses would probably have effects on output and employment per dollar of total budgetary cost that were close to those for this option. As is the case with large businesses, a fairly small share of the income of small businesses goes to lower-income households that would spend a large fraction of their additional income.[39]

Reducing Tax Rates on Repatriated Foreign Earnings

American multinational corporations pay U.S. tax on income from their foreign operations when the income is repatriated to the U.S. parent company as dividends, minus a credit for foreign income taxes paid when the income was earned. CBO analyzed a policy that would reduce the tax rate on repatriated income in 2012 to 5.25 percent from the current corporate tax rate of 35 percent; such a policy would be a repeat of a temporary policy that was last implemented in 2004 by the American Jobs Creation Act.

A temporary reduction in the tax rate of that magnitude would probably result in a large amount of repatriated income next year—as much as $700 billion, according to an estimate by the staff of the Joint Committee on Taxation.[40] By taking advantage of the one-year tax break, companies would be able to reduce the total taxes they pay to bring money back to this country, although they would pay more in taxes during 2012.

The government would collect more revenues next year but less in future years; the present discounted value of revenues would be reduced because of the tax break, creating a net cost to the government. As with the policy option allowing expensing for investment costs, this policy's effects are therefore estimated per dollar of the present value of the revenue effects of the policy (discounted at businesses' cost of debt and equity) instead of per dollar of total budgetary cost.

The short-term effect on U.S. output from such a policy would depend on the relative magnitude of several offsetting factors; CBO expects that the effect on output would probably be positive but much smaller than the net cost to the government. On the one hand, the reduction in tax liability would increase the value of the companies and thereby the wealth of their shareholders, which in turn would boost their spending to some extent. In addition, to the degree that firms are unable to finance profitable investments by borrowing or by using cash on hand, the reduction in the cost of accessing foreign earnings would increase U.S. investment. However, that effect is probably small because many of the firms that would be affected have substantial cash holdings and ready access to capital markets. On the other hand, overseas earnings that are held in foreign currencies would have to be converted to U.S. dollars in order to be repatriated. That demand for dollars would raise the exchange value of the dollar, reducing U.S. net exports and domestic output.[41]

CBO estimates that a one-year reduction in taxes on repatriated income would raise output cumulatively in 2012 and 2013 by something between a negligible amount and $0.20 per dollar of the present value of budgetary cost. CBO also estimates that the policy would boost FTE employment by up to one cumulative year per million dollars of net budgetary cost.

Fiscal Policy Options Involving Aid to State Governments or Spending on Infrastructure

CBO analyzed the following fiscal policy options involving purchases by the federal government or aid to state governments:

- Increasing aid to states for purposes other than infrastructure and
- Increasing spending on infrastructure.

Increasing Aid to States for Purposes Other Than Infrastructure

Many states have experienced a high degree of fiscal stress as a result of the recession. Leading up to fiscal year 2012, 38 states faced projected budget shortfalls. They closed those gaps in a variety of ways, including reducing government employment, increasing revenues, and reducing transfer payments to households; nevertheless, many states are anticipating further large budget gaps in the next few years. Adding to budgetary pressures, spending financed by the aid to state governments provided by ARRA for purposes other than infrastructure, which totaled over $200 billion from 2009 through 2011, is projected to drop sharply in 2012. CBO analyzed a policy to assist states by providing funding to state governments for a variety of purposes. Even if funding was intended for a specific activity, such as education, CBO anticipates that the availability of additional funds would both increase net state spending for the specified activity and affect other aspects of state budgets.[42]

Without further aid from the federal government, many states would have to raise taxes or cut spending by more than they would if aid were provided. Such actions would dampen spending by those governments and by households in those states, and more state and private jobs would be lost. Under current law, many states will probably have to take such steps on an ongoing basis during the next few years, so federal aid that was provided promptly would probably have a significant effect on output and employment in 2012 and 2013. Such aid could lead to some combination of fewer layoffs of state and local government employees, more hiring of such employees, more pay raises or fewer pay cuts for those employees, more government purchases of goods and services, increases in state safety-net programs, and lower state and local taxes than would occur without the federal assistance. But some of the federal aid would probably be used to replenish or avoid drawing down states' reserve funds; aid used in that way would not boost the economy in the short term. CBO estimates that providing aid to states for purposes other than infrastructure would raise output cumulatively in 2012 and 2013 by $0.20 to $1.00 per dollar of total budgetary cost (see Table 1 on page 28). CBO also estimates that the policy would add two to nine cumulative years of FTE employment in 2012 and 2013 per million dollars of total budgetary cost.

Increasing Spending on Infrastructure

ARRA provided about $60 billion for spending on water, transportation, and housing projects. CBO analyzed an option that would provide additional federal funding for infrastructure projects similar to those funded by ARRA.

Infrastructure spending directly increases employment because workers are hired to undertake construction projects. It also adds to demand for goods and services through purchases of material and equipment and through additional spending by the extra workers who are hired; as with other policy options discussed in this testimony, that increase in demand leads to further hiring. However, government spending on infrastructure projects could also cause private-sector spending to fall because of indirect crowding-out effects, as discussed earlier. In addition, CBO projects that states would reduce spending of their own funds on infrastructure by about one-half of any increase in federal outlays for that purpose.[43] One drawback of this option is that infrastructure projects often involve considerable start-up lags. Although some projects (such as highway repair and resurfacing) can be implemented relatively quickly, large-scale construction projects generally require years of planning and preparation. For example, building new transportation infrastructure that requires establishing new rights-of-way or developing and implementing alternative energy sources would probably have their biggest effects on output and employment after 2013. Indeed, trying to increase certain types of spending too quickly would raise the risk of making poor decisions about what specific projects should be supported. As a practical matter, the experience with ARRA suggests that the spending of infrastructure funds is slow: By the end of fiscal year 2009, seven and a half months after the legislation was enacted, less than 10 percent of the infrastructure funds provided by ARRA had been spent. Thus, most of the increases in output and employment from the option analyzed here would probably occur after 2012.[44]

CBO estimates that additional investments in infrastructure would raise output cumulatively in 2012 and 2013 by $0.10 to $0.70 per dollar of total budgetary cost. CBO also estimates that the policy would add one to six cumulative years of FTE employment in 2012 and 2013 per million dollars of total budgetary cost.

Longer-Run Effects

Over the long run, the nation's output depends on the size and composition of the capital stock, the quantity and quality of the labor force, and the nation's technological progress. Although the fiscal policy options analyzed here would increase output during the next few years, they would decrease output later because, by adding to federal budget deficits, they would reduce the amount of national saving and thus the size of the future capital stock. Because the policy options analyzed here are temporary, they would not generally have significant, lasting effects on the labor force or technology. However, to the degree that the policy options would reduce long-term unemployment in the next few years, they might improve participation in the labor force, employment, and productivity in later years.[45]

The reduction in output over the longer run that would result from the smaller capital stock could be offset by other changes in fiscal policy or by other effects of the short-run policy options. First, if future increases in taxes or cuts in government spending enabled the government to pay off the additional accumulated debt, then output in the longer run would not necessarily be diminished by the crowding out of investment caused by the short-run policies. However, if the future increases in taxes or cuts in spending reduced the returns from investing and thereby discouraged some future private saving, output would still be lower on net in the long run. Second, policy options that would raise government or private investment—such as expensing of investment costs or infrastructure spending—can raise output in the short run with less (or even no) negative longer-run impact on output because they tend to increase the stock of productive capital directly. CBO has not attempted to estimate such effects.

How Fiscal Policy Options Would Affect the Nation's Capital Stock

The size of the capital stock owned by residents of the United States depends on national saving, which is the sum of personal saving, business saving (that is, after-tax corporate profits not paid as dividends), and saving or dissaving (as reflected in budget surpluses or deficits) by the federal government and state and local governments. Federal budget deficits reduce national saving, so all other things being equal, an increase in those deficits would decrease that saving—resulting in a smaller capital stock owned by U.S. residents over time. Reductions in household or business saving would have the same effect. If the capital stock owned by U.S. residents was smaller, the amount of such capital invested overseas would also be smaller, and foreigners would tend to increase their investment in the United States (drawn by higher rates of return on the smaller stock of domestic capital), so the capital stock located in the United States would be diminished by less than the reduction in the capital stock owned by U.S. residents. Still, the smaller capital stock in the United States would lead to less output than would otherwise be possible because the labor force would have less capital to work with.

The impact of a fiscal policy option on the capital stock would depend partly on its effect on the federal budget deficit and partly on its effect on the saving of households, businesses, and state and local governments. In general, the more a policy option raised either government or private consumption in the short run—and thus the more it raised output in the short run—the more it would depress national saving. For example, cuts in taxes that boost consumption substantially would tend to decrease national saving (because the increase in government dissaving would not be offset very much by an increase in private saving), and cuts in taxes that are largely saved would tend to decrease national saving only a little (because the increase in government dissaving would be offset to a significant extent by higher private saving).

An Illustrative Example

To provide a rough idea of the potential magnitude of the long-run economic effects of policies to boost output and employment in the next few years, CBO considered a simple illustrative example: an increase in government spending on goods and services (such as office supplies or government salaries) in 2012. Such spending would tend to have larger negative long-run effects on output than the fiscal policy options discussed earlier, for several reasons:

- Increasing government spending would boost purchases of goods and services on a dollar-for-dollar basis—in contrast with tax cuts, only some of which would translate into increased household spending. The larger impact of government purchases on spending implies more crowding out in the long run.
- All of the increase in the federal deficit would occur in the first year, producing a larger cumulative impact on the government's interest payments than would more gradual policies.
- Under an assumption that the increase in government spending would not increase the productivity of private capital, it would not provide any long-run boost to output.

In estimating the effects of such a policy beyond the next few years, CBO used an enhanced version of a widely used model developed by Robert Solow. To illustrate a range of possible effects, CBO assumed that each dollar increase in the deficit would reduce domestic investment by 20 or 50 cents (reflecting different assumptions about the effects of deficits on both national saving and net borrowing from abroad). Those alternative assumptions would cause the policy to have, respectively, smaller and larger effects on future output. On that basis, CBO estimates that a deficit-financed increase in government purchases in 2012 would reduce GDP by an amount between slightly above zero and $0.10 in 2021 per dollar of total budgetary cost (with amounts measured in 2012 dollars). The specific policy options discussed in this testimony would have a smaller negative effect on GDP in 2021, as they would lead to a smaller decline in the U.S. capital stock per dollar of budgetary cost.

OTHER LEGISLATIVE POLICY OPTIONS FOR INCREASING ECONOMIC GROWTH AND EMPLOYMENT IN 2012 AND 2013

Lawmakers can influence economic growth and employment during the next two years by changing policies that do not involve, or whose scope extends well beyond, taxation and government spending.

For example, legislation could modify existing or proposed regulations, significantly alter the government's role in a particular sector of the economy, or change trade relationships with other countries. Other types of policy changes that do not require legislation, such as those related to monetary policy or those that can be implemented by federal agencies under current law, could also affect economic activity, but they are outside the scope of this testimony.

Society's decisions to regulate or not regulate certain activities in certain ways generally involve balancing the advantages and disadvantages of the regulations being considered. For example, properly designed regulations can provide benefits by reducing damage to people's health or the environment, reducing the risks posed to the economy by the financial system, or advancing other social goals. But in achieving those benefits, regulations generally impose costs on businesses and their workers and customers through restrictions on choices or forgone output and employment. Those costs can be weighed against the benefits. Similarly, society's decisions to have the government play a particular role in a particular sector of the economy and to engage in international trade under specified rules generally involve balancing the advantages and disadvantages of various courses of action.

How Changes in Regulations and Other Types of Policies Apart from Fiscal Policies Can Affect the Economy

Changes in regulations—whether those regulations were imposed directly by legislation or promulgated by federal agencies in implementing laws—and in other types of policies apart from fiscal policies could affect output and employment during the next few years as well as over a longer time span. Those effects could occur through their impact on businesses' incentives to invest and hire, on the prices that people pay for goods and services, on businesses' and people's expectations about their future income, on uncertainty about future government policies and economic conditions, and on other factors that affect economic behavior.

Effects on Incentives to Invest and Hire and on Prices

The short-run economic impact of changing a policy other than a fiscal policy depends importantly on how that change affects businesses' investment decisions. To start, consider the effect of imposing or strengthening a regulation, or raising a barrier to international trade. Such a change in policy can reduce businesses' incentives to invest. For example, adding to the length or complexity of a process for reviewing firms' activities or granting permits for new projects would generally reduce investment by imposing extra costs to comply with the process (which would reduce the return on investments), by increasing the probability that a project will not be approved, and by delaying the return on investments in projects that proceed.

In addition, changes in regulations that raise the cost of production for some firms may lead to increases in the prices of goods or services (such as energy) used as inputs by other firms, lowering the return on investments for those firms and therefore tending to reduce their investment. Moreover, strengthening trade barriers may negatively affect certain sectors of the economy and reduce the returns from investing in those sectors.

Yet, a change in policy of that sort can also increase investment in some ways. For example, requiring changes in production methods might necessitate investment in equipment or structures (such as pollution-control equipment) needed to comply with the rules. (Incentives to invest in other types of capital in the affected industries could be reduced, however, because those higher costs might lower firms' return on those other investments.) Similarly, strengthening trade barriers that protect certain sectors of the economy could increase the returns from investing in those sectors.

Eliminating or weakening a regulation or lowering a barrier to international trade can reverse or avoid those various effects. The net impact of such a policy change on investment depends on the relative sizes of those effects, which differ across policies. To the extent that eliminating or weakening a regulation or lowering a trade barrier led to greater business investment in the short term, it would tend to boost output and employment during that span (even if its economic effects in the medium term and long term were quite different). Conversely, to the extent that the policy change led to less investment in the short term, it would tend to decrease output and employment during that span (again, even if its medium-term and long-term economic effects were different).

Changes in policies apart from fiscal policies can also affect businesses' hiring decisions. A policy change that encourages firms to invest more or that increases the demand for their products indirectly encourages those firms to increase the size of their workforces. In the other direction, a policy change that discourages firms from investing or decreases the demand for their products can lead firms to lay off workers or decrease the size of their workforces through attrition. Moreover, a policy change can directly enhance or diminish firms' incentives to hire workers for a given amount of capital or demand for their products.

In addition to their effect on businesses, changes in policies apart from fiscal policies can affect the prices that people have to pay for goods and services and hence the real value of their income. For example, policy changes that increase energy prices reduce households' purchasing power, whereas policy changes that lead to lower prices on goods and services raise households' purchasing power.

Changes in regulations and other policies apart from fiscal policies that directly affect investment or hiring by firms or directly affect consumer spending also have indirect effects, some of which tend to be positive, and some of which tend to be negative.

Consider policy changes that would boost firms' investment or hiring or people's spending. On the one hand, additional spending resulting from such policies would generate profits and wages in other firms, some of which would be spent by the recipients, further increasing output. But any additional spending spurred by those policies could also crowd out other economic activity, making the net increase in activity small or nonexistent. The extent of such crowding out depends importantly on the overall level of economic activity. Under current economic conditions, CBO projects that such indirect effects, on net, probably strengthen policies' direct effects.

Effects on Expectations and Uncertainty

Changes to policies apart from fiscal policies can also affect output by changing people's expectations about their future income. For example, policies that improved businesses' expectations about the demand for their products and their income in the future would increase the value of the businesses and, therefore, the wealth of their owners; that effect would boost consumer spending to a modest extent during the next few years and beyond.[46] Similarly, policies that improved people's expectations about their future income would lead to an increase in current spending by some households.[47]

Household spending can also be affected by people's expectations about the prices of goods and services, which can be influenced by changes in regulations and other policies. However, because the effect of most such policy changes on future prices would be small and uncertain, most people probably would respond only to a limited extent—particularly in the current economic environment.

Changes to regulations and other policies—or the prospect of them—can also affect the degree of uncertainty faced by businesses and households, which will in turn affect their spending. Some changes would decrease uncertainty about future government policies and economic conditions. For example, eliminating regulations that impose extensive review processes would reduce uncertainty about the prospects for investment projects. Similarly, reversing policies whose implementation will require the issuance of significant new regulations could diminish uncertainty about future prices of inputs, about the demand for certain products, and about the ways that some markets or sectors of the economy will operate in the future. However, some changes to regulations and other policies would heighten uncertainty. For example, eliminating regulations that are designed to meet a requirement of current law without repealing the law itself could increase uncertainty because businesses and people would not know what alternative approach to meeting that requirement might be implemented in the future.

To the extent that policy changes reduce uncertainty, they would tend to increase businesses' investing and hiring and households' spending; to the extent that policy changes increase uncertainty, they would tend to have the opposite effects.

Potential Economic Effects of Changes in Particular Types of Policies Apart from Fiscal Policies

For this testimony, CBO considered changes in regulations and other policies in several areas:

- Energy and the environment,
- The financial sector,
- The health care sector, and
- International trade.

Estimating the near-term effects on overall economic activity of most regulations or other policies apart from fiscal policies is exceedingly difficult, and few analytic tools are available for that purpose. Accordingly, the agency did not attempt to quantify the effects of specific changes in policies of this sort with any precision. Instead, CBO focused on whether selected changes in policies besides fiscal policies would probably increase or decrease output and employment during the next few years.

Importantly, in focusing on the near-term aggregate economic effects of policy changes, this discussion does not speak to other considerations that are critical in assessing such policies. Those considerations include the long-term effects on the economy, on people's health, and on the environment, as well as the many other priorities at the core of the policies.

Some changes in policies that CBO considered would probably raise output and employment during the next few years; other changes would probably lower output and employment; and some changes would have effects on economic activity whose sign is difficult to determine. However, in CBO's judgment, the economic effects of the specific policy changes discussed below probably would be too small or would occur too slowly to significantly alter overall output or employment in the next two years. The policy changes examined here are meant to be illustrative rather than exhaustive; many other possible policy changes, which might have larger or smaller economic effects, could be considered.

Energy and the Environment

Projects to increase the production of energy are typically subject to review by multiple levels of government. Federal agencies generally focus on compliance with national performance standards and on infrastructure that crosses state boundaries, such as pipelines and electric power transmission lines. Federal agencies also determine the conditions under which the private sector can develop resources on public lands, such as the Outer Continental Shelf and national forests. Those review processes generally aim to limit damage to health and the environment from economic activity, but they also affect the amount and pace of investments in the energy sector. For example, the federal approval process may delay or prevent the launching of projects that, if ultimately approved and undertaken, would result in significant investment and production. In addition, the prospect of such delays and the risk of projects' being blocked deter some projects from being proposed at all.

The federal government could increase employment and output during the next few years by hastening or relaxing the approval process for energy projects or by expanding opportunities to develop resources on public lands. However, the short-term effects of such changes would probably be small relative to the size of the overall economy for several reasons. First, state and local governments strongly influence the siting of energy facilities within their boundaries, and the federal government does not control the actions of those governments. Second, even if additional projects were approved in the next few years, many of them would not commence in earnest for several years. Finally, energy production accounts for only a small percentage of overall output, so incremental gains in that sector would have only a modest effect on the economy as a whole.

Another set of federal regulations that might be changed are environmental regulations. Consider, for example, the Environmental Protection Agency's (EPA's) regulations regarding emissions from coal-burning power plants, industrial boilers, and process heaters (such as industrial furnaces used in steelmaking). The regulations—designed primarily to meet the requirements of the Clean Air Act—pertain to hazardous air pollutants (including mercury) and emissions of sulfur dioxide and nitrogen dioxides, which help create airborne particulates and ozone. Those regulations demand costly investment during the next few years in scrubbers and particulate filters, especially at certain older power plants that lack emissions controls. EPA has estimated that regulated firms might make more than $50 billion in capital investments, spaced out over several years, to comply with the requirements. Delaying or eliminating those regulations would result in firms' delaying the investments in scrubbers and particulate filters they would otherwise have undertaken during the next few years, which would tend to decrease investment and output.

However, if those regulations were eliminated or their implementation delayed, firms might, instead, make additional investments in other equipment. Moreover, the reduced cost of production stemming from the lessening of regulation would increase the returns from investing in this sector and might thereby prompt other investments. Also, delaying or eliminating those regulations might boost spending by businesses and households by postponing or obviating an increase in the price of electricity that would otherwise occur, thus raising the return on investment of businesses that purchase electricity and increasing other purchases by households.

On balance, CBO expects that delaying or eliminating those regulations regarding emissions would reduce investment and output during the next few years, because the response to the factors that would tend to boost investment under those circumstances would probably be smaller than the response to the factors that would reduce investment. One reason for that conclusion is that the amount of investment in power plants other than that spurred by those regulations is expected to be relatively small—adding less than 1 percent to total generating capacity each year between 2013 and 2035, according the Energy Information Administration. Another reason for that conclusion is that the price increases that will probably result from those regulations—EPA estimates that one of the regulations will increase customers' electric bills by about 4 percent—are not expected to occur for several years, so they probably will not have an appreciable effect on household spending in the next few years.

Another possible approach to increasing investment in the energy sector in the next few years is to reduce uncertainty about future energy and environmental regulations. For example, quicker rulemaking by federal agencies might speed investment by affected firms, other things being equal. However, quicker action might increase the likelihood of errors in the process. Moreover, when markets have already adapted to an existing policy, and a change in policy would require agencies to revise regulations in the future, such a change might lead to greater uncertainty and therefore decrease investment until it became clear how the new policy would be implemented.

The Financial Sector

Changing certain regulations that push up borrowing costs and reduce access to credit for some borrowers could increase investment, consumer spending, output, and employment during the next few years. Such regulations are typically instituted in an effort to improve the safety and soundness of the financial system and thereby reduce the risk of financial crises of the sort that the nation recently experienced. As a result, any short-term economic benefits of loosening or repealing financial regulations may involve trade-offs with the potential cost of hindering progress toward those other goals.

Last year's major financial legislation (the Dodd-Frank Wall Street Reform and Consumer Protection Act [P.L. 111-203]) will have significant effects on the government's regulation of the financial sector, and one possible policy change would be to repeal or modify that legislation. CBO has not estimated the effects of such actions on the economy over the next two years or in the longer term. One specific aspect of that legislation that might be changed would be provisions that could lead to regulations raising capital requirements for banking institutions. Higher capital requirements will increase costs for those institutions, and those higher costs—to some degree—will be passed along to borrowers in the form of higher interest rates. A higher cost of borrowing will reduce investment. However, for two reasons, repealing or postponing implementation of the provisions of that legislation leading to higher capital requirements might not affect borrowing costs and investment very much in the next few years. First, financial regulators might increase capital requirements even in the absence of legislation—for example, as part of the Basel Capital Adequacy Accord (Basel III) negotiations for a revised international regulatory framework for banks— unless a new law expressly forbade such a change.[48] Second, banking institutions might increase their capital in response to market pressures even in the absence of the legislation (and, indeed, many have already increased their capital).

Legislative changes in financial regulatory policy might also affect investment by altering the degree of uncertainty about such policy. For example, reversing certain provisions of the Dodd-Frank legislation would reduce uncertainty about the new regulations that might be instituted to comply with those provisions. However, making further changes in regulatory policy so soon after the major changes enacted last year might accentuate uncertainty about future regulatory policy.

The Health Care Sector

The federal government affects health care spending and the provision of health care services in many ways. Examples include the Medicare and Medicaid programs, tax preferences for employer-sponsored health insurance, outlays for veterans' health care, investment in medical research, and the regulation of health care products such as drugs and medical devices. Last year's major health care legislation (the Patient Protection and Affordable Care Act of 2010 [P.L. 111-148] and provisions related to health care in the Health Care and Education Reconciliation Act of 2010 [P.L. 111-152]) will fundamentally alter the market for health insurance and employers' options and responsibilities for obtaining health insurance for their employees over the next several years.

One possible policy change in this area would be to repeal or modify last year's health care legislation. CBO has not estimated the effects of such actions on the economy over the next two years.[49] Such an analysis would be difficult and highly speculative because many of the provisions of that legislation will not go into effect until 2014, and so, much of the legislation's economic impact in the next two years will stem from businesses' and people's expectations and uncertainty about what will happen if and when the legislation is fully implemented. Specifically, repealing or modifying the legislation would probably have a variety of effects on investment, employment, and output in the near term. For example, the law provides an incentive for expansion in the health care industry to meet the higher demand for health care services that will arise from the greater number of people with health insurance. However, the legislation also lowers Medicare's payment rates for certain health care services, which reduces the incentive for certain investments in the health care industry. Whether the net effect of those aspects of the legislation is higher or lower investment in the health care industry during the next few years is unclear, and therefore whether repealing or modifying the legislation would raise or lower such investment in the near term is unclear as well. The legislation might also affect investment and hiring outside the health care industry by changing businesses' expected spending on employer-sponsored health insurance and thus businesses' expected labor costs. However, changes in businesses' spending on health insurance for their workers will probably be largely offset, for most workers, by changes in other forms of compensation for those workers; that is, changes in businesses' spending on health insurance will alter the mix of compensation but probably not have a significant effect on overall labor costs for most workers.[50] Therefore, CBO does not expect that the legislation will have a large effect on investment and hiring outside the health care industry during the next two years. Repealing or modifying the legislation could also affect the economy in the next few years by changing households' and businesses' uncertainty about the future. The cost and availability of health insurance has long been a source of considerable uncertainty, and some provisions of the legislation reduced aspects of that uncertainty. At the same time, there is currently a great deal of uncertainty about how the law will be implemented and how the health insurance market, the health care market, and the labor market will respond to specific provisions of the legislation—such as the mandate for individuals to purchase health insurance, the penalties for employers that do not offer appropriate coverage, and the reductions in certain payment rates under Medicare. Therefore, repeal or modification of the legislation would increase certain aspects of uncertainty and remove others. To the extent that such changes, on balance, reduced uncertainty, they would probably boost spending, investment, and hiring in the next few years; to the extent that such changes, on balance, increased uncertainty, they would have the opposite effects.

International Trade

Recently enacted free-trade agreements with South Korea, Colombia, and Panama are expected to increase investment and hiring by U.S. exporters and by businesses facing lower prices for the imported goods and services they buy, and to increase spending by households facing lower prices for the imported products they buy. However, investment and hiring by some businesses whose products compete with imports could be reduced.

Further free-trade agreements would tend to have similar effects. Over the long run, the net effect of such free-trade agreements on U.S. output is probably positive. During the first few years, however, further agreements' effects on output or on employment could be either positive or negative because of temporary dislocations as economic activity shifted between industries and firms. In any event, agreements with individual countries would generally not have much effect on the overall U.S. economy in the next few years. That is the case partly because trade between the United States and most other individual countries is a small share of U.S. economic activity. And it is the case partly because the development and approval of free-trade agreements is usually a multiyear process, and even once agreements are implemented, industries' and firms' adjustments in response tend to take several years.

End Notes

[1] See Congressional Budget Office, *Options for Responding to Short-Term Economic Weakness* (January 2008); and the Statement of Douglas W. Elmendorf, Director, Congressional Budget Office, before the House Committee on the Budget, *The State of the Economy and Issues in Developing an Effective Policy Response* (January 27, 2009).

[2] See Congressional Budget Office, *The Budget and Economic Outlook: An Update* (August 2011).

[3] CBO has not published new estimates of the paths for potential GDP and the output gap since August.

[4] For an analysis of the cost of losing a job in an economic downturn, see Congressional Budget Office, *Losing a Job During a Recession*, Issue Brief (April 2010).

[5] See Congressional Budget Office, letter to the Honorable Chris Van Hollen providing CBO's estimate of the portion of the federal deficit that is due to the current underutilization of capital and labor resources in the economy (October 4, 2011).

[6] Weak growth in outlays by state and local governments will also slow economic growth in those years, but that effect will be largely offset by slow growth in those governments' collections of tax revenues because of the modest recovery.

[7] In estimating the effects of ARRA, CBO selected low and high estimates of the effects of each provision of the law; those estimates were chosen to encompass most economists' views about the effects of that type of provision. For a discussion of CBO's estimation methods, see Congressional Budget Office, *Estimated Impact of the American Recovery and Reinvestment Act on Employment and Economic Output April 2011 Through June 2011* (August 2011). The low ends of the ranges described here are smaller than those shown in CBO's August report, reflecting further analysis of the multiplier effects of changes in federal taxes and spending. CBO's next report on ARRA, which will be issued later this month, will incorporate those changes.

[8] For more information about automatic fiscal stabilizers, see Congressional Budget Office, *The Effects of Automatic Stabilizers on the Federal Budget* (April 2011).

[9] The AMT is intended to curtail the extent to which higher-income people can reduce their tax liability through the use of preferences in the tax code. CBO anticipates that the impact of higher taxes under the AMT will largely be delayed until 2013, when most of those additional taxes will be paid if no further legislation limiting the reach of the AMT is enacted.

[10] To reflect the high degree of uncertainty that accompanies estimates of the economic impact of fiscal policy, CBO used a range of assumptions about the extent to which changes in taxes and government spending affect the demand for goods and services, budget deficits affect private investment, and changes in marginal tax rates on labor income affect the labor supply. For more information about some of those assumptions, see Congressional Budget Office, *The Macroeconomic and Budgetary Effects of an Illustrative Policy for Reducing the Federal Budget Deficit* (July 2011); and for a discussion of estimation methods, see Congressional Budget Office, *An Analysis of the President's Budgetary Proposals for Fiscal Year 2012* (April 2011).

[11] A basis point is one-hundredth of a percentage point.

[12] The additional growth in federal debt under those alternative assumptions would also increase the risk of a fiscal crisis; see Congressional Budget Office, *Federal Debt and the Risk of a Fiscal Crisis*, Issue Brief (July 2010).

[13] See the Statement of Douglas W. Elmendorf, Director, Congressional Budget Office, before the Joint Select Committee on Deficit Reduction, *Confronting the Nation's Fiscal Policy Challenges* (September 13, 2011).

[14] See the Statement of Douglas W. Elmendorf, *The State of the Economy and Issues in Developing an Effective Policy Response* (January 27, 2009).

[15] CBO estimates that the rate of unemployment that could be reached without raising the rate of inflation, which is to say the rate of unemployment stemming from sources other than the business cycle, is currently about 6 percent. In the agency's estimation, that rate will decline over the coming decade, enabling the unemployment rate ultimately to fall below 6 percent without spurring inflation. For further discussion, see Congressional Budget Office, *The Budget and Economic Outlook: An Update* (August 2011), pp. 45–46.

[16] For a summary of the literature on the effects of partial expensing in the early 2000s, see Congressional Budget Office, *Options for Responding to Short-Term Economic Weakness.*

[17] See John B. Taylor, "An Empirical Analysis of the Revival of Fiscal Activism in the 2000s," *Journal of Economic Literature*, vol. 49, no. 3 (September 2011), pp. 686–702.

[18] See National Conference of State Legislatures, *State Budget Update: Summer 2011* (September 2011).

[19] For further discussion, see Congressional Budget Office, *The Budget and Economic Outlook: An Update* (August 2011), pp. 23–29; and the Statement of Douglas W. Elmendorf, *Confronting the Nation's Fiscal Policy Challenges* (September 13, 2011).

[20] See N. Gregory Mankiw and Matthew Weinzierl, "An Exploration of Optimal Stabilization Policy," *Brookings Papers on Economic Activity* (Spring 2011), pp. 209–249.

[21] Most of the fiscal policy options assessed in this testimony are similar to those assessed in Congressional Budget Office, *Policies for Increasing Economic Growth and Employment in 2010 and 2011* (January 2010).

[22] For a recent example of that approach, see Congressional Budget Office, *Estimated Impact of the American Recovery and Reinvestment Act on Employment and Economic Output from April 2011 Through June 2011.*

[23] See Nicholas Bloom, "The Impact of Uncertainty Shocks," *Econometrica*, vol. 77, no. 3 (May 2009), pp. 623–685.

[24] One might attempt to calculate the budgetary cost per FTE-year for different policies by inverting the number of cumulative years of full-time employment per million dollars of budgetary cost that is reported below. However, such calculations could be misleading for two reasons. First, for many of the options considered here, employment is affected beyond 2013 (in part because effects on employment lag behind those on GDP). Second, CBO's ranges of estimated effects on GDP (and thereby employment) are chosen to be centered relative to the distribution of possible outcomes, but the inverses of those ranges are not necessarily centered relative to the distribution of the inverses of those outcomes.

[25] See Congressional Budget Office, *Policies for Increasing Economic Growth and Employment in 2010 and 2011* (January 2010).

[26] In addition, the earlier publication reported cumulative effects on GDP over a five-year period rather than over the one- and two-year periods shown in this publication. In most cases, the shorter period in this analysis implies smaller cumulative estimated effects.

[27] This policy differs from the similar policy that CBO analyzed in January 2010 primarily as to when households would receive the payments. Under the policy discussed here, most of the credits would be received in the second quarter of 2012. Under the policy analyzed previously, the credits would have been paid evenly throughout 2011—a year after the policy was implemented and during a period when the Federal Reserve was projected to begin to offset some of the economic effects of the policy. Primarily for that reason, the estimated effects on output and employment of the policy analyzed here are larger than those shown in CBO's January 2010 report.

[28] See Federal Housing Finance Agency, "FHFA, Fannie Mae, and Freddie Mac Announce HARP Changes to Reach More Borrowers" (press release, Washington, D.C., October 24, 2011).

[29] For a discussion of the costs and benefits of a stylized refinancing program, see Mitchell Remy, Deborah Lucas, and Damien Moore, *An Evaluation of Large-Scale Mortgage Refinancing Programs*, Congressional Budget Office Working Paper 2011-4 (September 2011).

[30] Portions of that projected budgetary cost were calculated on a present-value basis.

[31] The losses that would be incurred by the Treasury, Fannie Mae, and Freddie Mac stemming from additional refinancing were estimated on a present-value basis, while the losses that would be incurred by the Federal Reserve were estimated on a cash basis. That approach is consistent with how the financial transactions of those entities are reflected in CBO's budget projections.

[32] This approach differs from the one that CBO used in its January 2010 analysis of fiscal policy options, which incorporated an assumption that households would respond to an extension of the AMT patch as having a temporary effect on their income. The current approach yields a greater effect on output and employment.

[33] This approach differs from that used in CBO's January 2010 analysis of fiscal policy options, which projected that households would respond to an extension of the tax cuts as though those changes would have only a temporary effect on their income. The current approach implies a greater effect on output and employment.

[34] For 2011, the 2010 tax act reduced the payroll tax paid by employees from 6.2 percent to 4.2 percent.

[35] HIRE included two provisions targeted toward unemployed workers. Employers were exempted from paying their share of OASDI taxes (6.2 percent) from March 19, 2010, through December 31, 2010, for every person whom they hired who had been employed for 40 hours or less during the preceding 60 days, and were also eligible for a $1,000 retention credit for each of those workers retained for at least one year.

[36] Since its January 2010 analysis of fiscal policy options, CBO has updated its estimate of a key parameter for this option—the ratio of payroll increases to total payroll at firms that increase their payroll—to incorporate new data about payroll growth and improved projections of that growth. The current approach implies a slightly smaller effect on output and employment.

[37] For further discussion, see Congressional Budget Office, letter to the Honorable Robert P. Casey Jr. providing CBO's assessment of a policy option to reduce payroll taxes for firms that increase their payroll (February 3, 2010).

[38] Taxable income from C corporations is subject to the corporate income tax, and that income can be taxed again at the individual level after it is distributed to shareholders or investors. Income from S corporations generally is treated as personal income: It is subject only to the individual income tax, and it is taxed at the personal income tax rates of the businesses' owners. Businesses also can be established as partnerships or sole proprietorships. Their income is generally taxed at the individual income tax rates of their owners.

[39] For estimates of the proportion of small business income received by taxpayers having $50,000 or less of adjusted gross income, see Department of the Treasury, *Methodology to Identify Small Businesses and Their Owners,* Office of Tax Analysis Technical Paper 4 (August 2011), www.trea-sury.gov/resource-center/tax-policy/tax-analysis/Documents/OTA-T2011-04-Small-Business-Methodology-Aug-8-2011.pdf.

[40] Letter from Thomas A. Barthold, Chief of Staff, Joint Committee on Taxation, U.S. Congress, to the Honorable Lloyd Doggett, April 15, 2011, *http://doggett.house.gov/images/ pdf/jct_repatriation_score.pdf.*

[41] CBO estimates that the effects on investment and net exports would be small and roughly offsetting, so the effects of the policy on output and employment would be determined by the increase in spending by shareholders. A further effect not included in this analysis is that, after the tax rate returned to 35 percent, companies would tend to reduce the rate at which they repatriated foreign income to the extent they expected the temporary tax reduction to be repeated in the future.

[42] In projecting how fast such federal aid would be disbursed, CBO relied heavily on the experience with grants to states provided under ARRA for purposes other than infrastructure or Medicaid. Most of those grants were related to education, with a small portion directed to other state and local spending programs; the timing of the disbursement of grants in those two categories was similar. Federal outlays for grants to states for Medicaid would be disbursed significantly faster, but the impact of those grants on state spending and revenue policies would lag behind the federal disbursements because it would take time for states to enact legislation to alter their policies in response.

[43] In its January 2010 analysis, CBO did not incorporate such an offset. That partial offset is consistent with evidence about states' behavior. The reduced state spending on infrastructure would, in turn, relieve pressure on state budgets in the same way as would additional federal aid to states for purposes other than infrastructure, allowing states to reduce revenues or increase other spending. Incorporating those effects on state policies slightly reduces the estimated effects of federal infrastructure spending on output and employment relative to CBO's earlier estimates because aid to states for other purposes is estimated to have smaller economic effects, on average, than infrastructure spending.

[44] In addition to its effect on demand, well-chosen infrastructure spending can also increase the productivity of private activities (by reducing traffic congestion, for example). However, any such effect on total output would be small over the 2012–2013 period.

[45] See Ben S. Bernanke, "The Near- and Longer-Term Prospects for the U.S. Economy" (address given at the Federal Reserve Bank of Kansas City Economic Symposium, Jackson Hole, Wyoming, August 26, 2011).

[46] The overall effect on consumer spending may not be positive if the increase in shareholders' wealth is offset by a direct cost to others that would decrease their spending—as would be the case, for example, for a decrease in the minimum wage.

[47] See Jesús Fernández-Villaverde, Pablo Guerrón-Quintana, and Juan F. Rubio-Ramírez, *Supply-Side Policies and the Zero Lower Bound,* Working Paper No. 11-47 (Philadelphia, Pa.: Research Department, Federal Reserve Bank of Philadelphia, October 2011), www.philadelphiafed.org/ research-and-data/publications/working-papers/2011/wp11-47.pdf.

[48] The Basel Committee on Banking Supervision provides a structure through which developed countries can cooperate on issues relevant to supervising banks, including setting capital requirements. Regulators in each of

the participating countries decide whether and how to implement the standards set by the committee. The implementation of increased capital requirements under Basel III is to be phased in over six years.

[49] CBO has analyzed the effects of that legislation later in the coming decade on individuals' decisions about whether and how much to work and employers' decisions about hiring workers. The agency estimates that the legislation will, on net, reduce the amount of labor used in the economy by a small amount—roughly half a percent—primarily by reducing the amount of labor that workers choose to supply. If the legislation did not affect the average number of hours worked per employed person, CBO projects that it would reduce household employment in 2021 by about 800,000. However, because the legislation will probably affect average hours worked among those employed, the effect on employment will be somewhat different. The reduction in the amount of labor used in the economy is largely attributable to the substantial expansion of Medicaid and the provision of subsidies that will reduce the cost of health insurance for some people; those provisions of the legislation will not go into effect until 2014. For further discussion, see Congressional Budget Office, *The Budget and Economic Outlook: An Update* (August 2010), pp. 48–49.

[50] Some exceptions to that general statement are discussed in Congressional Budget Office, *The Budget and Economic Outlook: An Update* (August 2010), pp. 48–49.

In: Recovery after Recession: Select Research and Analyses ISBN: 978-1-62417-777-4
Editors: Drew Symmes and Amanda Zulpo

Chapter 5

ARE RECOVERIES FROM BANKING AND FINANCIAL CRISES REALLY SO DIFFERENT?*

Greg Howard, Robert Martin and Beth Anne Wilso

ABSTRACT

This paper studies the behavior of recoveries from recessions across 59 advanced and emerging market economies over the past 40 years. Focusing specifically on the performance of output after the recession trough, we find little or no difference in the pace of output growth across types of recessions. In particular, banking and financial crisis do not affect the strength of the economic rebound, although these recessions are more severe, implying a sizable output loss. However, recovery does change with some characteristics of recession. Recoveries tend to be faster following deeper recessions, especially in emerging markets, and tend to be slower following long recessions. Most recessions are associated with a slowing, if not outright decline in house prices, but recessions with large declines in house prices also tend to have slower recoveries. Long recessions and those associated with poor housing-market outcomes can lead to sustained output losses relative to pre-crisis trends. Consistent with microeconomic studies showing permanent income loss to job-losing workers during recessions, we find that the sustained deviation in output from trend is associated with a reduction in labor input, especially linked to declines in employment and labor-force participation following recessions. On net, our results imply that the output/employment gap following a severe, long recessions is considerably smaller than is typically assumed by standard macro models, which in turn may have substantial implications for macroeconomic policy during recoveries.

I. INTRODUCTION

More than two years after the date the NBER set for the end of the U.S. recession, U.S. employment growth remains sluggish, the housing market is moribund, and GDP has barely exceeded its pre-recession peak. Thus, attention is increasingly focusing on the determinants

* This Discussion Paper was released by the Board of Governors of the Federal Reserve System, November 2011.

and characteristics of recoveries. Although research on the causes and types of recessions is legion, there has been surprisingly little academic work that concentrates on recoveries.[1] That said, two stylized facts have been frequently cited in the current policy discussion. The first is that recoveries from banking and financial crises are typically slow, reflecting impaired financial intermediation and the need for structural adjustment (see Cerra and Saxena (2008) and Reinhart and Reinhart (2010)). The second is that the rate of growth following deep recessions is typically faster than average, given pent-up demand and large stocks of underutilized labor and capital. As the Great Recession was both a banking and financial crisis and associated with a deep decline in output, these stylized facts imply different trajectories for output growth in this recovery.

To address this uncertainty and to gain greater insight into the nature of recoveries, defined as output growth following recession troughs, we examine quarterly data on GDP over the past 40 years for almost 60 countries, split roughly evenly between the advanced and the emerging market economies, resulting in observations on 271 recessions. Classifying recessions according to whether or not they included a banking or financial (B&F) crisis we find, in contrast to earlier work, that there is little distinction in the pace of recovery across recession types. Although recessions associated with B&F crises are typically more severe, the subsequent recoveries are not particularly unusual. Earlier work, finding the opposite, does so because it characterizes the pace of recoveries by averaging growth starting from the pre-recession cyclical peak rather than the recession trough, thus confounding the strength of the recession with the behavior of the recovery.

We do, however, find that, independent of whether a recession is associated with a banking or financial crisis, the depth and duration of the recession do have some predictive power for the pace of recoveries. Deeper recessions are associated with slightly stronger growth during the first three years of recovery.

Recessions of greater duration are linked to slower post-trough performance. Also, recessions with large house price declines—a common but not omnipresent feature of long recessions—tend to recover slower than other recessions.

Because banking and financial crises are often both deep and long, these effects on the pace of recovery balance out, leading post-trough growth to be about average and implying that output declines during such severe recessions are not made up quickly. We confirm and extend earlier work showing that severe recessions are associated with sustained negative gaps in the level of output from pre-crisis trend and show that these gaps are attributable to reductions in the utilization of labor – particularly through employment and labor force participation rates.

Until recently in the United States, GDP growth was about on pace with the average recovery in the advanced economies. However, recently the path of output has veered below the average recovery and is well below what would be predicted given the depth and duration of the Great Recession. However, once the impact of the severe decline in housing prices is accounted for, the recovery becomes less surprising. In addition, the composition of the recovery has been unusual.[2]

Exports and non-residential investment have outperformed the median recovery so far, but consumption, housing, and employment have languished. Looking more closely at these components, we find surprising strength in consumption of goods, in particular large durable goods such as cars and household furniture which one might think would be particularly restrained in this recovery. On the other hand, services consumption in almost every category is weaker than ever before in a post-war U.S. recovery. Likewise, even compared with other —jobless— recoveries, the weakness in employment is omnipresent and extreme.

Following this introduction, section II of the paper describes the dataset and recession classification system used. Section III presents our results, provides robustness checks, and contrasts our work with previous findings. Section IV focuses on characterizing and comparing the current U.S. recovery with past U.S. experience. Section V concludes.

II. Data and Methodology

For our cross-country comparisons, our database contains an unbalanced panel of quarterly GDP data for 59 countries – 26 advanced economies (AEs) and 33 emerging market economies (EMEs) – from 1970 (or whenever we begin to have quarterly GDP data) to present. Most data are from national sources, and a full list of countries can be found in appendix A. For comparability across countries, recessions are classified as two consecutive quarters of negative GDP growth. If a single quarter of positive growth occurs surrounded by a recession on either side, it is included in the recession. The pre-recession peak is defined as the last quarter before the beginning of a recession while the recession trough is the last quarter of the recession. As will be discussed further, we check the robustness of our results using a variety of other recession-dating methodologies found in the literature including the Bry-Boschen procedure for quarterly data (henceforth called the BBQ method) as described by Harding and Pagan (2002).[3]

Using our definition of recession, our sample contains 271 recessions; 137 occurring in the advanced economies and 134 in the emerging market economies (table 1). If the Great Recession is excluded, the sample of recessions is reduced to 224 episodes (116 AE and 108 EME). The greater number of AE recessions reflects the fact that quarterly GDP data are available for those countries earlier than for most of the EMEs. (See appendix B for data range for each country in our sample.)

In our analysis, we divide our sample by the type of economy – emerging market or advanced – and by type of recession. For comparability with earlier work, we match up the list of banking and financial crises found in IMF work by Laeven and Valencia (2008) with the list of recessions from the above procedure to identify if the downturn coincides with a currency, banking, or debt crisis.[4] Laeven and Valencia identify crises in the year of occurrence. For each recession, if a crisis occurred in a year during which the recession began or was ongoing, or if the recession began in the first or second quarter of a year immediately following a crisis, it was classified as being related to that crisis. Using this method, we identify 8 recessions in the advanced economies and 39 recessions in the emerging economies as being related to a crisis.

We also classify housing price slumps for a smaller sample of OECD countries for which we have a long time series of quarterly data on house prices. For these countries, we identify cycles in real house prices. Because the housing market is highly cyclical, most recessions are associated with periods of real house price decline. We identify periods of severe housing market stress as those associated with declines in real house prices above the median. We identify 35 recessions associated with severe housing slumps in the advanced economies. A list of countries, recession dates, and recession types is found in appendix A.

As with other work in this area, much of our analysis will be in the form of butterfly charts, allowing us to compare the behavior of output around cyclical downturns across numerous recessions and countries. In our case, however, instead of indexing the output series for each recession to be 100 at the pre-recession peak, we index the level of GDP to 100 at the date of the recession trough. This allows us to isolate the trajectory of the recovery, which is the key focus of our paper. We typically look at the 12 quarters before and after the trough. Because we have observations on so many recessions, it is not informative to chart individual recessions for most of our analysis. To summarize the cross-country experience, we calculate the mean value of output at each quarter across recession observations to construct the average path of GDP before and after the trough. Our results are not qualitatively different if medians are constructed. Using means allows us to create standard error bands around our average output paths.

III. RESULTS

A. Banking and Financial Crises

As a first look, we construct the average path of GDP around recession troughs for our entire sample, excluding the Great Recession (figure 1). On average in a recession in our sample, output falls 41/2 percent from the pre-recession peak to the trough.[5] GDP then rises at an average annual pace of 33/4 percent for the next three years, putting the level of output roughly 12 percent higher than at the trough. Splitting the sample between advanced economies and emerging market economies (figure 2), shows, not surprisingly, that the EMEs have more extreme cycles, both in terms of the severity of recessions and the rapidity of recoveries. For the average EME recession, output falls 61/2 percent from peak to trough, compared to 21/2 percent for the AEs. And the average annual pace of EME recovery is 5 percent over the three years following the trough, almost 2 percentage points faster than that in the AEs, leaving the level of output in the EMEs about 6 percentage points higher than that in the advanced economies.

As mentioned earlier, we have classified recessions by type, depending on whether they were associated with banking and financial crises. Over our sample, excluding the current recession, 8 advanced economies have experienced B&F crises out of a sample of 116 – or roughly 61/2 percent of all AE recessions.[6] The frequency of banking and financial crises is a much higher 36 percent (or 39 out of 108) for the emerging market economies. Because of this, and the more pronounced behavior of output around EME recessions, we separate our sample into advanced and emerging market economies throughout the paper so country composition does not distort our conclusions.

As seen in figures 3 and 4, the pace of output growth upon exiting a recession, shown in the region to the right of the recession trough, is remarkably similar for both the advanced and emerging economies. Recoveries from banking and financial crises appear identical in pace to recoveries from other types of recessions. Table 2 presents the results of regressions of the level of GDP one, two, and three years after the trough on a constant and a dummy for whether the crisis was associated with a banking and financial crisis. For both the advanced economies and the emerging markets, the coefficient on banking and financial crises comes in highly insignificant. There appears to be little evidence that the pace of output differs in recovery depending on whether the recession is related to a banking and financial crisis.

This result is surprising given the stylized fact and the standard interpretation of the previous empirical work (Reinhart and Reinhart, 2010; Reinhart and Rogoff, 2009; Claessens et al., 2008 and Terrones et al, IMF WEO, 2009) that finds that recoveries from banking crises are slow.[7] A key reason for the divergence in results is that earlier analysis has indexed the level of GDP to the pre-recession peak, rather than the trough. As can be seen in figures 3 and 4, there are significant differences in the severity of recessions associated with B&F crises. The red lines in the region to the left of the trough are all higher and fall more sharply. Indeed, running similar regressions on the level of GDP one, two, and three years *prior* to the trough show that the coefficient on banking and financial crises is large and significantly positive in most cases – indicating a sharper decline during the recession for B&F crises (table 3). Indexing to the peak confounds the strength of the recession and the behavior of the recovery, as can be seen when we re-index our data to the pre-recession peak (figures 5 and 6). Our results are consistent with findings that banking and financial crises are associated with greater declines in output and slower returns to pre-crises levels or trends, but this is because the recessions were deeper rather than because of disparities in the pace of recovery.

To confirm that indexing is central to our differences with the previous literature, we also ran robustness tests using the alternative methods of dating recessions and country samples for the AEs used in earlier work. Figures 7 and 8, display the output paths around the trough for the various samples of AE countries experiencing B&F crises found in Reinhart and Rogoff or Terrones et al. for both the two-quarter and the BBQ method of dating recessions. For the Reinhart and Rogoff recessions (excluding the Great Depression), the average path of GDP after a recession for B&F crises follows closely or is even stronger than our own, while the Terrones sample is just a touch weaker. To a first order, differences in recession classification and country sampling do not appear to alter our results. Figures 9 and 10 present similar results for the emerging economies, though only for Reinhart and Rogoff, as Terrones et al. does not cover emerging economies.[8]

B. Housing Slowdowns

Given the collapse in housing markets in a number of countries during the recent recession, we also looked at historical experiences with recoveries associated with severe slumps in housing markets. Our analysis is limited to the 18 advanced economies for which we could obtain reasonable historical data on housing markets and we define housing slumps simply in terms of changes in real house prices using quarterly OECD data starting in 1970.

The quarterly house price data are volatile, so to define a housing price slump we smooth each country's data using an HP filter with the low parameter of 100 and then look for local maxima and minima in the smoothed series. Returning to the unsmoothed data with the dates of the local peaks and troughs, we calculate the duration and depth of house price declines across the sample. Our methodology identifies 57 periods of house price declines, covering a significant portion of countries and time periods (occasionally across multiple recessions). For the United States (figure 11), this process identified four periods of real house price decline: the mid-1970s, the early 1980s, a brief period around 1990, and the most recent downturn. To classify a severe housing slump, we pick only the more sizable declines, those above the median. (For the United States, only the current housing slump would be classified as severe.) In these cases, the decline in real house prices is greater than 19 percent. They last for an average of 61/2 years and fall an average of 33 percent.

Our paper focuses on the cyclicality of GDP, not real house prices, so our final step is matching housing slumps to recessions. We do this simply: if any quarter of the recession overlaps with any quarter of the housing slump, we classify the recession as associated with a severe housing slump. There are 35 such recessions.

Dividing the OECD sample into recessions associated with severe housing slumps and those without reveals some interesting patterns. In particular, as shown in figure 12, housing-slump recessions tend to be longer and deeper and recoveries from these recessions are significantly slower. Table 4 runs a simple regression showing similar results.

C. Depth and Duration

Our result that the pace of growth after the trough of recessions associated with financial crises are similar to other recessions is somewhat surprising and leads to questions about what we know about recoveries following severe recessions more generally. In particular, how accurate is the second stylized fact that deep recessions are associated with faster bouncebacks? To address the questions, we characterize all recessions in terms of their depth – the decline in the level of GDP from peak to trough – and duration – the number of quarters from peak to trough. Figures 13 and 14 present histograms of the depth of the recessions in our sample for the advanced and emerging market economies, along with selected summary statistics, excluding the Great Recession. As mentioned above, the average decline in output for the AEs is 2.6 percent, with 12 percent of recessions associated with declines of more than 5 percent. The right tail is even more elongated for the EMEs, with the average decline being 6.4 percent, but 17 percent of the sample seeing output loss of 10 percent or greater. Figures 15 and 16 present the same analysis for recession duration. Not surprisingly, for both sets of countries, there is a mass of recessions lasting 2 quarters (the duration of output decline that defines a recession in our work).

For the advanced economies, the average recession length is about 3 quarters with almost 30 percent of the sample experiencing output declines for a year or more. For the EMEs, the duration is more extreme. The average EME recession lasts a year, and 45 percent of recessions last more than a year with one, that for post-Soviet Russia, of almost 6 years.

In Figures 17 through 20, we construct butterfly charts around the trough for recessions that are above the top 25th percentile in depth and duration and below the bottom 25th percentile for the AFEs and EMEs. In terms of recession depth, the charts certainly suggest that deeper recessions are associated with sharper bouncebacks than shallower recessions for both types of countries. The average level of output is 5 percent higher three years after a deep recession in the AEs and the EMEs. The results are different for long recessions. Here the average recovery appears slightly weaker following long recessions in the advanced economies, especially in the first few years. For the EMEs, there appears little difference between recoveries following long recessions than those following short recessions.

To provide a bit more rigorous look at this, table 5 presents the results of regressions of the level of GDP in the advanced economies one, two, and three years following a recession trough on the depth and duration of the recession, a dummy for whether the recession is associated with a banking or financial crisis, and a constant. Unlike with banking and financial crises, both depth and duration significantly affect the path of recovery, particularly in the first year. For example, for every 1 percentage point increase in recession depth, the level of output one year after the trough is a little over 1/2 percentage point greater. In contrast, a recession that is 1 quarter longer is associated with a similar-sized reduction in the pace of recovery. Over time, the drag from a longer recession appears to dissipate while the level of output is still roughly 1/2 percentage point higher following deep recessions. The results are even stronger for regressions on EME recessions (table 6). For these economies, a quarter longer recession is associated with a 1 percentage point lower level in output a year after the trough and 11/2 percentage point lower level in output three years later. In contrast, a 1 percentage point greater decline in the level of output during the recession is associated with a 1/2 percentage point higher level of output rising to 3/4 percentage point greater level by year three of the recovery. In all three versions, the coefficients on length and depth come in statistically significantly and with opposite signs.

In the previous literature, financial and banking crises have been linked to severe recessions – implying both deeper and longer downturns – which may explain why we are failing to get statistically significant effects of banking and financial crises – these impacts may be cancelling each other out. To check this, we take a closer look at the relationship between banking and financial crises and severity of recessions. Figures 21 and 22 present scatterplots of the depth and duration of recessions, again dividing countries by whether they are considered advanced or emerging market economies. Individual banking and financial crises are represented by the yellow dots and all other recessions are captured by the black dots. The vertical and horizontal lines represent the average duration and depth of recessions, respectively—yellow lines capturing the averages for banking and financial crises and black lines the average duration and depth for all other recessions. What was somewhat surprising to us is that banking and financial crises are not universally longer and deeper. Judging by the distance between the yellow and black lines, for the AEs, B&F crises tend to be longer but not much deeper than all other types of recessions. The reverse is true for the EMEs. For these economies, B&F recessions are associated with deeper but not much longer recessions. Table 7 details the summary statistics behind these charts. Prior to the Great Recession, the correlation between length and depth was .36 for the AEs and a much stronger .67 for EMEs.

D. Implications

What do our results imply should be the pace of the current recovery? To show this, we use the coefficients from our three regressions above to predict the pace of recovery at 4, 8, and 12 quarters past the trough based on observed depth and duration in the current recession[9]. Figures 23 through 24 illustrate the results of this exercise. The solid black line represents the pace of recovery predicted for all AEs and EMEs, respectively, given the average depth and duration of the Great Recession and the red line represents the path of actual average AE or EME GDP in the current recovery. The pace of recovery in the AEs appears to be underperforming while that in the EMEs seems right on track.

Turning to the United States, figure 25 compares the current U.S. recovery to past recoveries in the advanced economies. Although the U.S. Great Recession was longer and deeper than almost all previous U.S. and advanced economy recessions and was accompanied by extreme financial disruptions, the U.S. recovery aligned well with average AE recoveries until the first half of 2011 when the pace of recovery slowed sharply. However, figure 26 shows that the actual path of recovery is well below what would be predicted by our simple model of depth and duration, suggesting other factors, possibly related to the financial crisis, may be at play this time around.[10] One could ask if generalization from overall AE experience to the U.S. economy is appropriate given its relatively high average growth rate and greater flexibility. In simple tests, however, we were unable to find compelling evidence that U.S. recoveries are typically faster than AE recoveries in general (tables 8 and 9).

E. Permanent versus Transitory, or Does the Economy Ever Actually "Recover"

Despite the differences in recovery rates we have highlighted above for recessions that are long or deep, recovery rates across recessions are still quite similar. This implies that long and deep recessions are associated with large and sustained losses to output. In particular, the economy will not return to its long-term trend, implying a persistent gap between the pre-crisis trend and the post-crisis level of output. This result is consistent with Cerra and Saxena (2008) which finds that large output losses associated with financial crises are highly persistent.

Our work also suggests that large declines in output over long periods of time can have more permanent effects on the level of output. For example, using the regression results for the advanced economies, the pace of recovery is the same after a recession of 2 quarters duration that results in a 2 percent decline in output and one of twice that length and duration – suggesting a greater potential permanent loss in output from the more severe recession.

To press this result further, we conduct a series of exercises to test whether output returns to pre-recession trend levels. To do this, we face both a conceptual and a practical challenge. Often, macroeconomic data are detrended using HP or Kalman filters. Both of these techniques are two-sided moving average filters. This implies that the view of the past changes as the data evolves. In particular, and of great importance here, these detrending tools cannot accommodate a permanent deviation from trend. For this reason, we choose to use a simple exponential trend which can accommodate such long-lasting deviations. Even with this methodology, determining the appropriate pre-recession trend is somewhat tricky, to the extent that banking and financial crises are associated with bubbles or positive deviations from trend prior to the crisis. To avoid including the bubble in our trend, we calculate the four-year average growth rate for each country, two years prior to the peak, thus excluding the often rapid period of growth before the crisis. (The results are similar using average growth calculated over different pre-peak intervals.)

Having calculated a pre-recession trend, we then examine GDP as a percentage of this trend (figures 27 and 28) for the average recession and from particularly mild and severe recessions. Average GDP in the advanced economies never recovers to trend, even for short and shallow recessions. However, the average recession in the emerging economies does return to trend, and exceeds trend for short and shallow recessions. But, as for the AE recessions, for deep and long EME receeesions, GDP does not drift back toward 100 percent of the pre-crisis trend, even after 10 years. For both AEs and EMEs, deep and long recessions lead to a sustained loss from pre-recession trend of about 8 to 10 percent after 10 years. While varying the specification of our regressions or the definition of pre-crisis trend can modify these loss estimates, these exercises all suggest a more sustained hit to output from severe recessions.

Another way of testing if GDP returns to its pre-crisis trend is to evaluate whether growth rates immediately after recessions differ from long-run average growth. We have examined this, first, by constructing scatterplots for the AE and EME countries of average growth over the sample for each country and average pace of growth three years after a recession trough (figures 29 and 30). If growth in recoveries proceeds at about average pace, then the points should line up close to the 45 degree line, indicating no quick return to pre-recession trend levels. In these charts, average growth seems very close to the pace of growth during recoveries. We also include a variable in our depth and duration regression to capture average pre-recession growth. It is possible that countries with faster trend growth experience faster growth coming out of recoveries. If these countries are also associated with greater propensity (or less) to experience banking and financial crises, then our estimates of post-trough growth may be biased. As seen in in table 10, pre-crises growth rates come in statistically insignificant – suggesting the average pace of growth prior to the recession does not affect the post-recession recovery rate.

Shifting back to our comparison with Cerra and Saxena, they find that B&F crises lead to permanent losses in output. Given our results on depth and duration, one might ask whether their result is purely a reflection of the depth and duration of the downturns associated with financial crises or is there something special about financial crises above and beyond the contour of the downturn which leads to permanently lower output? There are differences in methodology and data between the two studies – Cerra and Saxena restrict their analysis to the initial shock stemming from the first year of a banking crisis, focus solely on banking crises (treating currency and debt crises as separate), use simulations from VAR analysis to estimate the impact of banking crises, and compare banking crises to non-crisis growth performance whereas we draw comparisons to other recessions. Despite these differences, we can shed some light on this question.

Using the sample of non-crisis recessions, we regress the level of post-trough GDP on the depth and duration of the crisis, similar to table 5, but with a sample restricted to non-crisis recessions and of course without the B&F crisis explanatory variable. This gives us a prediction for the recovery given a recession of a certain depth and duration. We use the model to create a prediction for a recovery after a non-B&F related recession that has the same depth and duration of an average B&F crisis. Finally, we compare the prediction to the average of actual outcomes of B&F crises. Figures 31 and 32 show that the average recovery and the prediction are almost identical. There appears to be nothing inherently special about banking and financial crises that creates more of an output loss than similarly sized recessions unassociated with crises. Combining this simple experiment with our earlier results, we conclude that any recession of similar magnitude to a B&F crisis may lead to sustained losses in the level of output.

F. A Simple Look at What Doesn't Recover

Our work above suggests that the level of GDP, particularly after long and deep recessions, does not recover to its pre-crisis trend even five years after the start of a recession, thus it is important to understand what is driving this sustained output loss. In general, even for the advanced economies, it is a challenge to get comparable quarterly time series data across countries to allow a more granular look at post-recession behavior. One exception is a dataset developed by and detailed in Ohanian and Raffo (2011) which contains quarterly information on total hours, labor-force participation, employment, and average weekly hours for 15 OECD countries from 1960 to the 2010.[11] With these data we can examine the broad supply-side components of output – total hours and output per hour – to see where the weakness in overall GDP lies following a recession. Figure 33 shows, for the smaller sample used here, the average behavior of the level of GDP as a percentage of pre-recession trend – divided into those that were particularly severe (in the top 25th percentile of depth and duration) and all others. In both cases, the level of output fails to return to the pre-recession trend, with the gap being particularly sizable (about 71/2 percent) for severe recessions. Figures 34 and 35 break output down into total hours and output per hour for both sets of recessions. Interestingly, for typical recessions, the loss in output is a reflection of declines in both productivity and labor input. In contrast, for severe recessions, the sustained deviation in the level of output from trend is more than entirely accounted for by a loss in total hours – productivity actually increases relative to trend.

We next decompose total hours into labor-force participation, the employment rate, and average weekly hours (figure 36 through 38). Interestingly, whereas the workweek returns and even exceeds its pre-recession trend relatively quickly, employment and labor-force participation rates remain depressed – particularly after long and deep recessions. These results suggest the decline in output relative to pre-crisis trend, especially after severe recessions, is importantly concentrated in a reduction in the utilization of labor. For particularly bad recessions, the reduction in the employment and labor force participation rates is sustained even five years after the pre-recession peak.

IV. The Current U.S. Recovery in More Detail

With the general knowledge of the features of recoveries in hand, we can now turn to characterizing the current U.S. recovery in more detail. The butterfly chart in figure 39 shows the evolution of U.S. GDP around the trough of every recession since 1947, separating the 1980s downturn into two recession periods.[12] The thick black line denotes the current recession. Only the downturn in 1980 had a more sluggish pace of recovery two years after the trough.

This anemic post-recession performance is not a reflection of weak outcomes in the manufacturing sector. After falling dramatically in the recent recession industrial production (figure 40) has since climbed at an about-average pace and real exports (figure 41) have surged nearly 25 percent. Non-residential investment (shown in figure 42) tells a similar story. The fall in investment was larger than in any previous recession, leaving a tremendous gap between the current level and the peak, but the pace of investment growth during the recovery has been on the high end of the more recent historical experiences.

On the other hand, unusually poor recovery is evident in consumption and housing. The level of real private consumption (figure 43) has fallen behind every recession except the

1980 double dip. Residential investment remains below its level at the trough of the recession (figure 44) and house prices have underperformed all previous recoveries (figure 45).

A number of factors appear to be contributing to these areas. Credit growth, even outside of mortgage lending, has fallen further since the recession trough (figure 46) – undoubtedly reflecting tighter lending conditions but also weak demand. Consumer sentiment has also improved little over the past two years (figure 47) as income growth has been particularly slow (figure 48) and employment has languished (figure 49). Consumption performance has shown some variation – with goods consumption, especially for durables and motor vehicles, picking up at about on average pace (figures 50 to 52) but services consumption is markedly weaker than in previous recoveries (figure 53). Employment growth has been weak across the board but like consumption, relatively worse in in the services industries than the goods industries (figure 54 and 55). Also of note is the unusual behavior of state and local employment which was rising at a relatively slow pace prior to the recession and has shown declines matched only by the recession in 1980, with little hope of improvement going forward (figure 56). The policy response in this recovery has been mixed. Monetary policy, even excluding long-term asset purchases and other non-traditional programs, has been larger than in most previous recoveries with the real federal funds rate (figure 57) remaining in negative territory two years after the recession trough. In contrast, government expenditures (figure 58), which had risen sharply during the recession, has leveled off noticeably since then especially compared with earlier recoveries. Further, although revenue fell more than in other recessions, the revenue growth following the recession is on the high end of previous recoveries (figure 59). Finally, we apply similar supply-side analysis to the United States as above to the OECD countries.[13] Re-indexing to the peak and taking deviations from a simple exponential pre-recession trend, shows that 21/2 years after the recession trough the level of output in the United States is strikingly below trend (figure 60). This gap is driven entirely by a lack of hours (figure 61), as labor productivity has returned to trend (figure 62). As with the OECD results more generally, this hours gap reflects a downshift in labor force participation and employment rather than the workweek (figure 63 to 65).

CONCLUSION

We take away several key points from our work on recoveries. First, whether a recession is associated with a banking or financial crisis does not have a statistically significant effect on the pace of growth following recession troughs. This result surprised us and raises questions for future research about the exact channels through which banking and financial crises affect growth.

In comparison, as might be expected, recoveries from recessions associated with severe housing downturns are found to be slower. Second, the depth and duration of a recession does matter for recovery speed. Deeper recessions are associated with faster post-trough recoveries, in line with the view that pent-up demand and underutilized resources can contribute to a sharp snapback.

In contrast, longer recessions are associated with slower post-trough growth, possibly reflecting skill and capital deterioration as recessions drag on. Banking and financial crises are associated with more severe recessions – deeper in the case of emerging market economies and longer in the case of the advanced economies – but do not appear to impose additional restraint to recoveries beyond the depth and duration. Currently, the emerging market economies are recovering as would be predicted given the depth and duration of their Great Recession experiences, but the advanced economies, including the United States, are lagging. Third, we expand on earlier work in the literature that finds evidence that recessions, especially severe recessions, are associated with persistent negative deviations in the level of GDP from pre-crisis trend.

This deviation appears to importantly reflect the lower utilization of labor, particularly a decline in employment and labor force participation rates from earlier trend levels. Going forward, it will be important to examine these results in line with what we know from the micro labor literature about skill deterioration, hysteresis, and long-term unemployment. Finally, we may need to reexamine the assumptions in many of our macro models that output levels eventually return to trend or reevaluate the concept of trend.

For the United States, the current recovery has been weaker than would have predicted based on the depth and duration of the recession alone. Without question, the labor market has performed particularly weakly – with especially tepid employment growth and a sharp decline in labor force participation. These developments raise questions about the financial and fiscal channels that affect labor demand and about the role of policy in the face of long and deep recessions.

REFERENCES

[1] Cerra, Valerie and Sweta Chaman Saxena, —Growth Dynamics: The Myth of Economic Recovery," *American Economic Review,* 2008, 98:1, p. 439-457.

[2] Claessens, Stijn, M. Ayhan Kose, and Marco E. Terrones, —What Happens During Recessions, Crunches, and Busts?" *IMF Working Paper,* WP/08/274, December 2008.

[3] Harding, Don and Adrian Pagan, —Dissecting the Cycle: a methodological investigation," Journal of Monetary Economics, 2002, vol 49, p 365-381.

[4] Laeven, Luc and Fabian Valencia —Systemic Banking Crises: A New Database," *IMF Working Paper,* 08/224, November 2008.

[5] Lopez-Salido, David and Edward Nelson, — *Postwar Financial Crises and Economic Recoveries in the United States,"* mimeo, 2010.

[6] Ohanian, Lee E and Andrea Raffo, — *Hours Worked over the Business Cycles: Evidence from OECD Countries,* 1960-2010," mimeo, 2011.

[7] Romer, Christina and David Romer, — What Ends Recessions?" *NBER Macroeconomics Annual,* 1994, vol. 9, p13-80.

[8] Reinhart, Carmen M. and Vincent R. Reinhart, — *After the Fall" NBER Working Paper Series, Nuxmber* 16334, September 2010.

[9] Reinhart, Carmen M. and Kennth S. Rogoff, — *The Aftermath of Financial Crises," NBER Working Paper Series,* Number 14656, January 2009.

[10] Terrones, Marco E., Alasdair Scott, Prakash Kannan, —From Recession to Recovery: How soon and how strong?" *International Monetary Fund World Economic Outlook,* April 2009, Chapter 3.

Table 1.

Total		Advanced Economies	Emerging Market Economies
All			
Recessions	271	137	134
Excluding Great Recession of which ...	224	118	104
Banking or Financial Crisis	47	8	39
Housing Related	---	35	---

Table 2.

Advanced Economies	One year after		Two years after		Three years after	
	Coefficient	Std Error	Coefficient	Std Error	Coefficient	Std Error
B&F	-1.05	1.23	-0.28	1.57	1.30	1.78
Constant	103.99		106.48		108.75	
R-squared	0.00		-0.01		0.00	
Emerging Economies	One year after		Two years after		Three years after	
	Coefficient	Std Error	Coefficient	Std Error	Coefficient	Std Error
B&F	0.17	1.09	0.20	1.85	1.25	2.58
Constant	106.78		110.90		114.51	
R-squared	-0.01		-0.01		-0.01	

Table 2 is based on a simple linear regression of the form

$$\frac{GDP_{trough+x}}{GDP_{trough}} = \beta_0 + \beta_1 D_{B\&F} + \epsilon$$

where x is one, two, or three years, and $D_{B\&F}$ is a dummy variable for whether the recession was associated with a banking or financial crisis.

A * indicates confidence at the 95 percent level, and a ** indicates confidence at a 99 percent level.

Table 3.

Advanced Economies	One year prior		Two years prior		Three years prior	
	Coefficient	Std Error	Coefficient	Std Error	Coefficient	Std Error
B&F	0.84	1.11	3.20 *	1.30	3.98 *	1.67
Constant	101.28		98.76		95.67	
R-squared	0.00		0.04		0.04	

Emerging Economies	One year prior		Two years prior		Three years prior	
	Coefficient	Std Error	Coefficient	Std Error	Coefficient	Std Error
B&F	4.96 **	1.25	8.30 **	1.94	7.84 **	2.72
Constant	102.96		98.67		96.05	
R-squared	0.08		0.11		0.05	

Table 3 is based on a simple l i near regression of the form

$$100\frac{GDP_{trough-x}}{GDP_{trough}} = \beta_0 + \beta_1 D_{B\&F} + \epsilon$$

Table 4.

Advanced Economies	One year after		Two years after		Three years after	
	Coefficient	Std Error	Coefficient	Std Error	Coefficient	Std Error
Housing	-1.57*	0.71	-1.98*	0.83	-1.32	0.95
Constant	104.52		107.15		109.20	
R-squared	0.04		0.05		0.01	

Table 4 is based on a simple li near regression of the form

$$100\frac{GDP_{trough-x}}{GDP_{trough}} = \beta_0 + \beta_1 D_H + \epsilon$$

where D_H is a dummy variable for whether the recession was associated with a housing slump.

Table 5.

Advanced Economies	One year after		Two years after		Three years after	
	Coefficient	Std Error	Coefficient	Std Error	Coefficient	Std Error
Depth	0.64**	0.11	0.61**	0.15	0.42**	0.18
Duration	-0.62**	0.20	-0.52*	0.27	-0.19	0.32
B&F	-0.40	1.17	0.18	1.58	1.27	1.87
Constant	104.20		106.45		108.23	
R-squared	0.20		0.10		0.02	

Tables 5 and 6 are based on a simple linear regression of the form

$$100\frac{GDP_{trough+x}}{GDP_{trough}} = \beta_0 + \beta_1 D_{B\&F} + \beta_2 Depth + \beta_3 Duration + \epsilon$$

where Depth is a positive number measuring the fall in GDP during the recession as a percentage of peak GDP and Duration is the number of quarter from peak to trough.

Table 6.

Emerging Economies	One year after		Two years after		Three years after	
	Coefficient	Std Error	Coefficient	Std Error	Coefficient	Std Error
Depth	0.57 **	0.09	0.62 **	0.17	0.85 **	0.24
Duration	-1.07 **	0.21	-1.30 **	0.39	-1.61 **	0.55
B&F	-1.59	0.98	-1.60	1.85	-1.34	2.61
Constant	107.95		112.68		116.31	
R-squared	0.19		0.11		0.07	

Table 7.

Advanced Economies	Depth		Duration	
	M ean	Std Dev	M ean	Std Dev
B&F	3.66	4.07	5.13	2.75
Others	2.58	2.49	2.97	1.36
	p=.26		p=.00	

Emerging Economies	Depth		Duration	
	Mean	Std Dev	Mean	Std Dev
B&F	9.41	7.31	4.47	2.71
Others	4.92	5.94	3.71	2.80
	p=.00		p=.20	

Table 8.

Advanced Economies	One year after		Two years after		Three years after	
	Coefficient	Std Error	Coefficient	Std Error	Coefficient	Std Error
U.S. Dummy	-0.24	1.72	0.37	2.18	2.80	2.46
Constant	103.93		106.45		108.74	
R-squared	-0.01		-0.01		0.00	

Table 8 is based on a simple linear regression of the form

$$100\frac{GDP_{trough-x}}{GDP_{trough}} = \beta_0 + \beta_1 D_{US} + \epsilon$$

where D_{us} is a dummy variable for whether the recession occurred in the United States.

Table 9 is based on a simple li near regression of the form

$$100\frac{GDP_{trough+x}}{GDP_{trough}} = \beta_0 + \beta_1 D_{US} + \beta_2 Depth + \beta_3 Duration + \epsilon$$

Table 9.

Advanced Economies	One year after		Two years after		Three years after	
	Coefficient	Std Error	Coefficient	Std Error	Coefficient	Std Error
Depth	0.64 **	0.11	0.61 **	0.15	0.42 **	0.18
Duration	-0.65 **	0.19	-0.51 *	0.26	-0.11	0.30
U.S. Dummy	-0.32	1.52	0.34	2.06	2.87	2.42
Constant	104.25		106.41		107.95	
R-squared	0.20		0.10		0.03	

Table 10.

Advanced Economies	One year later		Two years later		Three years later	
	Coefficient	Std Error	Coefficient	Std Error	Coefficient	Std Error
Depth	0.50 **	0.13	0.45 *	0.20	0.27	0.24
Duration	-0.49 **	0.19	-0.41	0.28	-0.11	0.34
Pre-crisis Growth	-0.05	0.13	0.18	0.19	0.27	0.24
B&F	0.04	1.02	0.55	1.51	1.70	1.85
Constant	103.77		105.46		106.95	

Emerging Economies	One year later		Two years later		Three years later	
	Coefficient	Std Error	Coefficient	Std Error	Coefficient	Std Error
Depth	0.56 **	0.09	0.64 **	0.17	0.83 **	0.26
Duration	-1.11 **	0.21	-1.36 **	0.39	-1.71 **	0.58
Pre-crisis Growth	0.06	0.12	0.36	0.23	0.52	0.34
B&F	-0.15	1.01	1.78	1.91	2.56	2.84
Constant	106.96		110.00		112.77	

Tables 5 and 6 are based on a simple linear regression of the form

$$100\frac{GDP_{trough+x}}{GDP_{trough}} = \beta_0 + \beta_1 D_{B\&F} + \beta_2 Depth + \beta_3 Duration + \beta_4 Trend + \epsilon$$

where Trend is the 4 year average annual growth in the two years prior to the peak.

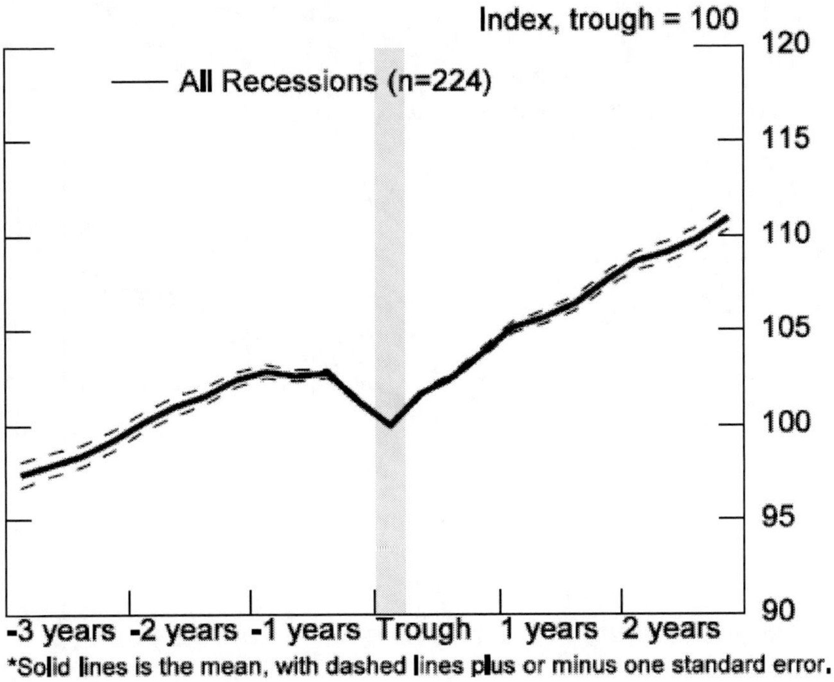

Figure 1. Recoveries in the entire sample.

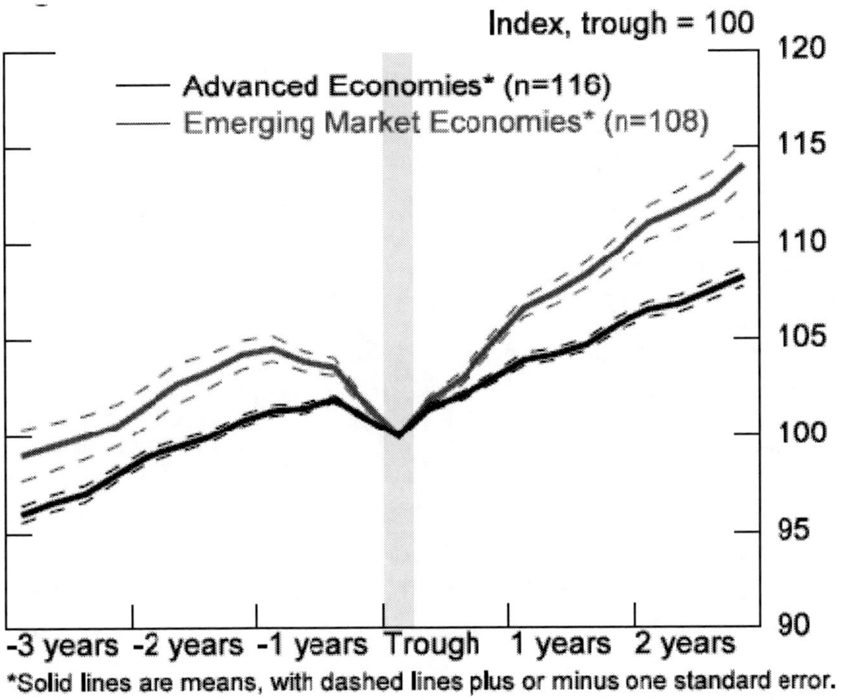

Figure 2. Recoveries.

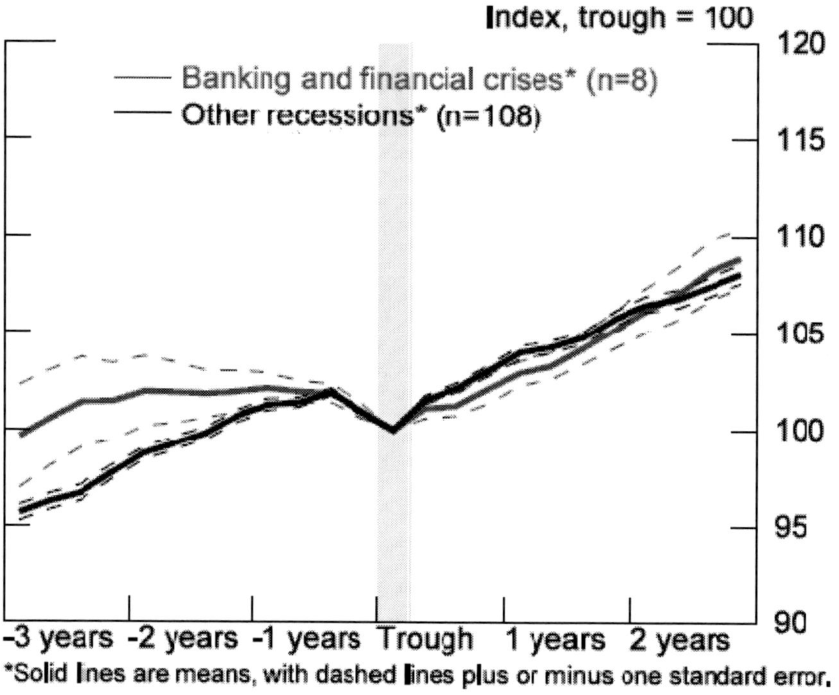

Figure 3. Recoveries in the Advanced Economies.

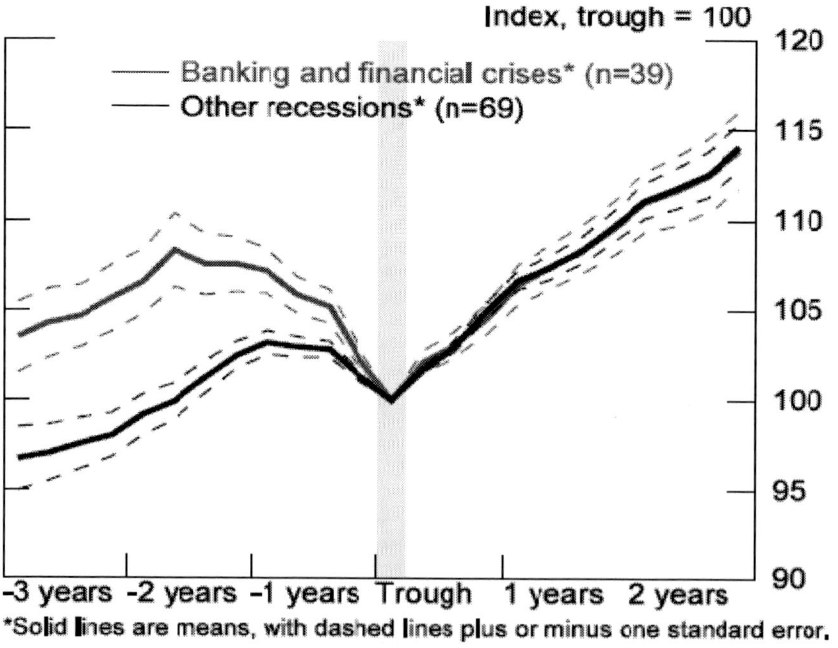

Figure 4. Recoveries in the Emerging Economies.

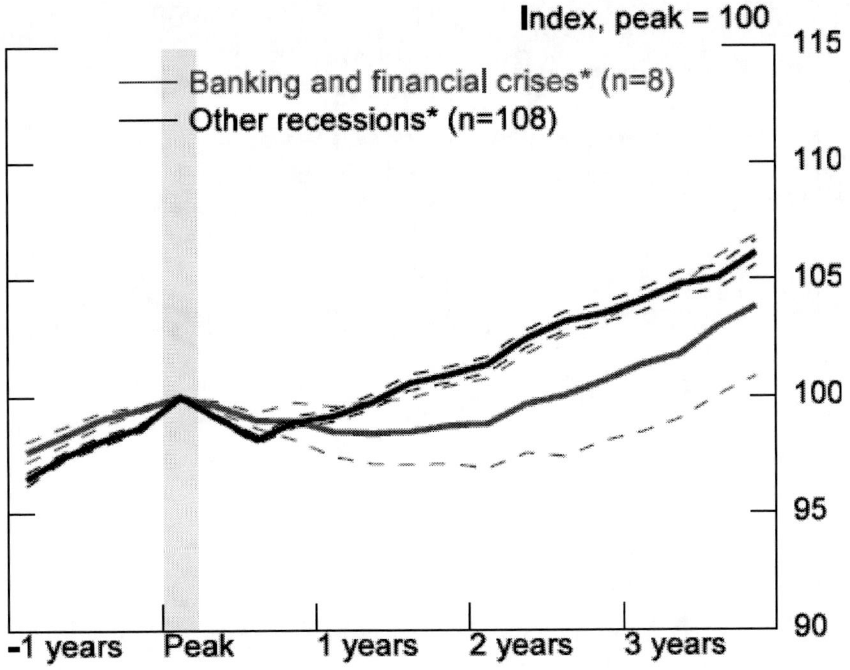

Figure 5. Recessions in the AEs, indexed to peak.

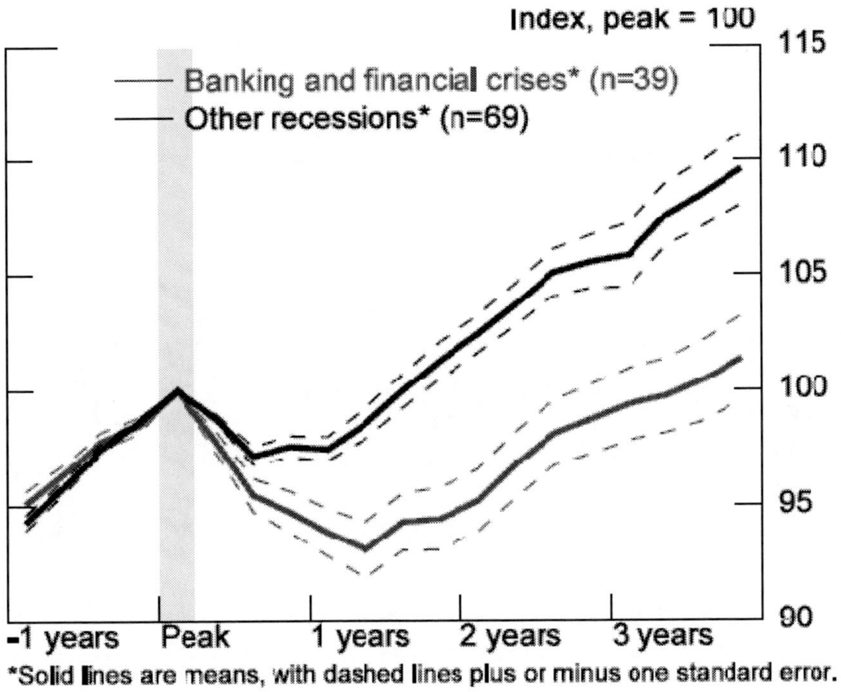

Figure 6. Recessions in the EMEs, indexed to peak.

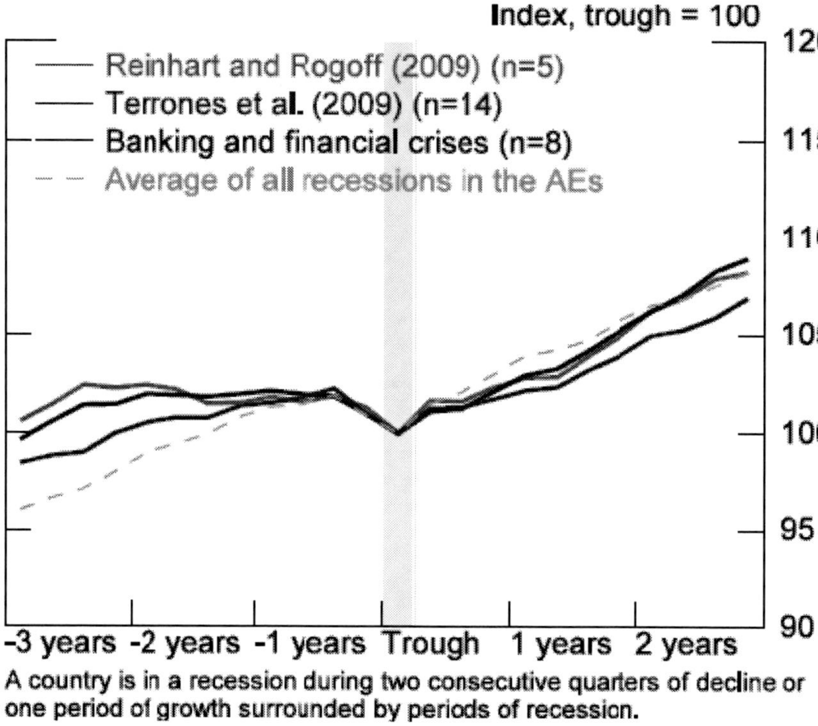

Figure 7. Two-quarter method of dating AE recessions.

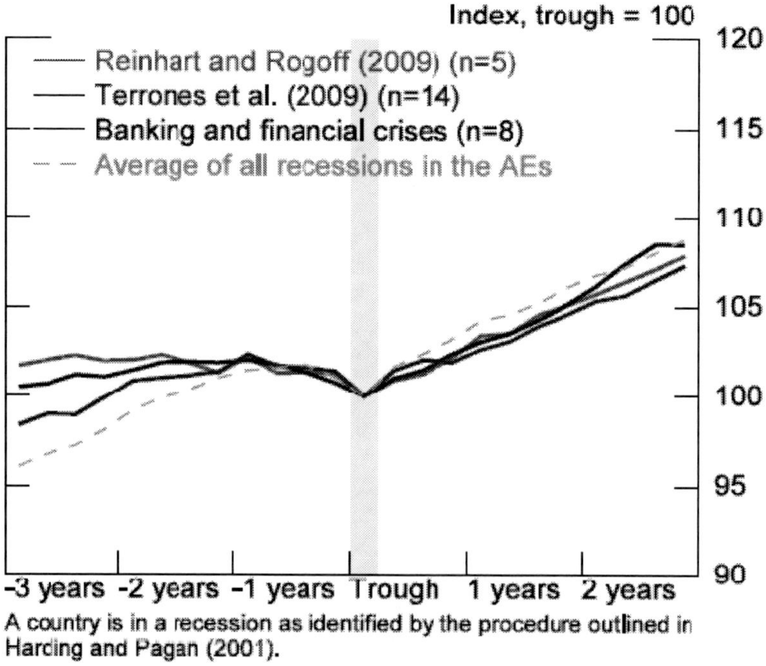

Figure 8. BBQ Method of dating AE recessions.

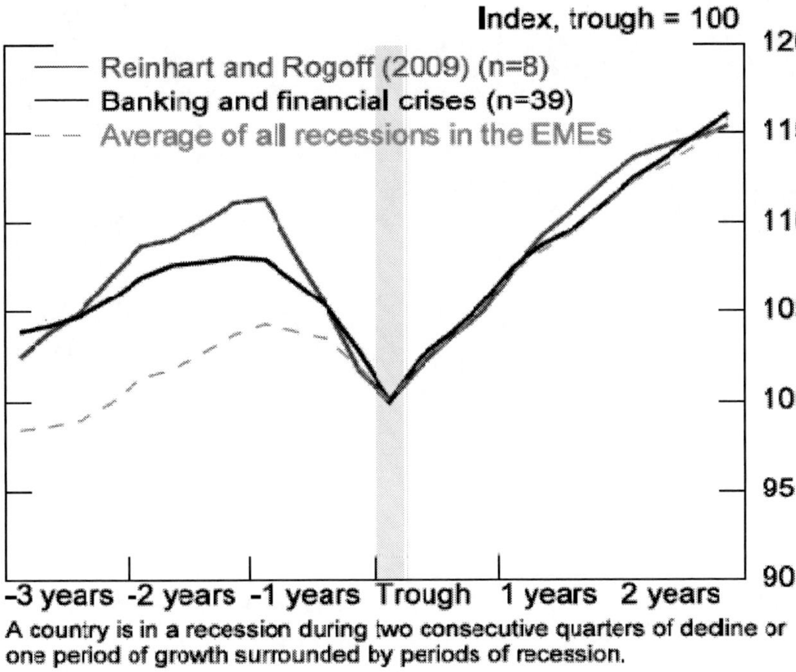

Figure 9. Two-quarter method of dating EME recessions.

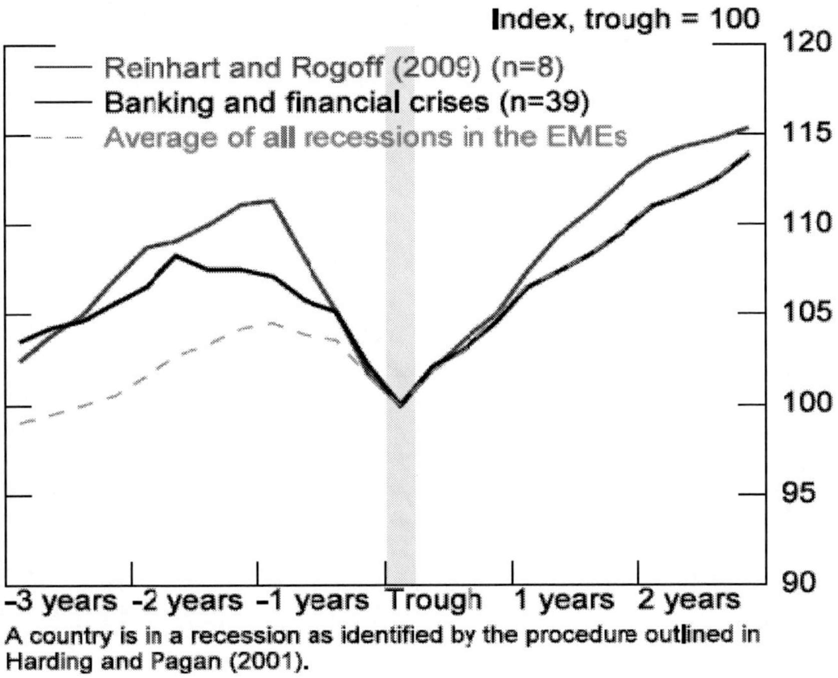

Figure 10. BBQ Method of dating EME recessions.

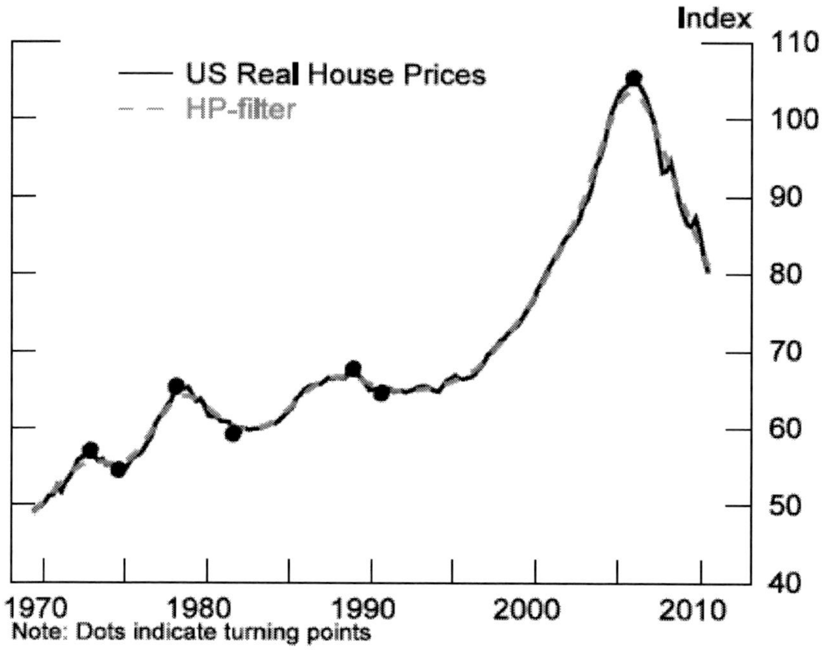

Figure 11. U.S. House Prices.

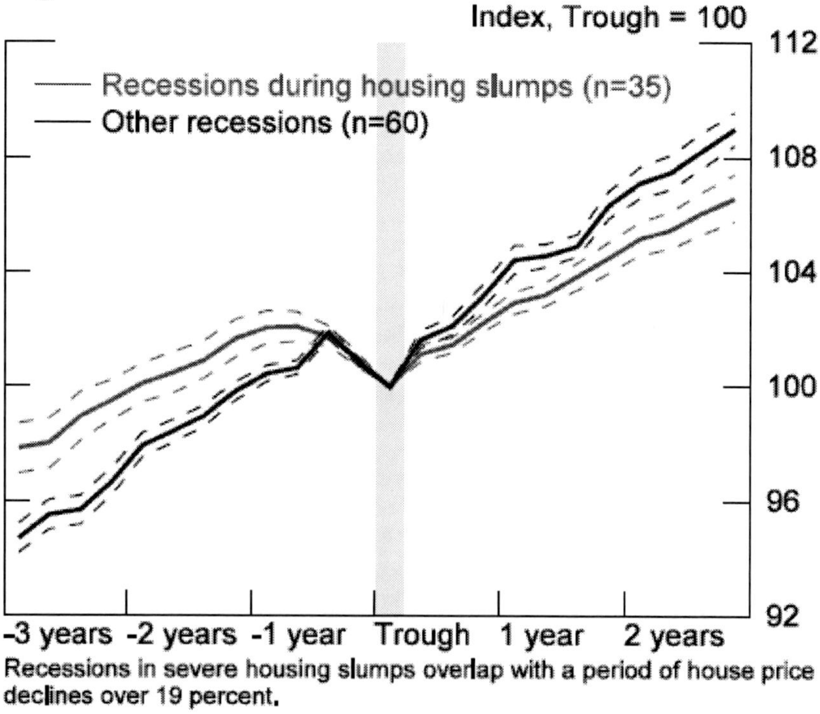

Figure 12. GDP in Select Advanced Economies.

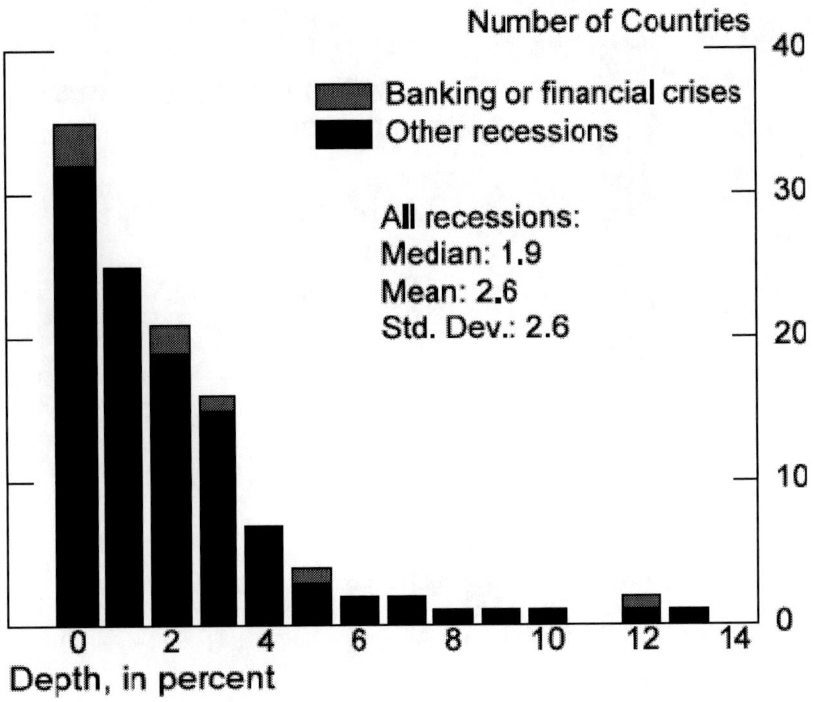

Figure 13. Recessions in the Advanced Economies.

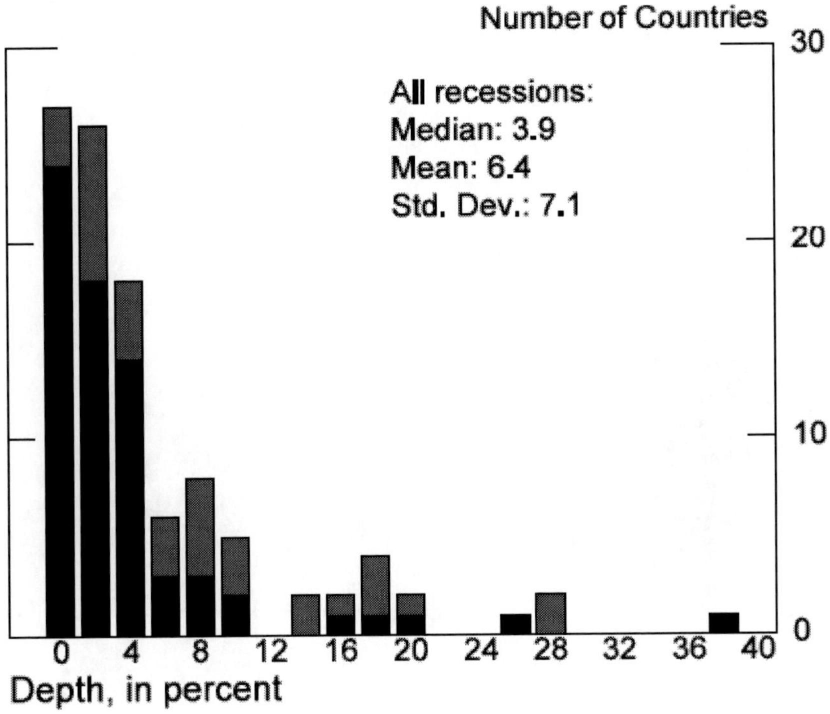

Figure 14. Recessions in the Emerging Economies.

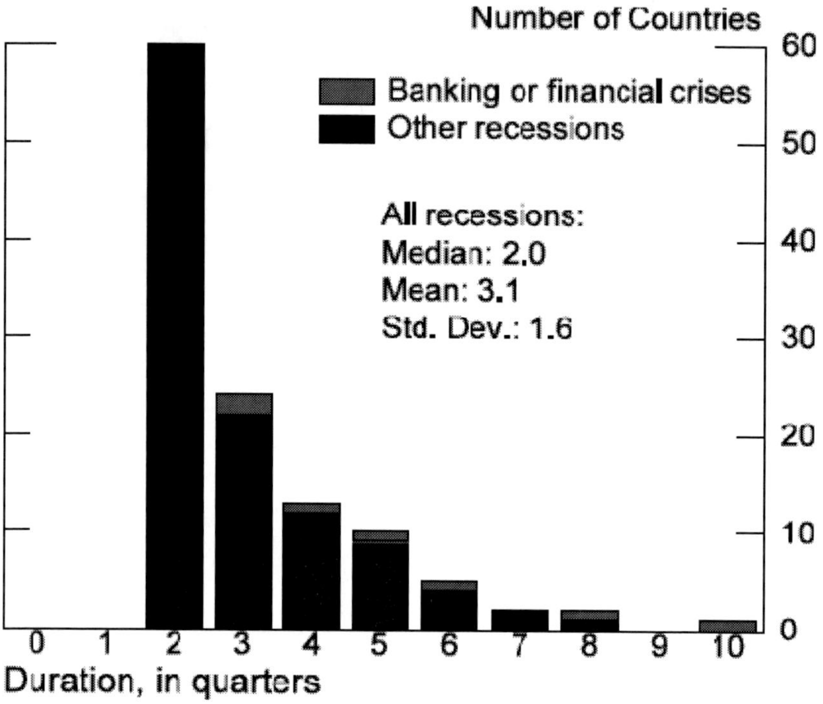

Figure 15. Recessions in the Advanced Economies.

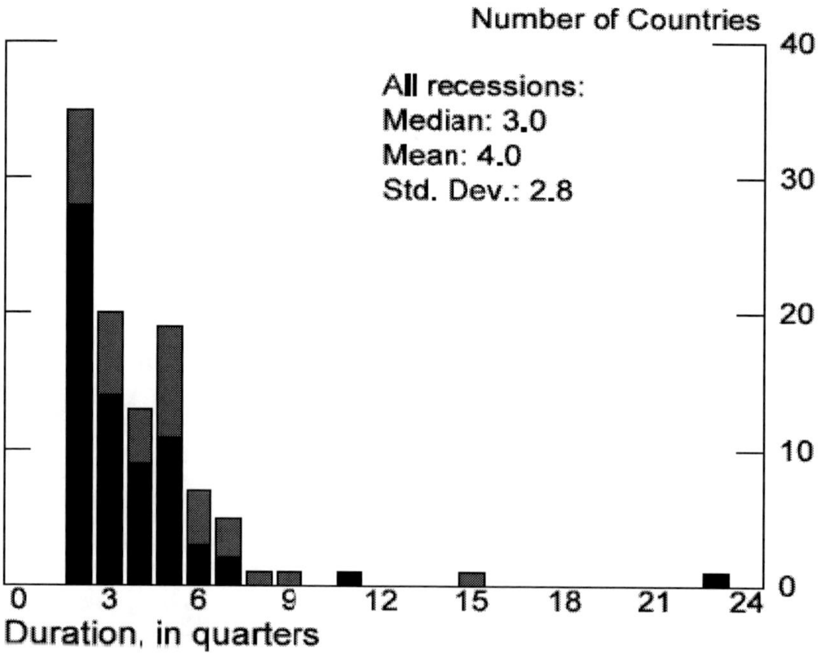

Figure 16. Recessions in the Emerging Economies.

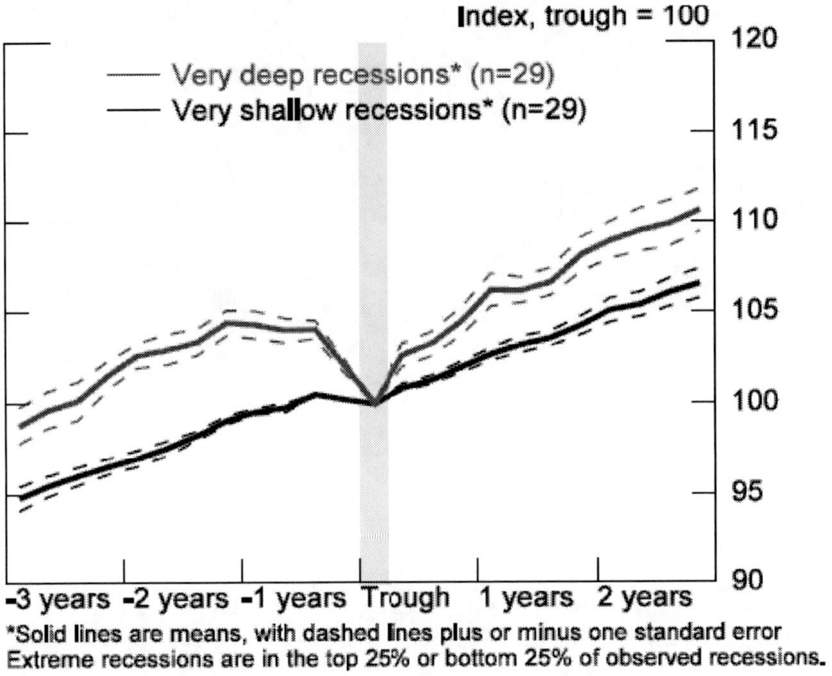

Figure 17. Recoveries in the Advanced Economies.

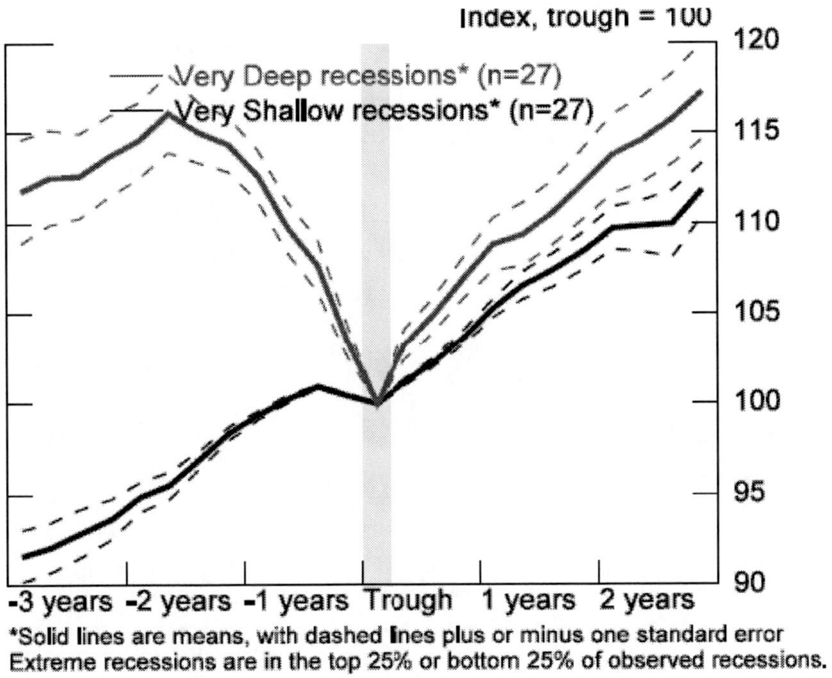

Figure 18. Recoveries in the Emerging Economies.

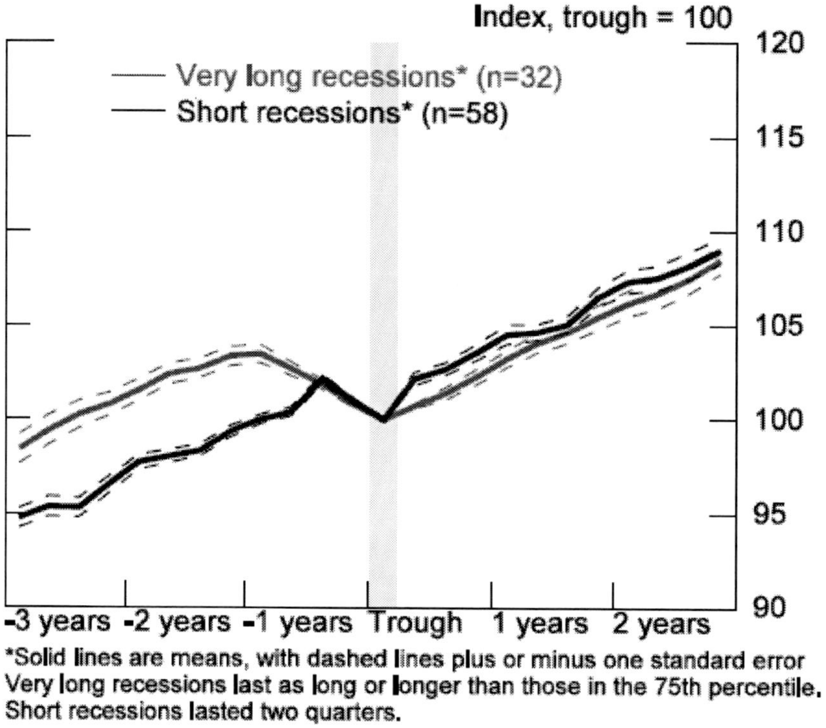

Figure 19. Recoveries in the Advanced Economies.

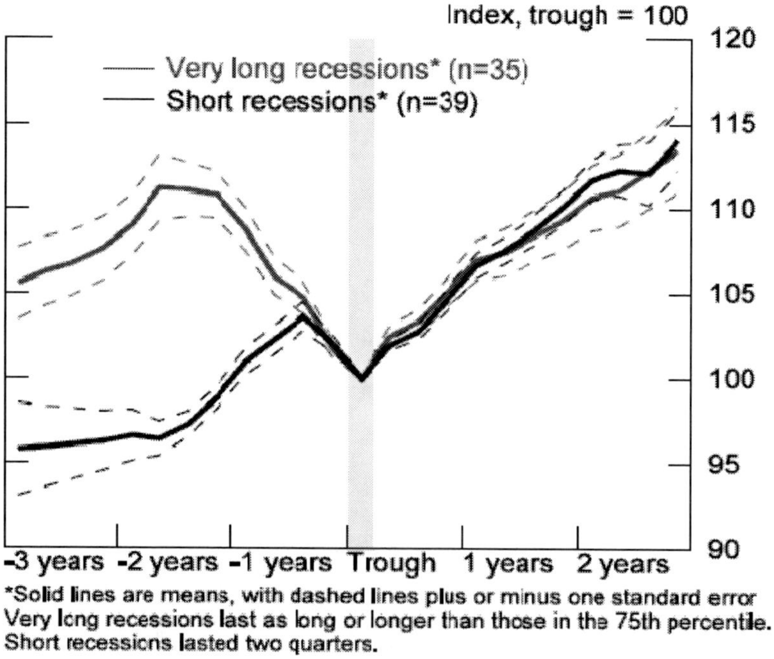

Figure 20. Recoveries in the Emerging Economies.

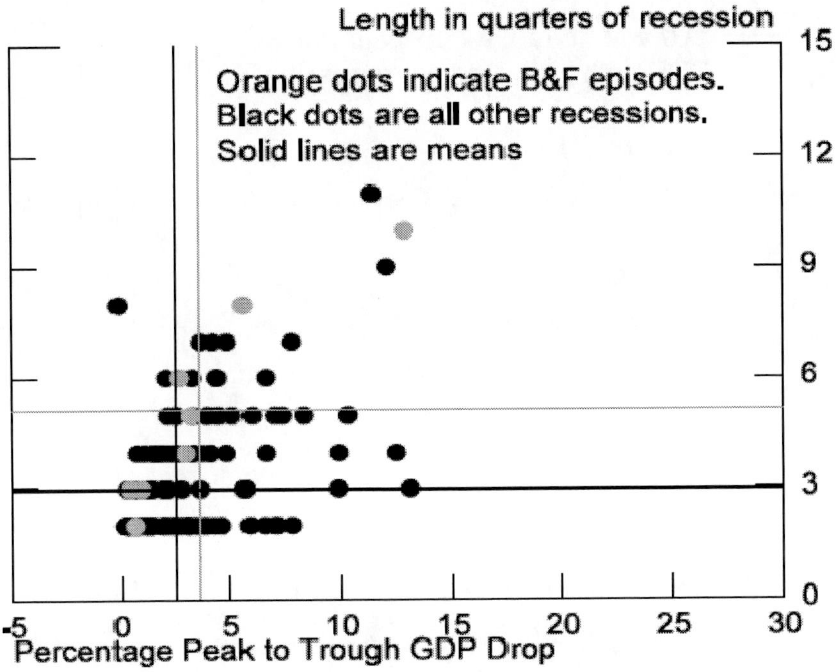

Figure 21. Recessions in the Advanced Economies.

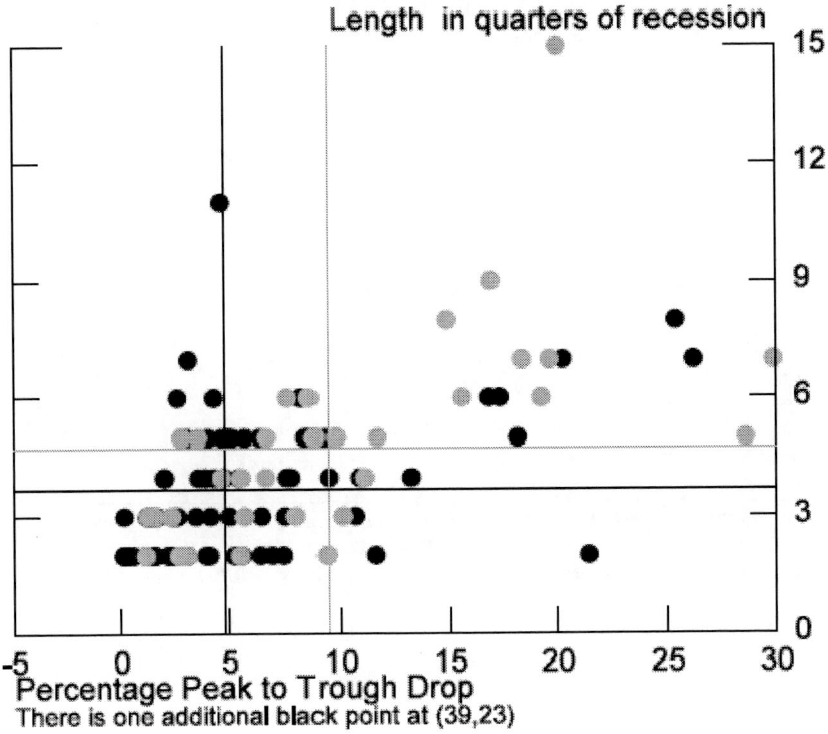

Figure 22. Recessions in the Emerging Economics.

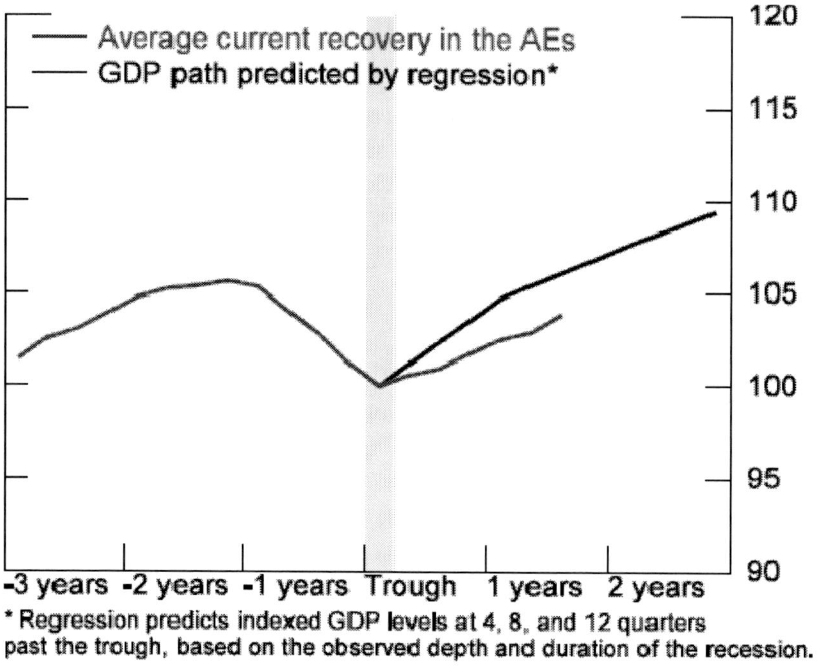

Figure 23. The Current AE recovery.

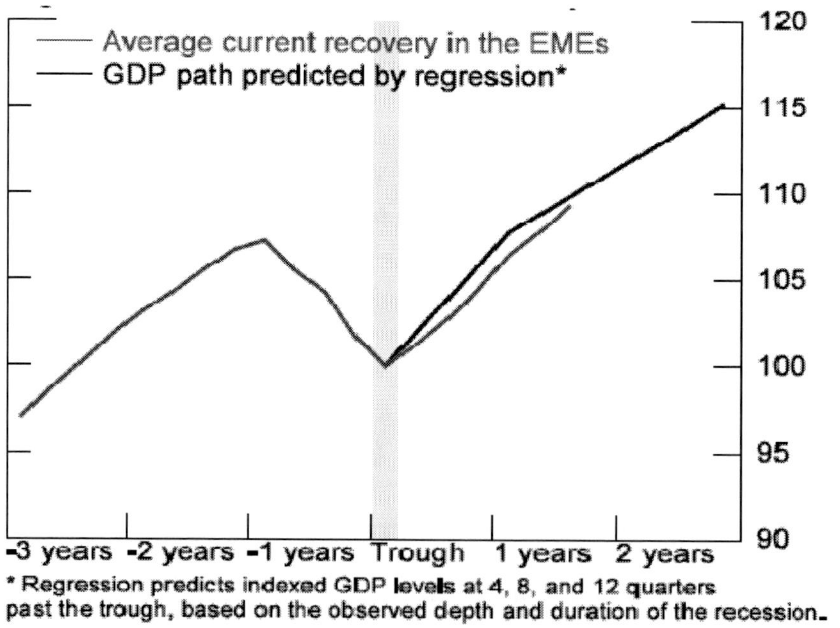

Figure 24. The Current EME Recovery.

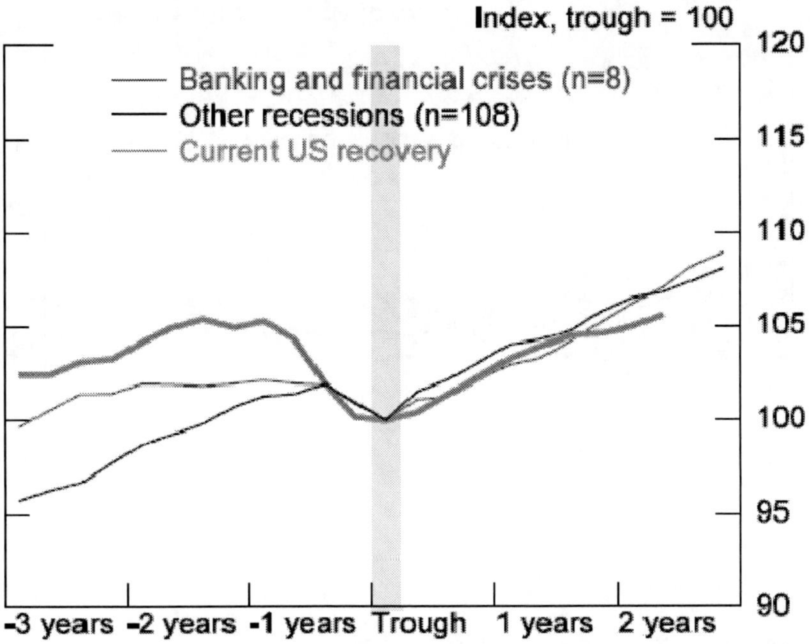

Figure 25. Recoveries in the Advanced Economies.

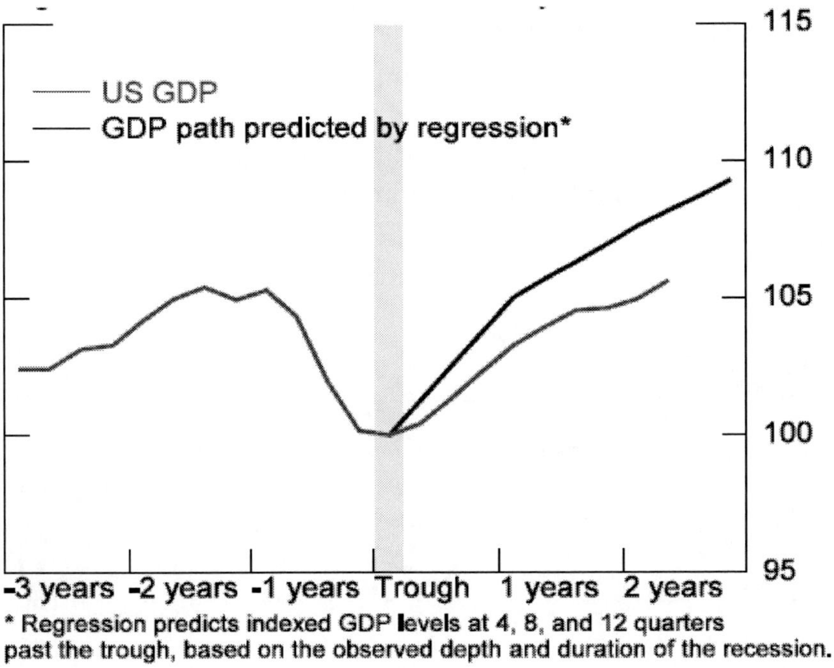

Figure 26. The Current U.S. recovery.

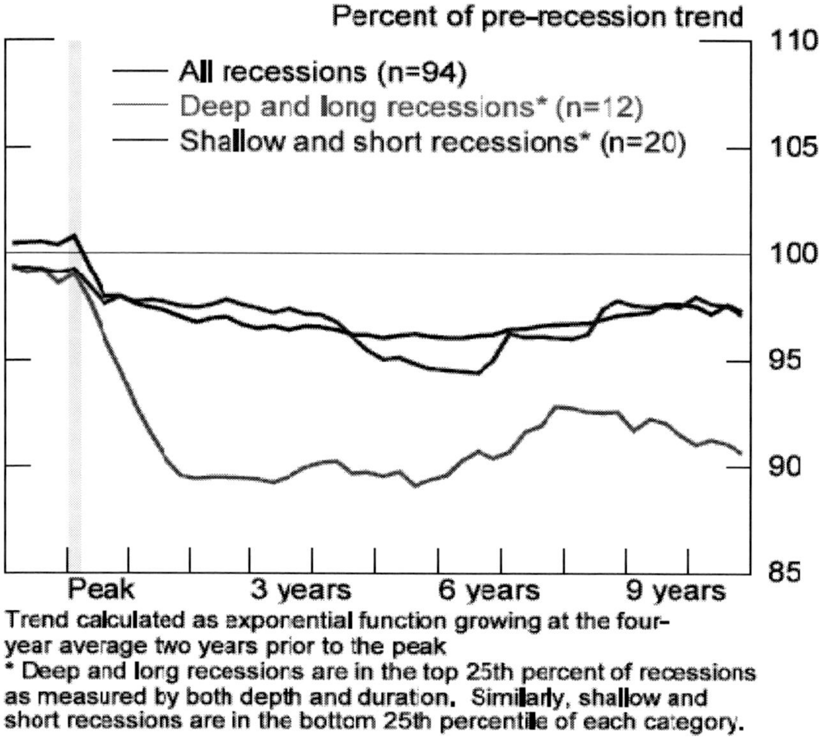

Figure 27. Recoveries in the Advanced Economies.

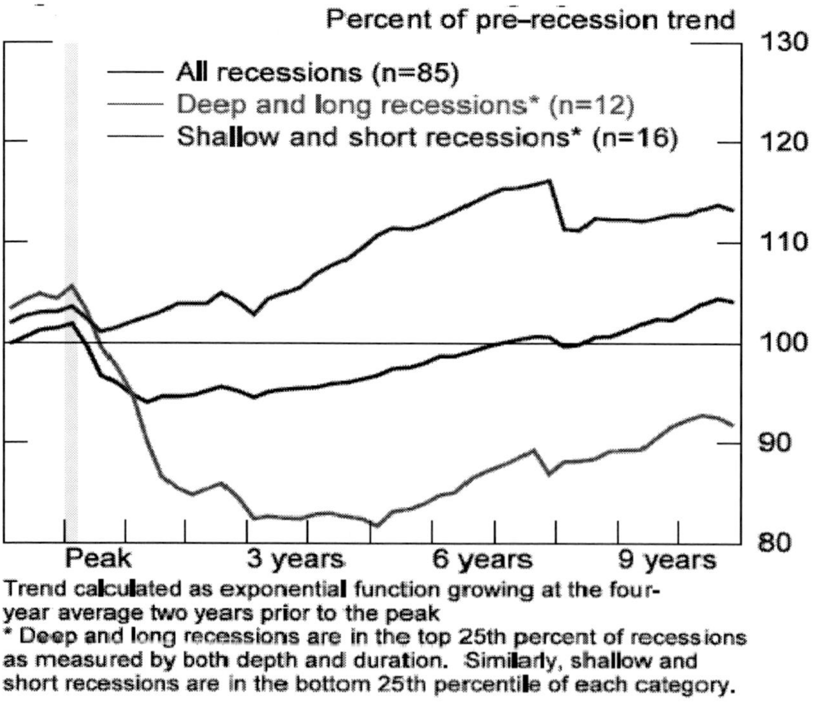

Figure 28. Recoveries in the Emerging Economies.

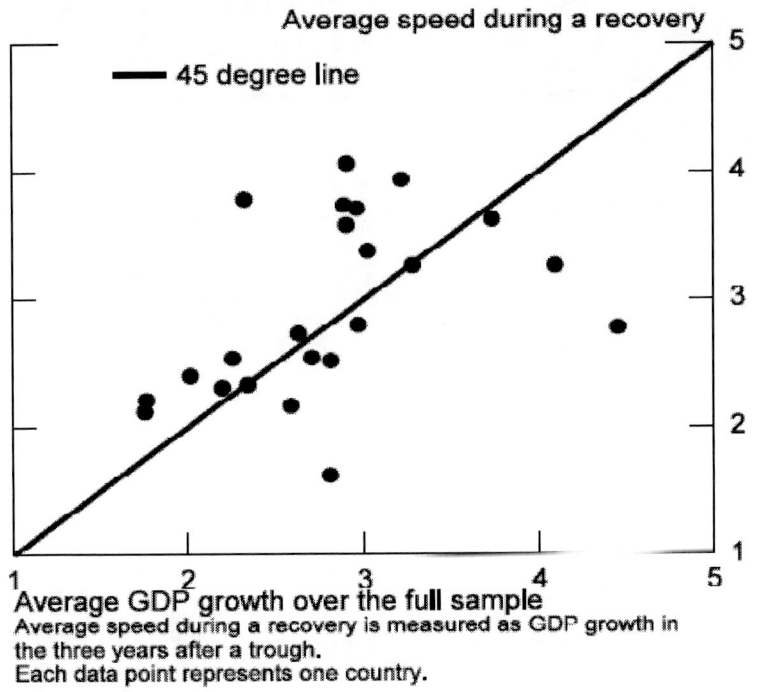

Figure 29. Growth Rates in the Advanced Economies.

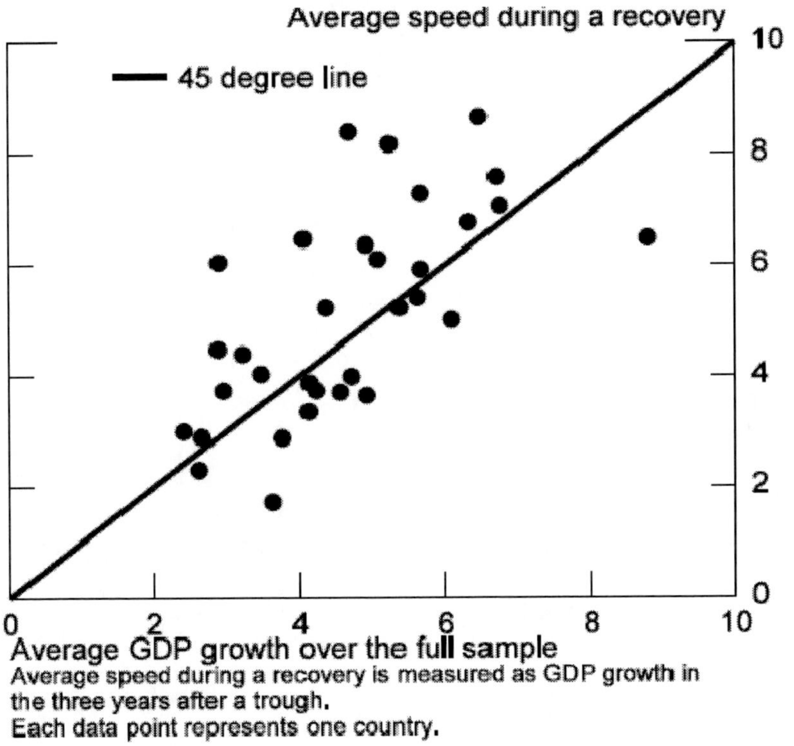

Figure 30. Growth Rates in the Emerging Economies.

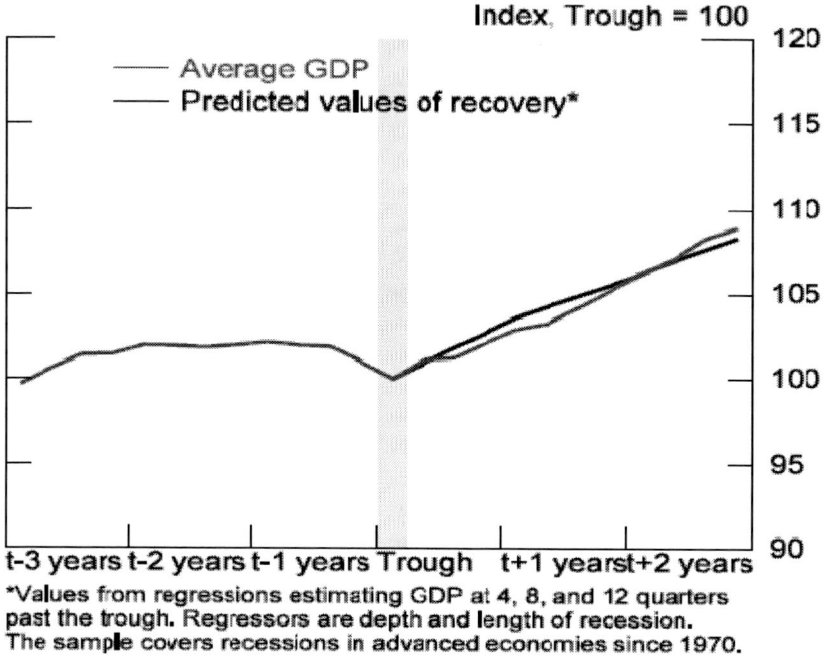

Figure 31. B&F crises in the Advanced Economies.

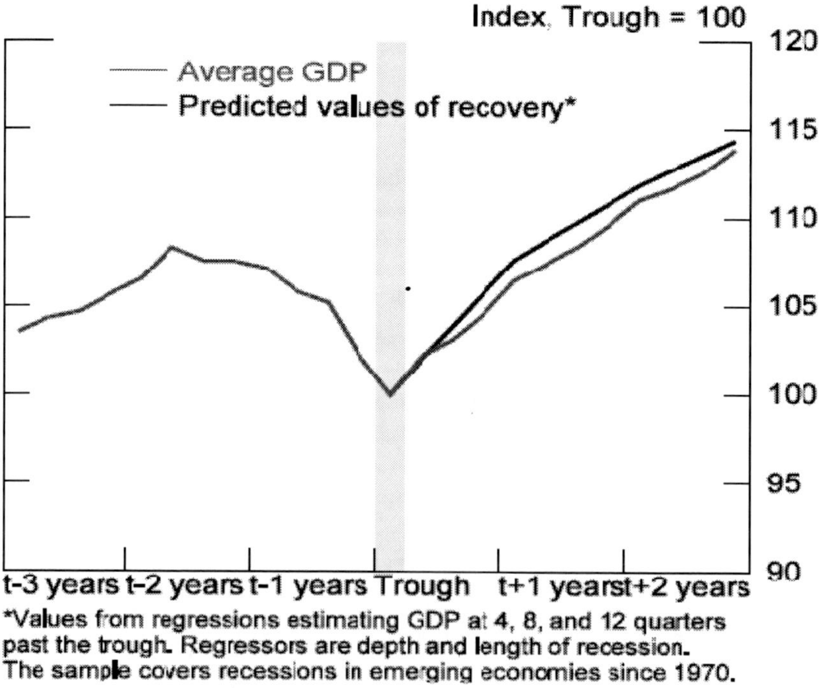

Figure 32. B&F crises in the Emerging Economies.

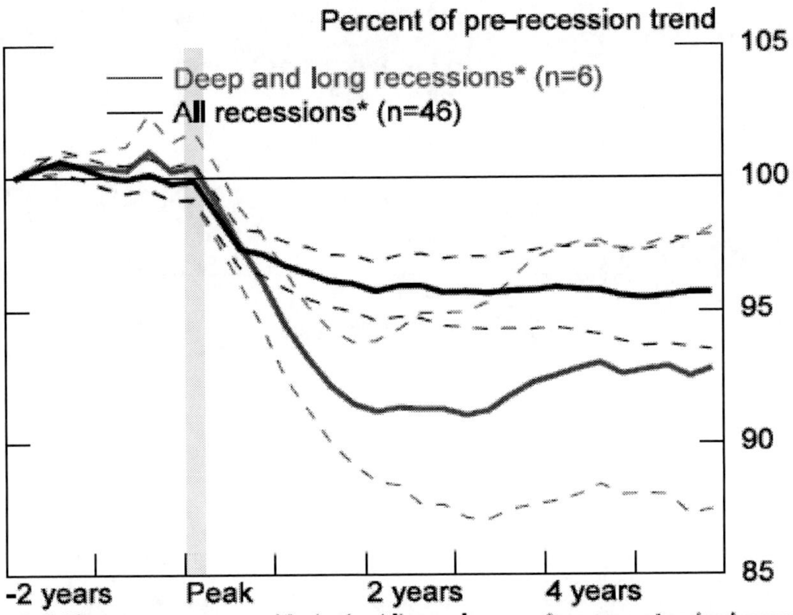

*Solid lines are means, with dashed lines plus or minus one standard error. Trend is exponential function growing at the 4-year average 2 years prior to the peak. Deep and long recessions are in the top 25th percent of recessions measured by depth and duration.

Figure 33. GDP in Select Advanced Economies.

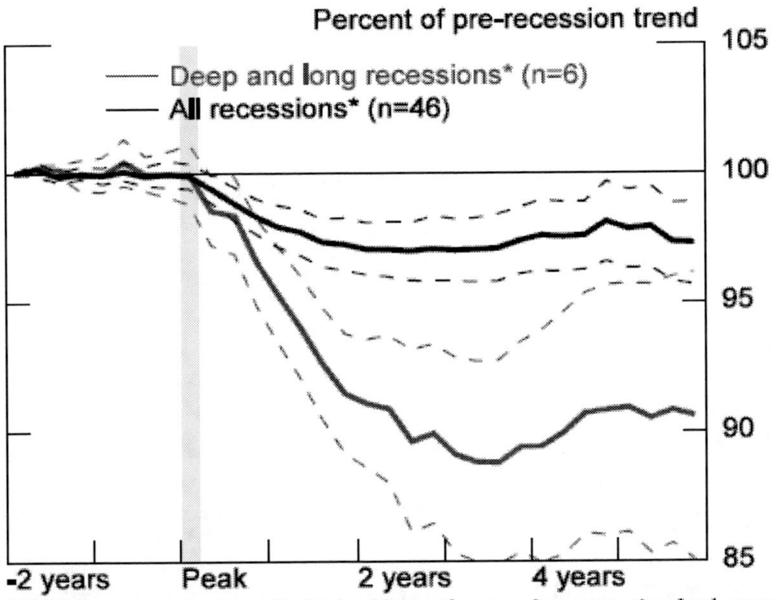

*Solid lines are means, with dashed lines plus or minus one standard error. Trend is exponential function growing at the 4-year average 2 years prior to the peak. Deep and long recessions are in the top 25th percent of recessions measured by depth and duration.
Data are from Raffo and Ohanian (2010).

Figure 34. Total Hours in Select Advanced Economies.

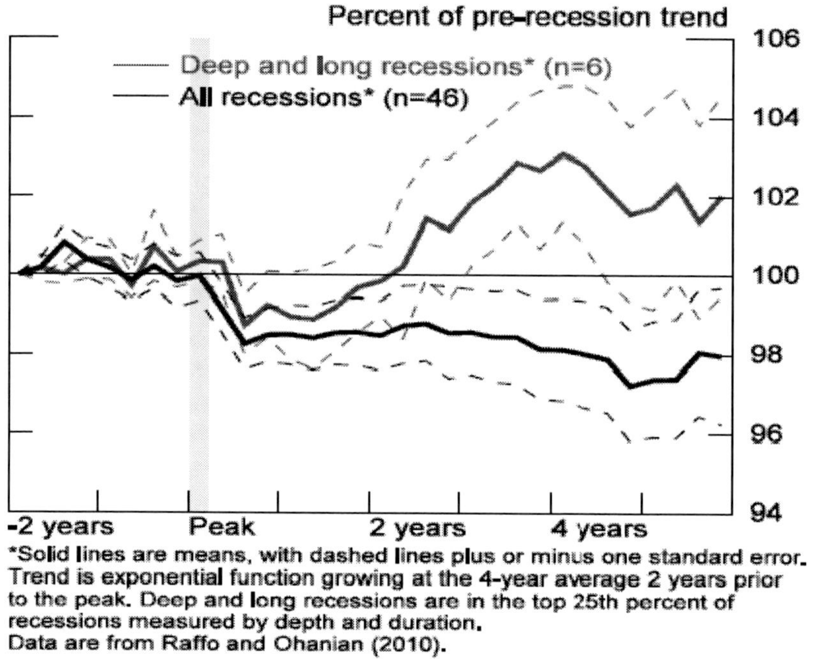

Figure 35. Output per Hour in Select AEs.

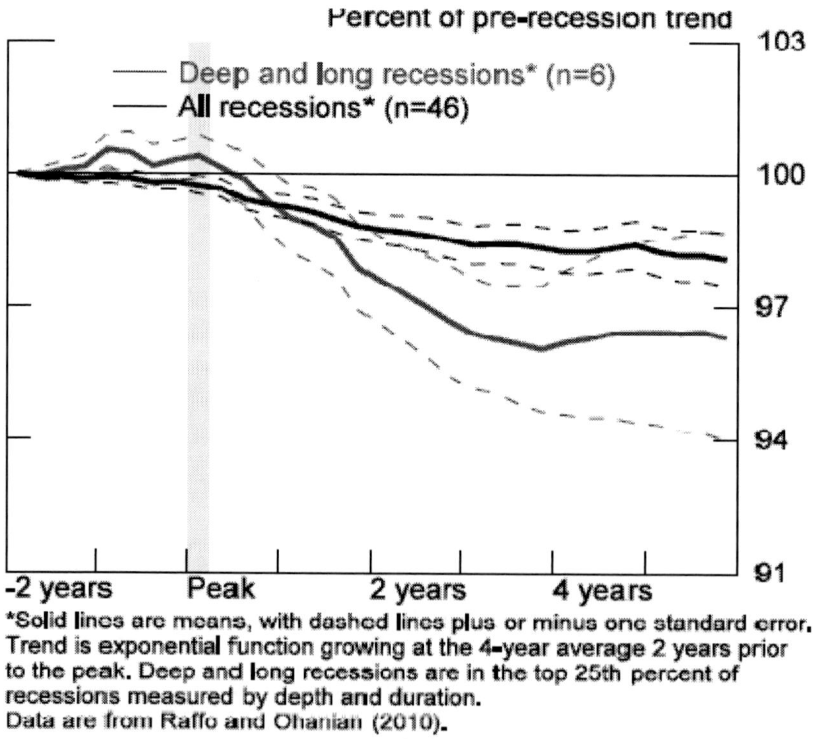

Figure 36. Labor Force Participation in Select AEs.

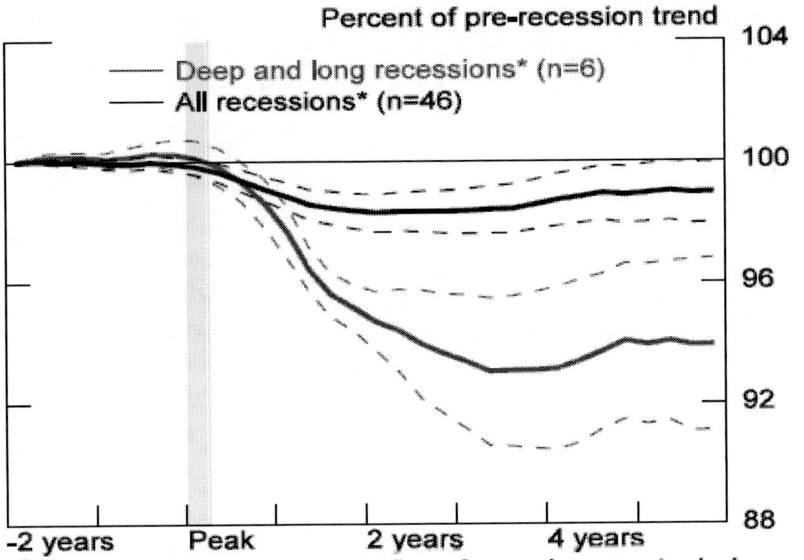

*Solid lines are means, with dashed lines plus or minus one standard error. Trend is exponential function growing at the 4-year average 2 years prior to the peak. Deep and long recessions are in the top 25th percent of recessions measured by depth and duration.
Data are from Raffo and Ohanian (2010).

Figure 37. Employment Rate in Select AEs.

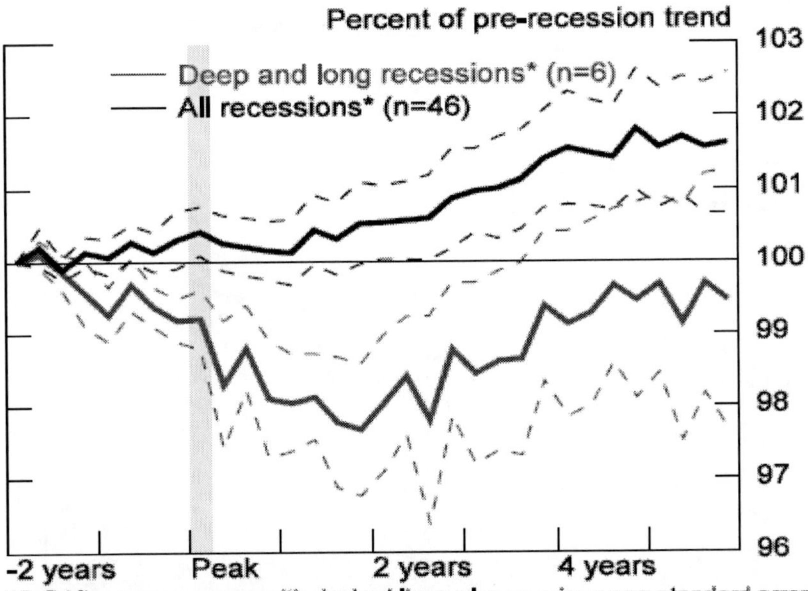

*Solid lines are means, with dashed lines plus or minus one standard error. Trend is exponential function growing at the 4-year average 2 years prior to the peak. Deep and long recessions are in the top 25th percent of recessions measured by depth and duration.
Data are from Raffo and Ohanian (2010).

Figure 38. Average Weekly Hours in Select AEs.

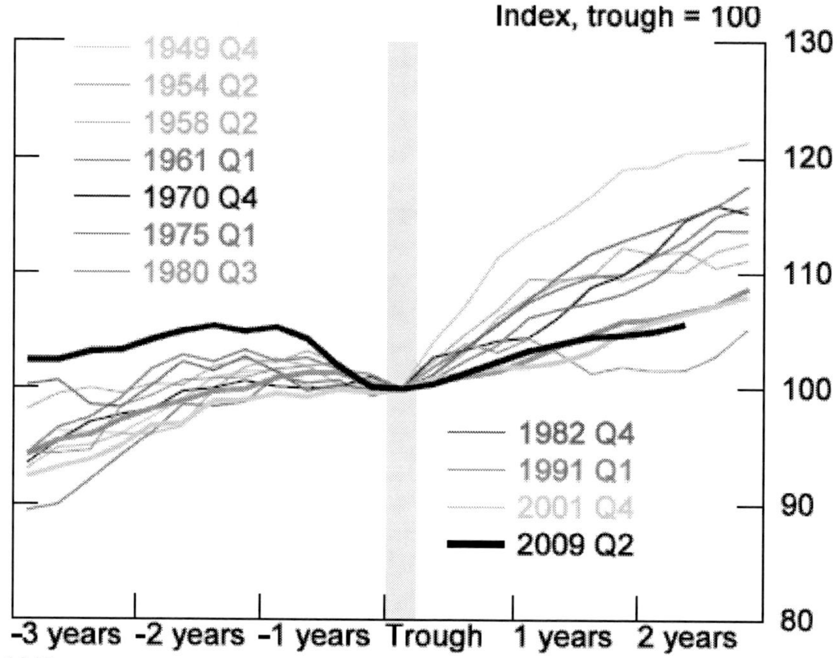

Note: Since 1947.

Figure 39. GDP During U.S. Recessions.

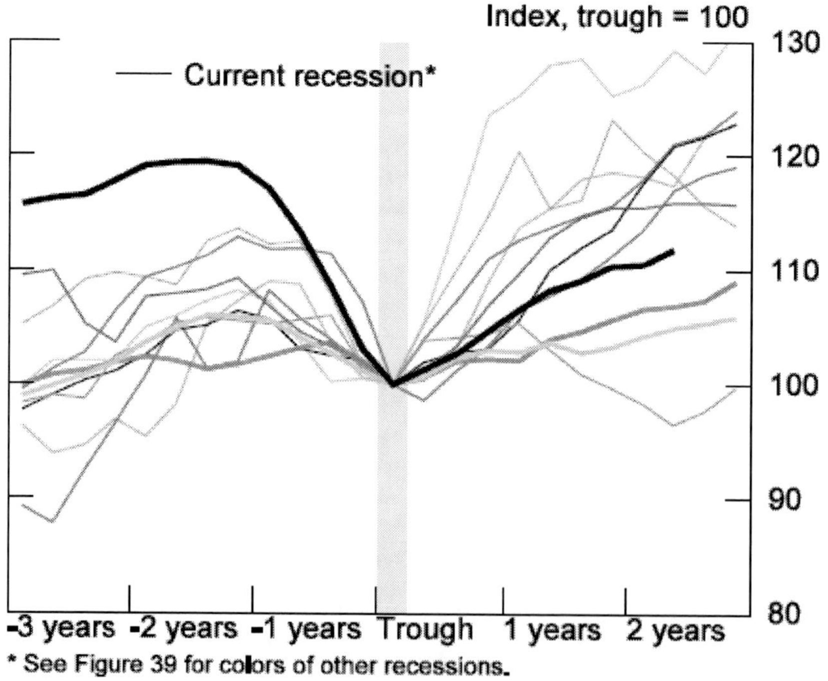

Figure 40. Industrial Production.

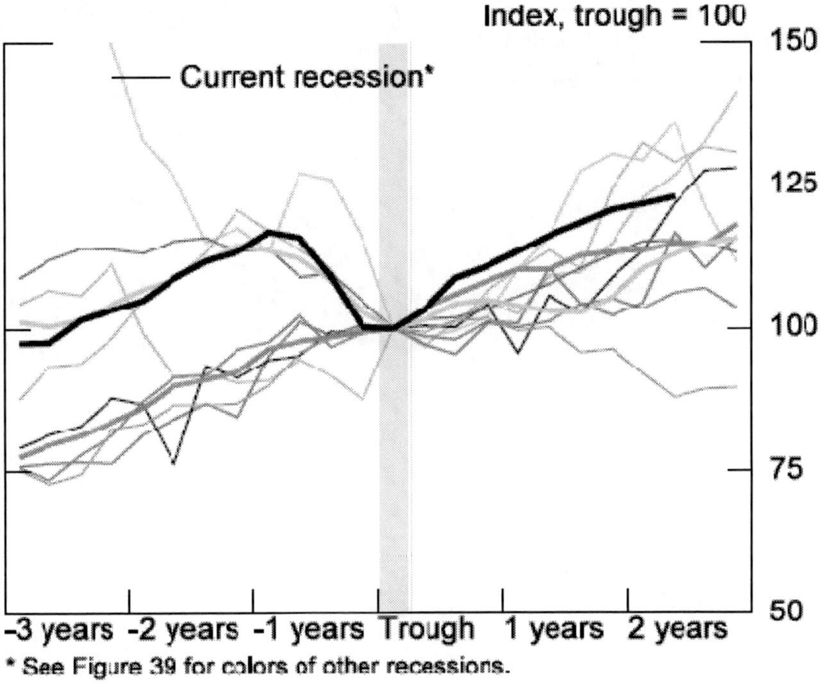

Figure 41. Real Exports.

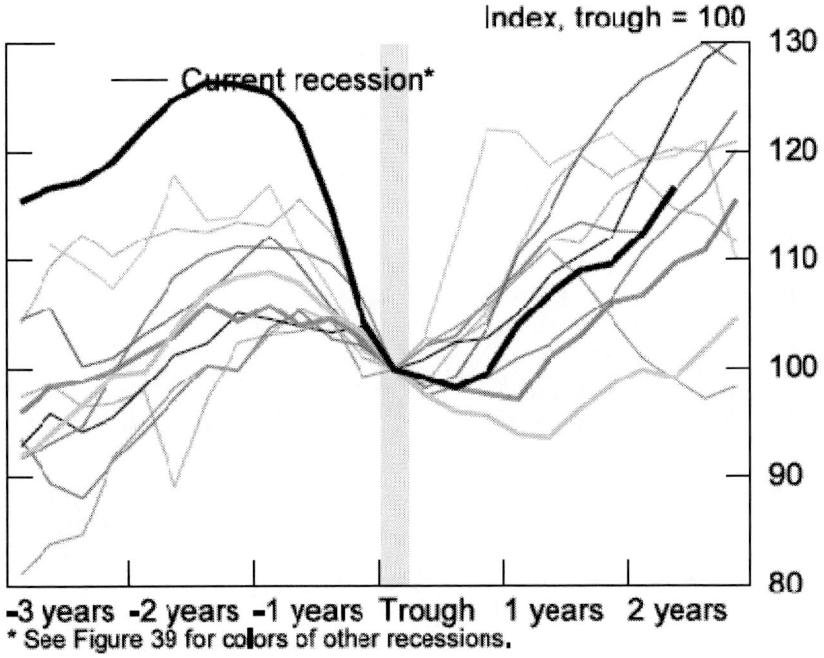

Figure 42. Non-residential Investment.

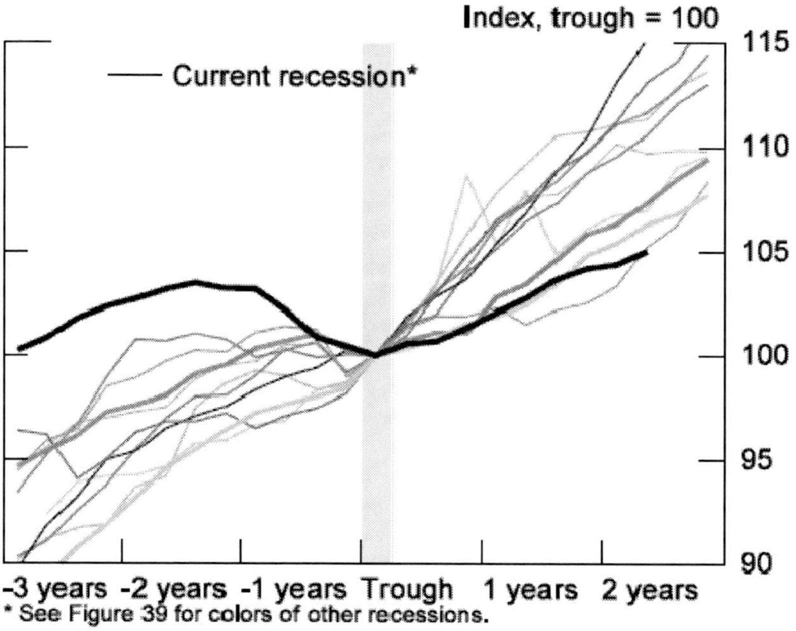

Figure 43. Private Consumption.

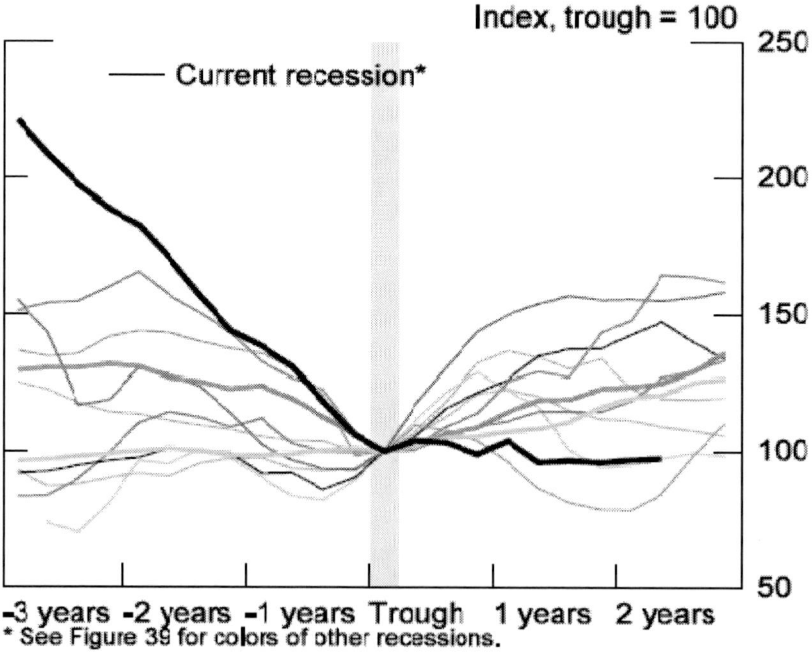

Figure 44. Residential Investment.

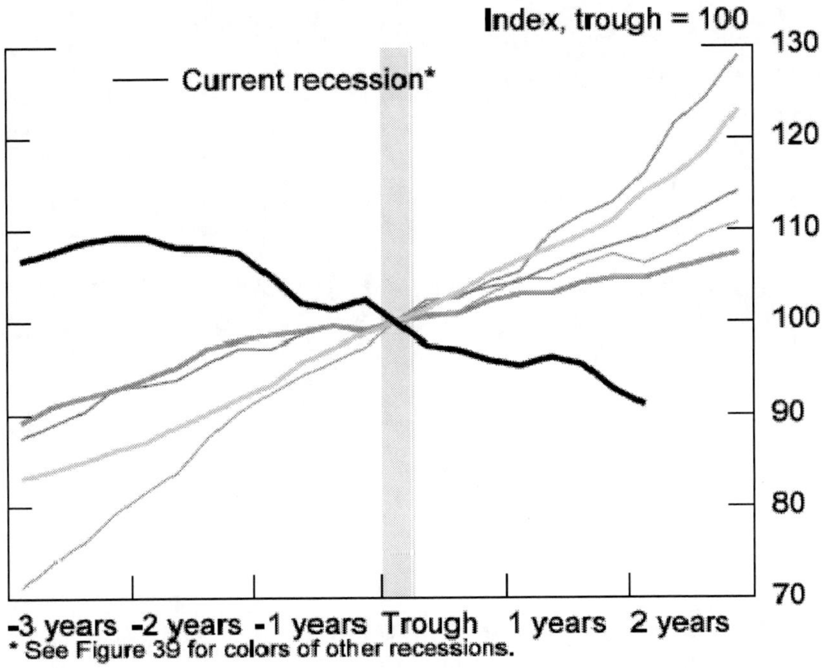

Figure 45. Housing Prices.

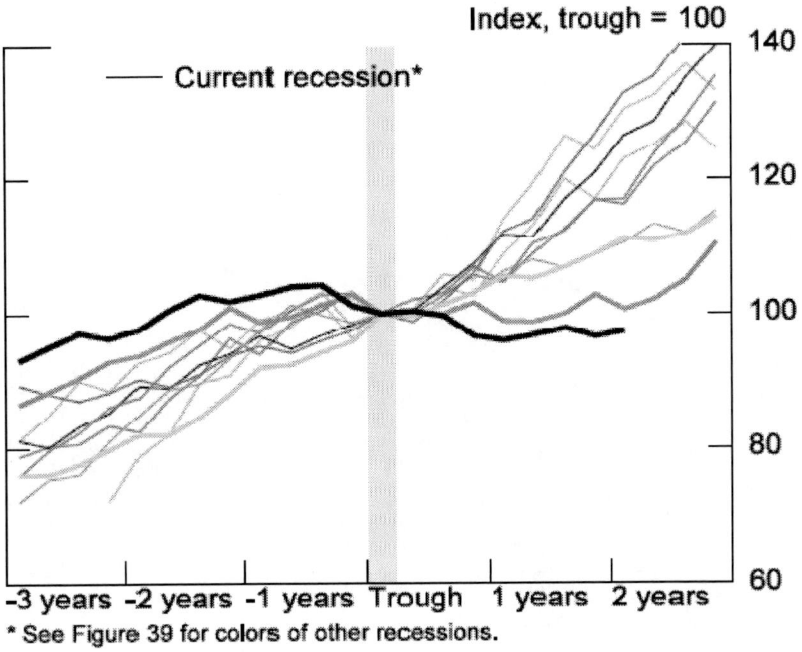

Figure 46. Consumer Credit.

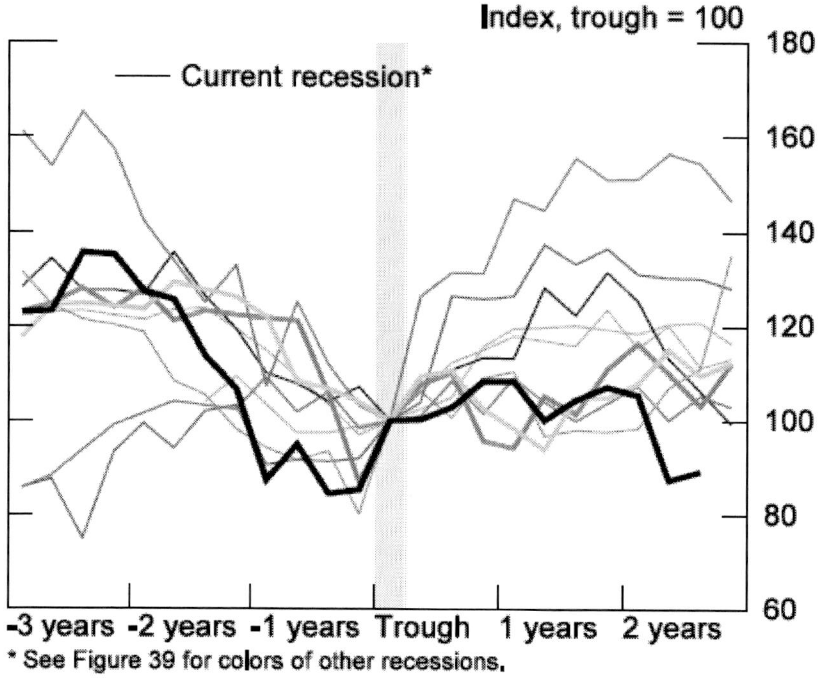

Figure 47. Consumer Sentiment (Michigan Index).

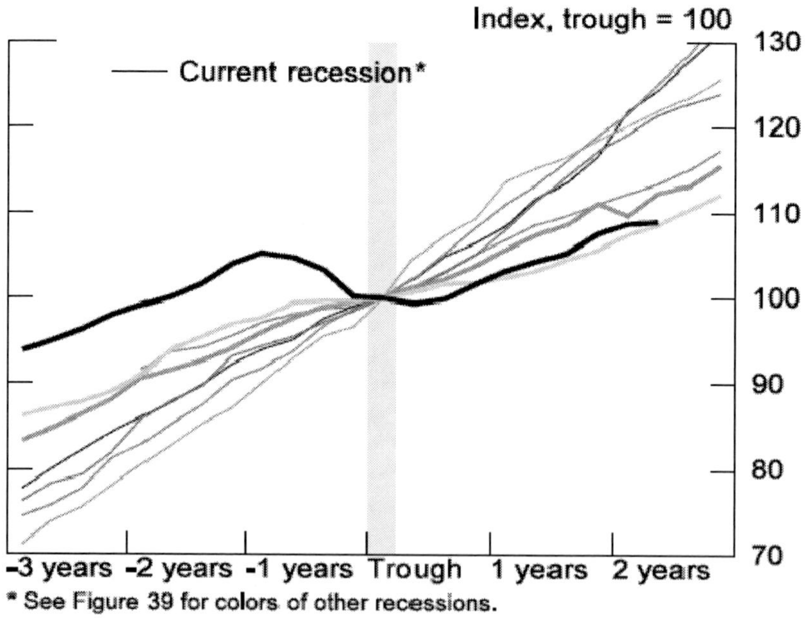

Figure 48. Personal Income.

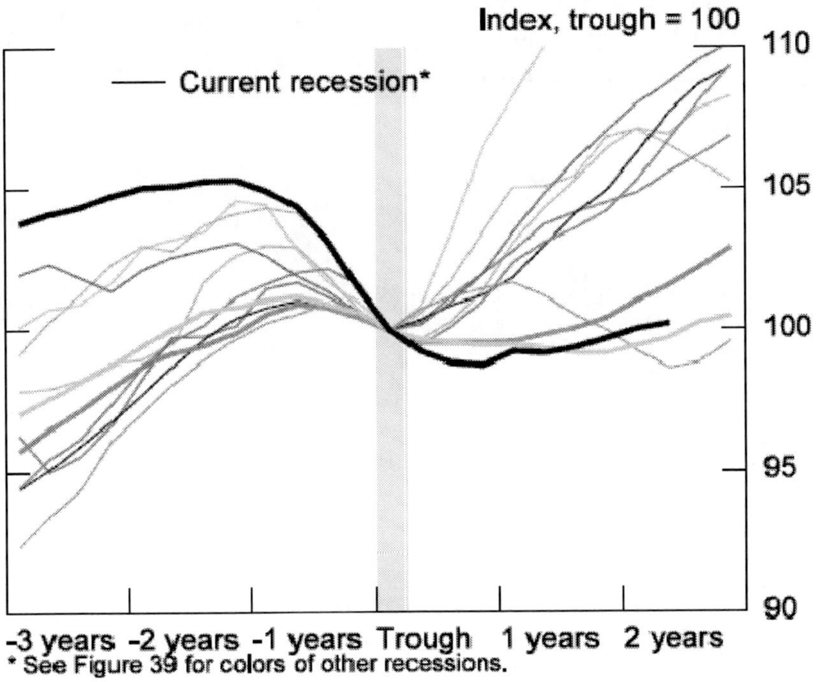

Figure 49. Employment.

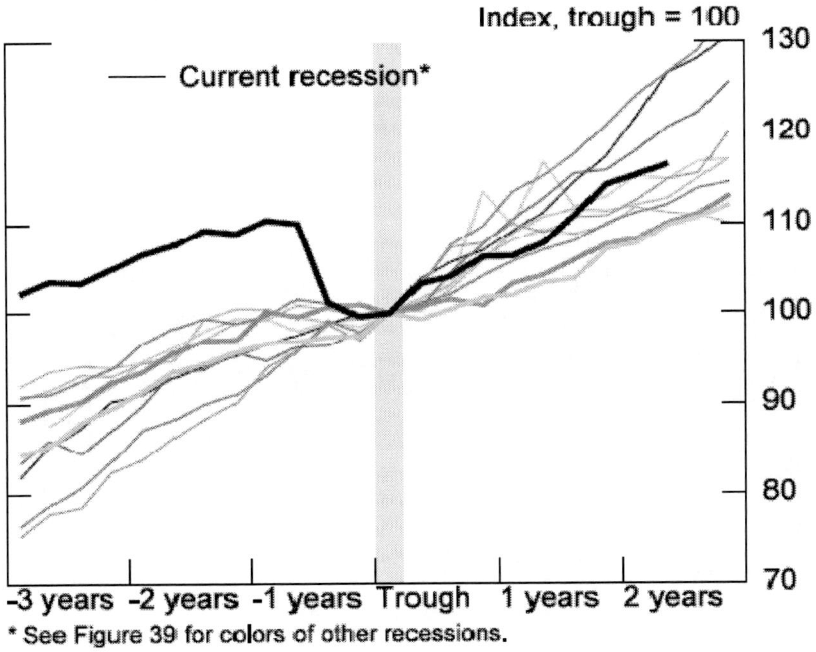

Figure 50. Goods consumption.

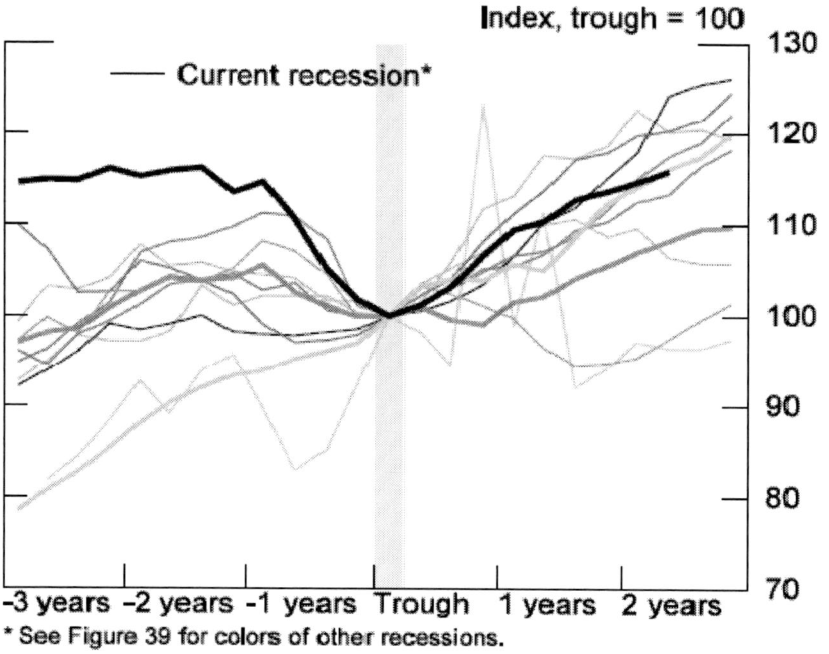

Figure 51. Household Durable Consumption.

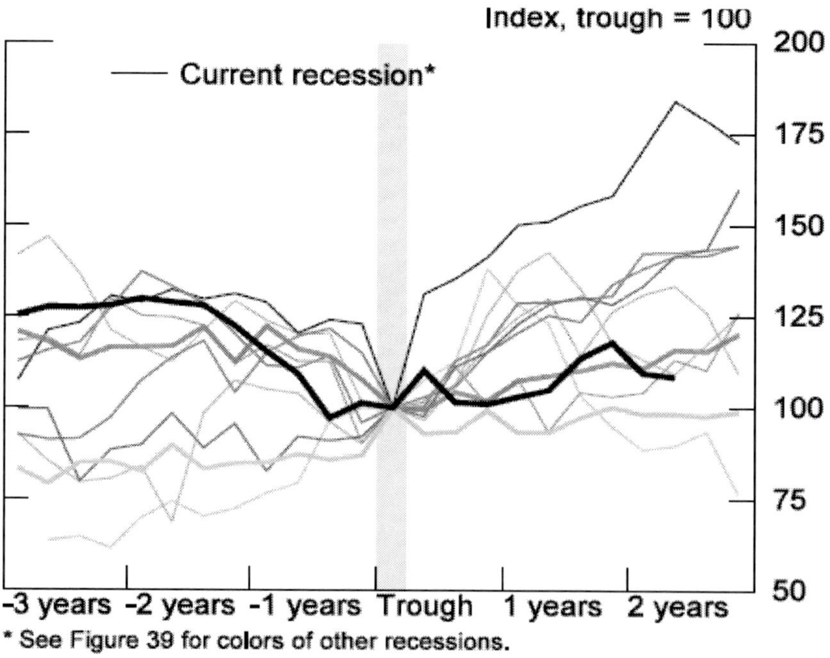

Figure 52. Motor Vehicle Consumption .

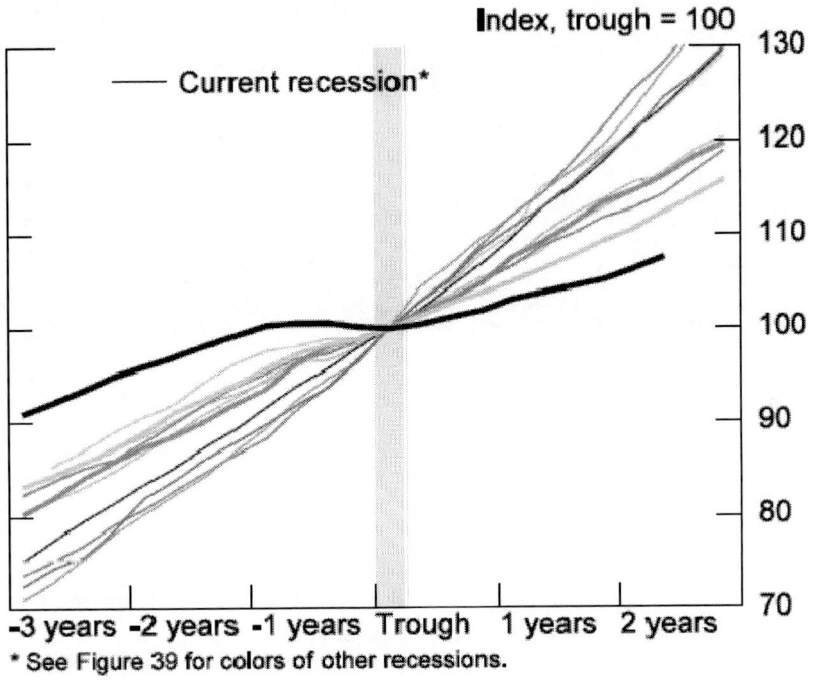

Figure 53. Service Consumption.

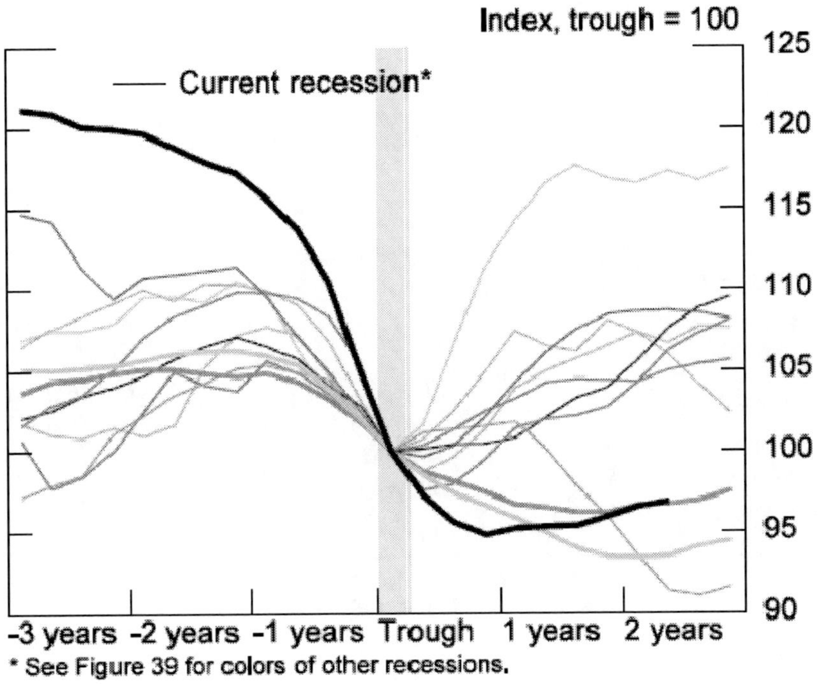

Figure 54. Goods-Producing Employment.

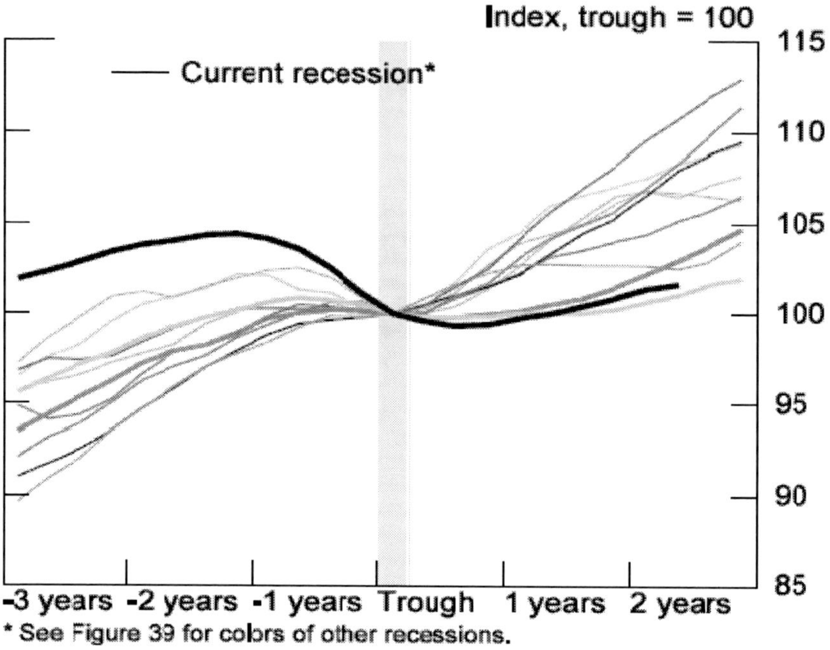

Figure 55. Private Service Providing Employment.

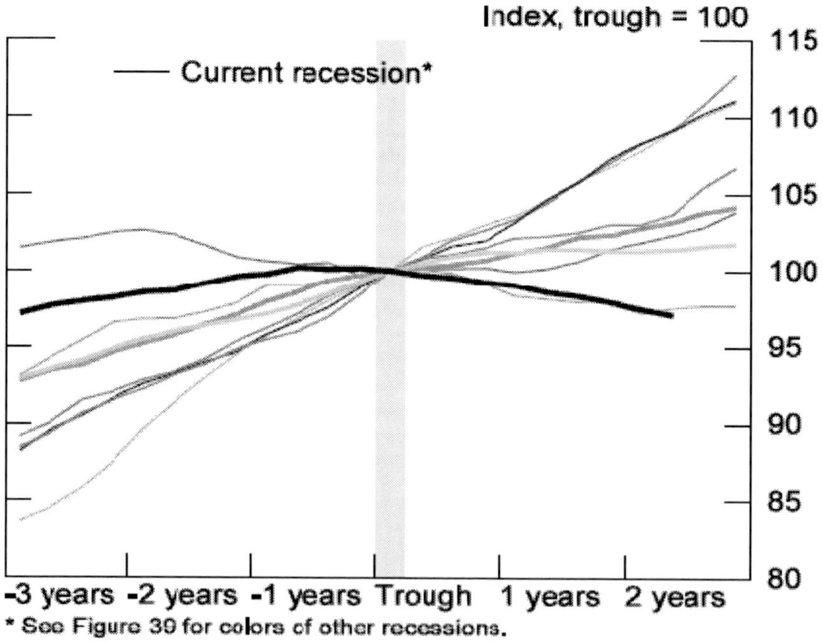

Figure 56. State and Local Government Employment.

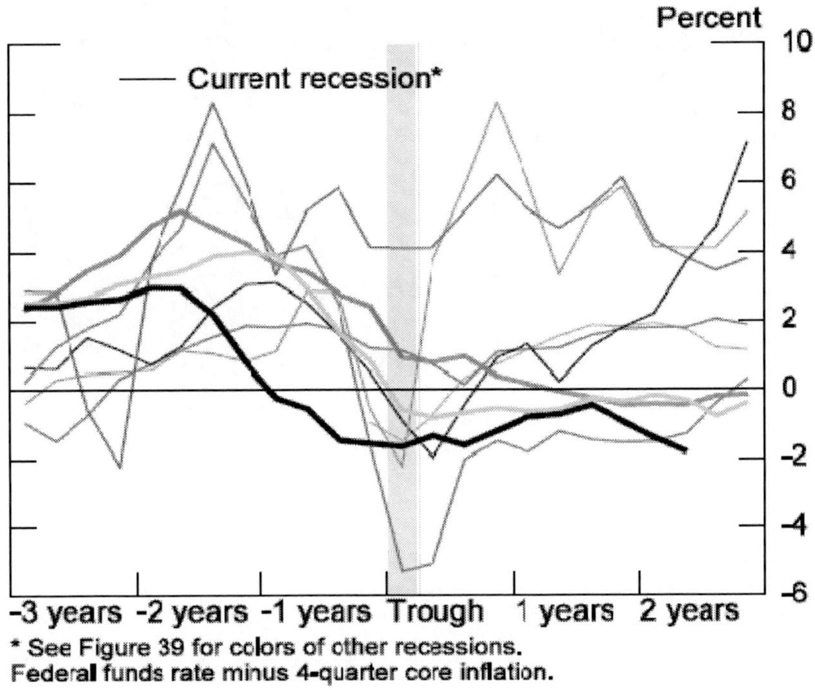

Figure 57. Real Federal Funds Rate.

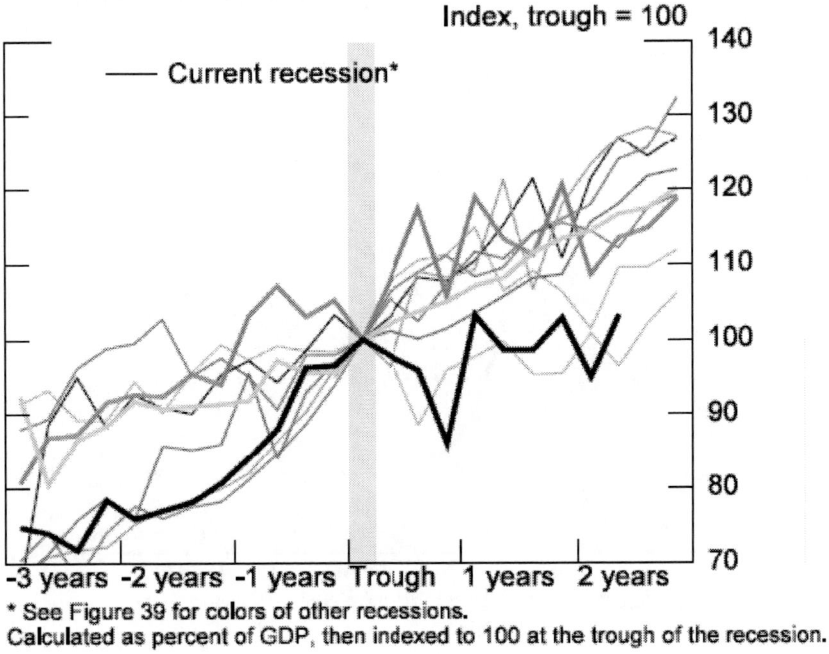

Figure 58. Government Expenditures.

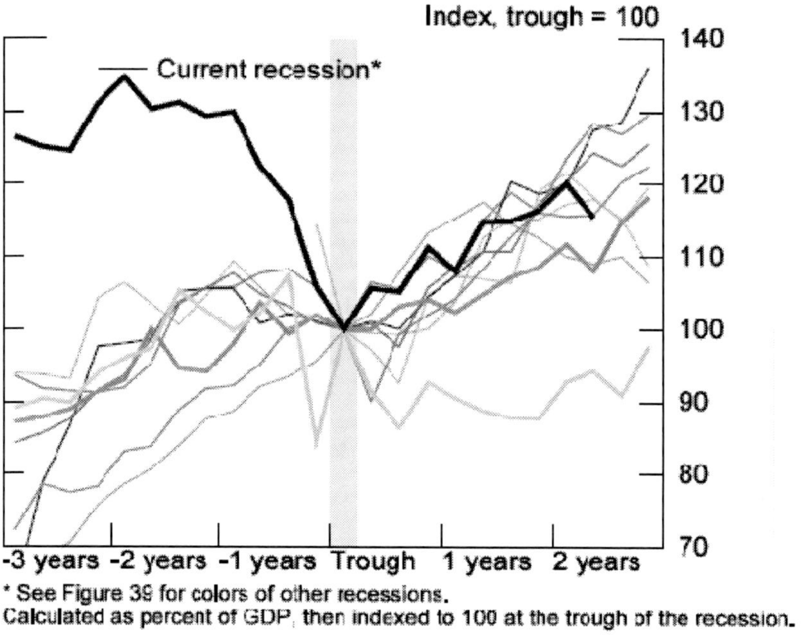

Figure 59. Government Revenue.

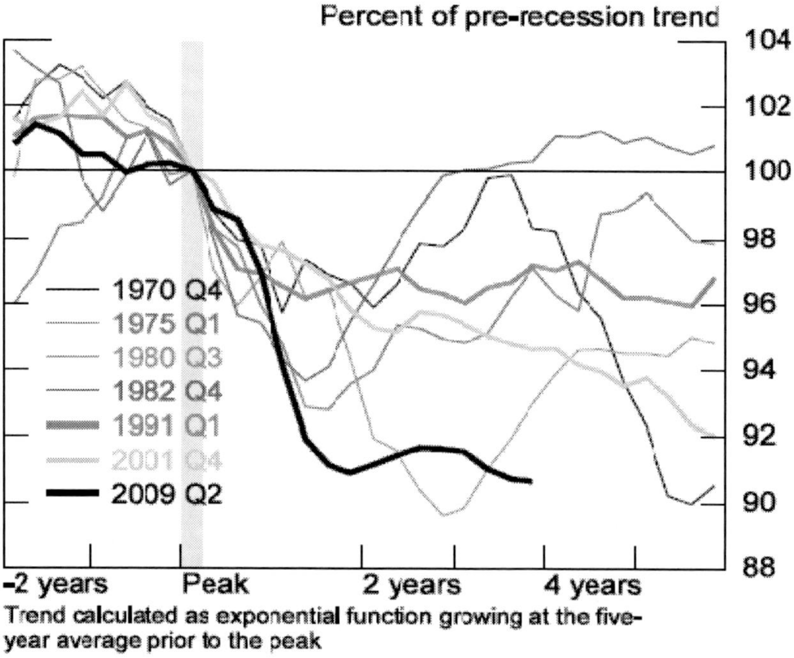

Figure 60. Gross Domestic Product.

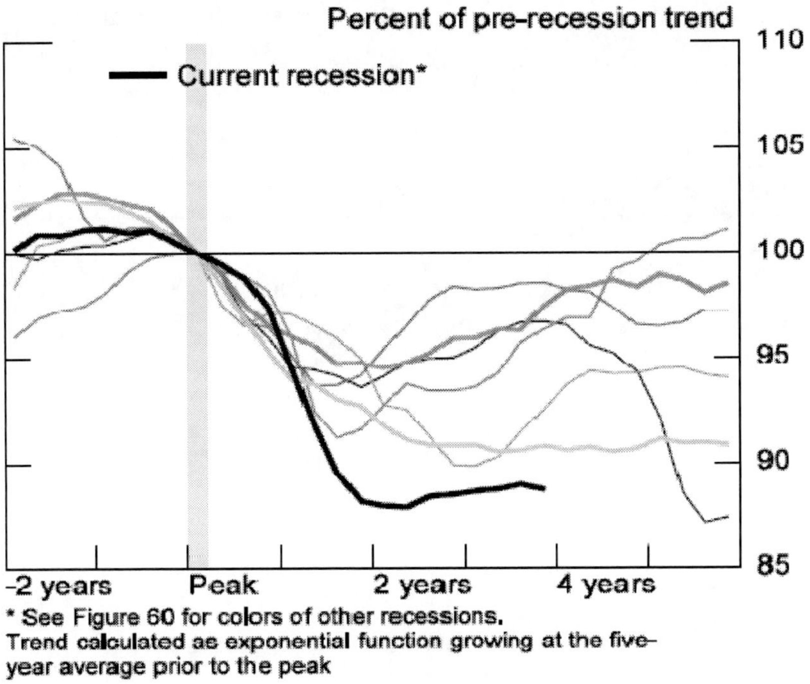

Figure 61. Total Hours.

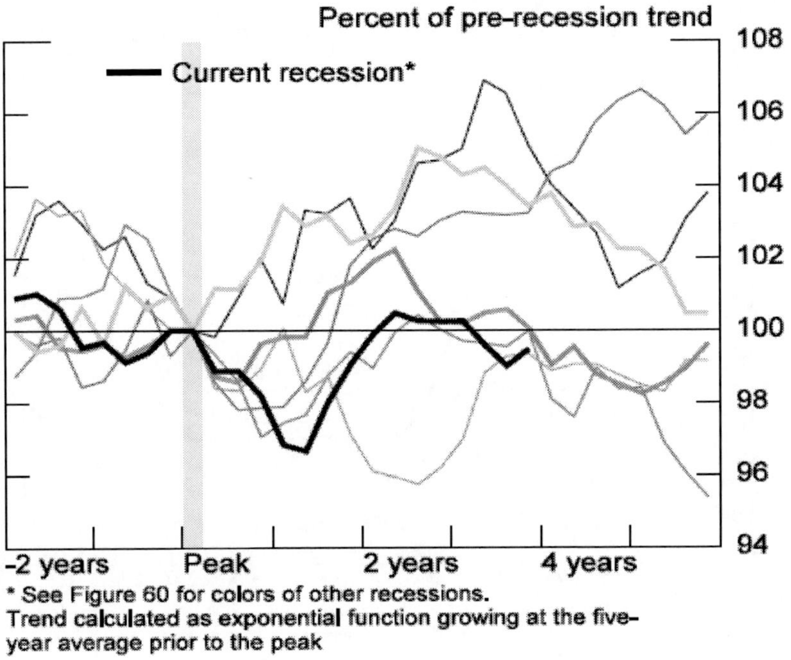

Figure 62. Output per Hour.

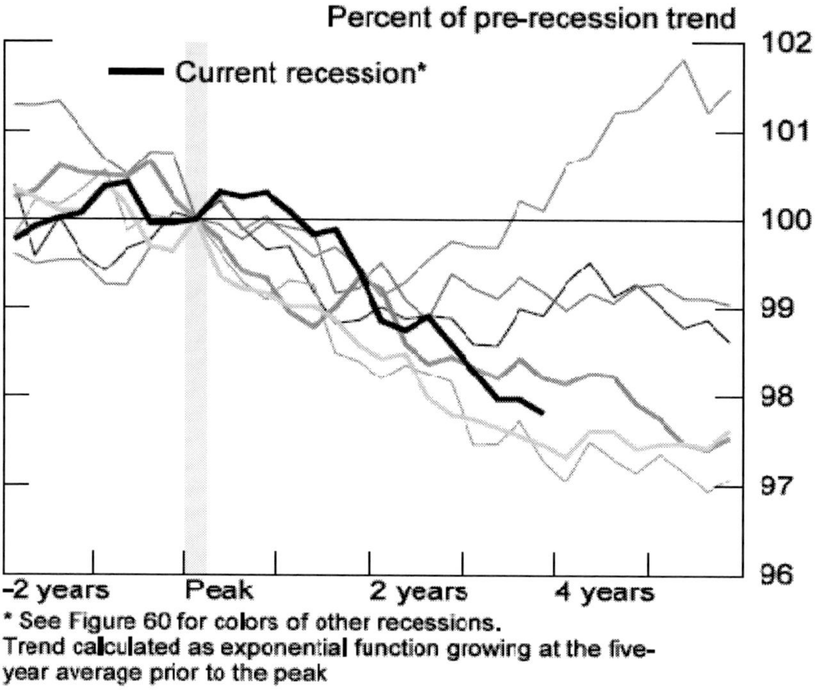

Figure 63. Labor Force Participation.

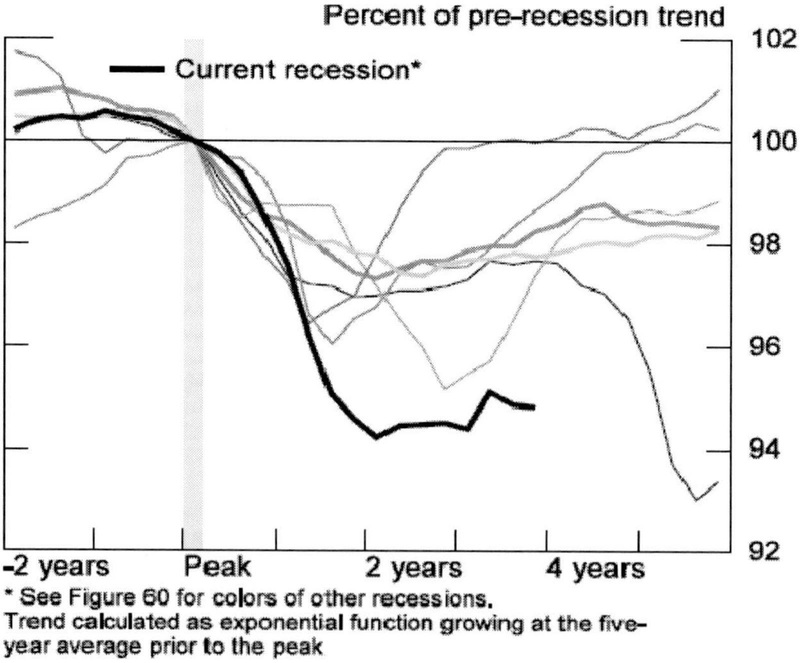

Figure 64. Employment Rate.

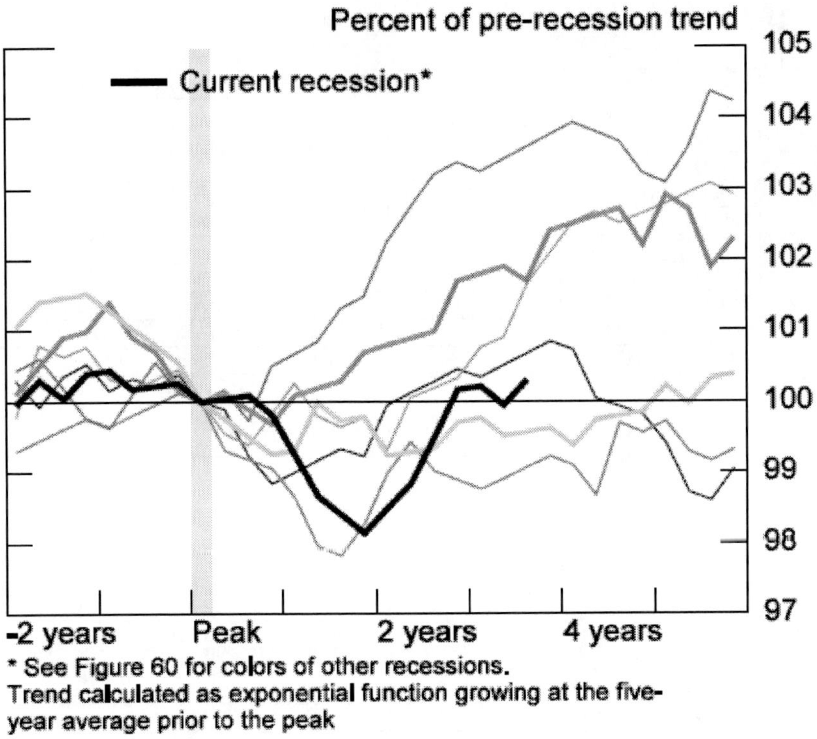

Figure 65. Average Work Week.

APPENDIX A. DATA BY EPISODE

Duration measured in quarters, Depth as a percentage of GDP. Recessions after 2007 are not categorized.

Country	Peak	Trough	IMF	Housing	AE/EME	Duration	Depth
Argentina	1974 Q4	1976 Q1	Currency		EME	5	3.6
Argentina	1977 Q2	1978 Q3			EME	5	4.9
Argentina	1980 Q3	1981 Q4	Banking, Currency		EME	5	9.8
Argentina	1984 Q4	1985 Q3			EME	3	10.7
Argentina	1986 Q3	1987 Q1	Currency		EME	2	2.7
Argentina	1988 Q1	1989 Q3	Banking		EME	6	15.6
Argentina	1992 Q3	1993 Q1			EME	2	3.9
Argentina	1994 Q4	1995 Q3	Banking, Currency, Debt		EME	3	5.7
Argentina	1998 Q2	2002 Q1	Banking		EME	15	20
Argentina	2008 Q3	2009 Q1			EME	2	1.5
Australia	1971 Q3	1972 Q1			AE	2	1.3
Australia	1975 Q2	1975 Q4			AE	2	2.4
Australia	1977 Q2	1977 Q4			AE	2	0.7
Australia	1981 Q3	1983 Q2			AE	7	3.7
Australia	1990 Q4	1991 Q2			AE	2	1.4
Australia	2000 Q2	2000 Q4			AE	2	0.6
Austria	1974 Q3	1975 Q2			AE	3	2

Appendix A. (Continued)

Country	Peak	Trough	IMF	Housing	AE/EME	Duration	Depth
Austria	1981 Q2	1981 Q4			AE	2	0.8
Austria	1982 Q2	1982 Q4			AE	2	0.4
Austria	1983 Q4	1984 Q2			AE	2	2
Austria	1992 Q3	1993 Q1			AE	2	0.8
Austria	2000 Q4	2001 Q3			AE	3	0.8
Austria	2008 Q2	2009 Q2			AE	4	4.8
Belgium	1974 Q2	1975 Q2			AE	4	2.8
Belgium	1976 Q3	1977 Q2			AE	3	0.8
Belgium	1979 Q4	1980 Q4		Housing	AE	4	2
Belgium	1982 Q3	1983 Q1		Housing	AE	2	0.7
Belgium	1992 Q3	1993 Q1			AE	2	1.9
Belgium	2001 Q2	2001 Q4			AE	2	0.5
Belgium	2008 Q2	2009 Q2			AE	4	4.1
Brazil	1980 Q4	1981 Q4			EME	4	7.8
Brazil	1982 Q3	1983 Q1	Currency, Debt		EME	2	5.5
Brazil	1987 Q1	1987 Q3	Currency		EME	2	3.1
Brazil	1988 Q1	1988 Q4			EME	3	3.5
Brazil	1989 Q4	1991 Q1	Banking		EME	5	8.9
Brazil	1991 Q3	1992 Q3	Currency		EME	4	4.7
Brazil	1995 Q1	1995 Q3	Banking		EME	2	2.9
Brazil	1998 Q2	1999 Q1	Currency		EME	3	1.6
Brazil	2001 Q1	2001 Q4			EME	3	1.2
Brazil	2008 Q3	2009 Q1			EME	2	5.6
Canada	1981 Q2	1982 Q4		Housing	AE	6	4.4
Canada	1990 Q1	1991 Q1		Housing	AE	4	3.3
Canada	2008 Q3	2009 Q2			AE	3	3.6
Chile	1971 Q4	1973 Q2	Currency		EME	6	8.6
Chile	1974 Q2	1975 Q4			EME	6	16.8
Chile	1981 Q2	1982 Q4	Banking, Currency		EME	6	19.2
Chile	1990 Q1	1990 Q3			EME	2	1.2
Chile	1998 Q2	1999 Q1			EME	3	4.1
Chile	2008 Q2	2009 Q2			EME	4	4.3
China	1971 Q2	1971 Q4			EME	2	0.2
China	1973 Q3	1974 Q2			EME	3	1.4
China	1975 Q3	1976 Q3			EME	4	4.7
Colombia	1982 Q2	1982 Q4	Banking		EME	2	1.2
Colombia	1998 Q1	1999 Q2	Banking		EME	5	6.7
Costa Rica	1995 Q3	1996 Q1			EME	2	2.7
Costa Rica	2008 Q1	2009 Q1			EME	4	3.6
Czech Republic	1996 Q4	1997 Q3	Banking		EME	3	2.4
Czech Republic	2008 Q2	2009 Q2			EME	4	4.8
Denmark	1973 Q3	1975 Q2			AE	7	4.2
Denmark	1976 Q4	1977 Q2			AE	2	0.3
Denmark	1979 Q4	1981 Q2		Housing	AE	6	3.3
Denmark	1986 Q3	1987 Q2		Housing	AE	3	0.6
Denmark	1992 Q3	1993 Q2		Housing	AE	3	1.9
Denmark	1997 Q2	1997 Q4			AE	2	1
Denmark	2000 Q4	2002 Q4			AE	8	-0.1
Denmark	2008 Q2	2009 Q3			AE	5	7.3
Estonia	1998 Q3	1999 Q2			EME	3	2.4
Estonia	2007 Q4	2009 Q3			EME	7	20.2
Finland	1971 Q2	1971 Q4			AE	2	0.3
Finland	1975 Q1	1975 Q4		Housing	AE	3	2.2
Finland	1980 Q3	1981 Q1			AE	2	2.7

Country	Peak	Trough	IMF	Housing	AE/EME	Duration	Depth
Finland	1990 Q1	1992 Q3	Banking	Housing	AE	10	12.8
Finland	2008 Q1	2009 Q2			AE	5	10.3
France	1974 Q3	1975 Q2			AE	3	2.8
France	1980 Q1	1980 Q3			AE	2	0.3
France	1992 Q1	1993 Q1			AE	4	1.1
France	2008 Q1	2009 Q2			AE	5	3.9
Germany	1974 Q3	1975 Q1			AE	2	3.4
Germany	1981 Q3	1982 Q4			AE	5	2.2
Germany	1985 Q3	1986 Q1			AE	2	1.2
Germany	1992 Q3	1993 Q1			AE	2	2
Germany	1995 Q3	1996 Q1		Housing	AE	2	0.7
Germany	2002 Q3	2003 Q2		Housing	AE	3	0.9
Germany	2004 Q1	2004 Q3		Housing	AE	2	0.2
Germany	2008 Q1	2009 Q1			AE	4	6.6
Greece	1973 Q3	1974 Q3			AE	4	12.4
Greece	1976 Q4	1977 Q2			AE	2	3
Greece	1979 Q2	1979 Q4			AE	2	3.1
Greece	1980 Q2	1981 Q1			AE	3	5.6
Greece	1981 Q3	1982 Q4			AE	5	4.6
Greece	1984 Q3	1985 Q1			AE	2	2.3
Greece	1990 Q1	1990 Q3			AE	2	7.1
Greece	1992 Q3	1993 Q1			AE	2	3.6
Greece	2000 Q1	2000 Q3			AE	2	1.1
Hong Kong	1973 Q4	1975 Q1			EME	5	4.9
Hong Kong	1981 Q4	1982 Q2			EME	2	2.9
Hong Kong	1984 Q2	1985 Q3			EME	5	4.1
Hong Kong	1988 Q4	1989 Q2			EME	2	1.3
Hong Kong	1995 Q1	1995 Q3			EME	2	0.4
Hong Kong	1997 Q3	1998 Q4			EME	5	8.8
Hong Kong	2000 Q4	2001 Q4			EME	4	2
Hong Kong	2002 Q4	2003 Q2			EME	2	2.5
Hong Kong	2008 Q1	2009 Q1			EME	4	7.6
Hungary	1995 Q1	1995 Q4			EME	3	1.2
Hungary	2008 Q1	2009 Q3			EME	6	8.3
Iceland	1982 Q2	1983 Q2	Currency		AE	4	3
Iceland	1987 Q4	1988 Q3			AE	3	1.3
Iceland	1991 Q1	1992 Q3			AE	6	4.4
Iceland	1997 Q3	1998 Q1			AE	2	1.4
Iceland	2003 Q1	2003 Q3			AE	2	4.3
Iceland	2008 Q1	2010 Q2			AE	9	12
India	1975 Q2	1976 Q1			EME	3	1.6
India	1978 Q1	1979 Q2			EME	5	8.6
India	1981 Q2	1981 Q4			EME	2	0.2
India	1983 Q4	1984 Q2			EME	2	1.3
Indonesia	1997 Q3	1998 Q4			EME	5	18.2
Ireland	1982 Q3	1983 Q2		Housing	AE	3	1
Ireland	1985 Q3	1986 Q2		Housing	AE	3	1.3
Ireland	2007 Q1	2009 Q4			AE	11	11.4
Israel	2000 Q4	2001 Q4			EME	4	3.9
Israel	2008 Q3	2009 Q1			EME	2	1.3
Italy	1974 Q2	1975 Q2			AE	4	3.7
Italy	1977 Q1	1977 Q3			AE	2	1.4
Italy	1982 Q1	1982 Q4	Currency	Housing	AE	3	0.9
Italy	1992 Q1	1993 Q1		Housing	AE	4	1.5
Italy	2001 Q1	2001 Q4			AE	3	0.6
Italy	2002 Q4	2003 Q2			AE	2	0.5

Appendix A. (Continued)

Country	Peak	Trough	IMF	Housing	AE/EME	Duration	Depth
Italy	2004 Q3	2005 Q1			AE	2	0.1
Italy	2008 Q1	2009 Q2			AE	5	7
Japan	1974 Q3	1975 Q1		Housing	AE	2	0.3
Japan	1997 Q1	1998 Q2	Banking	Housing	AE	5	3.2
Japan	2001 Q1	2001 Q4		Housing	AE	3	2.1
Japan	2008 Q1	2009 Q1			AE	4	9.9
Jordan	1998 Q1	1998 Q3			EME	2	1.2
Latvia	1992 Q1	1993 Q4	Currency		EME	7	29.9
Latvia	1994 Q3	1995 Q1			EME	2	3.1
Latvia	2007 Q4	2009 Q4			EME	8	25.4
Lithuania	2008 Q2	2009 Q4			EME	6	17.3
Luxembourg	1974 Q2	1975 Q3			AE	5	8.3
Luxembourg	1980 Q2	1981 Q2			AE	4	0.7
Luxembourg	2008 Q1	2008 Q4			AE	3	5.7
Malaysia	1974 Q3	1975 Q2			EME	3	1.3
Malaysia	1984 Q3	1985 Q3			EME	4	2
Malaysia	1997 Q4	1998 Q4	Banking, Currency		EME	4	11.1
Malaysia	2000 Q4	2001 Q2			EME	2	1.1
Malaysia	2008 Q2	2009 Q1			EME	3	6.5
Mexico	1982 Q2	1983 Q2	Banking, Currency, Debt		EME	4	5.5
Mexico	1985 Q3	1986 Q4			EME	5	4.6
Mexico	1987 Q4	1988 Q2			EME	2	1.3
Mexico	1994 Q4	1995 Q2	Banking, Currency		EME	2	9.4
Mexico	2000 Q3	2002 Q1			EME	6	2.6
Mexico	2008 Q1	2009 Q2			EME	5	8.5
Netherlands	1974 Q3	1975 Q2			AE	3	0.8
Netherlands	1980 Q1	1980 Q3		Housing	AE	2	2.5
Netherlands	2008 Q1	2009 Q2			AE	5	4.6
New Zealand	1970 Q1	1970 Q3			AE	2	4
New Zealand	1971 Q3	1972 Q1			AE	2	6.5
New Zealand	1973 Q1	1973 Q3			AE	2	7.8
New Zealand	1974 Q3	1975 Q2		Housing	AE	3	9.9
New Zealand	1977 Q2	1978 Q1		Housing	AE	3	13.1
New Zealand	1982 Q3	1983 Q1			AE	2	4.6
New Zealand	1984 Q1	1984 Q3			AE	2	3.2
New Zealand	1985 Q1	1985 Q3			AE	2	3.1
New Zealand	1986 Q3	1987 Q1			AE	2	7
New Zealand	1990 Q4	1991 Q2			AE	2	3.8
New Zealand	1997 Q3	1998 Q1			AE	2	1.4
New Zealand	2007 Q4	2009 Q1			AE	5	2.4
Norway	1977 Q3	1978 Q1			AE	2	5.9
Norway	1978 Q3	1979 Q2			AE	3	1.2
Norway	1980 Q1	1980 Q3			AE	2	2.5
Norway	1991 Q2	1991 Q4	Banking	Housing	AE	2	0.6
Norway	1992 Q3	1993 Q1		Housing	AE	2	1.4
Norway	2005 Q3	2006 Q1			AE	2	0.9
Norway	2008 Q2	2009 Q2			AE	4	2.5
Peru	1982 Q1	1983 Q4	Banking, Currency		EME	7	18.3
Peru	1985 Q1	1985 Q3			EME	2	7
Peru	1987 Q3	1989 Q2			EME	7	26.2

Country	Peak	Trough	IMF	Housing	AE/EME	Duration	Depth
Peru	1990 Q1	1990 Q3			EME	2	21.5
Peru	1992 Q1	1992 Q3			EME	2	5.2
Peru	1997 Q4	1999 Q1			EME	5	3.1
Peru	2000 Q1	2000 Q4			EME	3	5
Peru	2003 Q2	2003 Q4			EME	2	0.2
Peru	2008 Q3	2009 Q1			EME	2	2.6
Philippines	1983 Q2	1985 Q3	Banking, Currency, Debt		EME	9	16.9
Philippines	1990 Q3	1991 Q1			EME	2	1.4
Philippines	1997 Q4	1998 Q2	Banking, Currency		EME	2	2.8
Poland	2000 Q4	2001 Q2			EME	2	0.6
Portugal	1974 Q1	1975 Q2			AE	5	6
Portugal	1982 Q4	1984 Q2	Banking, Currency		AE	6	2.7
Portugal	1992 Q2	1993 Q3			AE	5	2.6
Portugal	2001 Q4	2003 Q2			AE	6	2.1
Portugal	2004 Q2	2004 Q4			AE	2	0.2
Portugal	2007 Q4	2009 Q1			AE	5	4
Russia	1989 Q2	1995 Q1			EME	23	39.1
Russia	1995 Q3	1996 Q3			EME	4	5.4
Russia	2008 Q2	2009 Q2			EME	4	10.9
Singapore	1984 Q4	1985 Q4			EME	4	2
Singapore	1997 Q4	1998 Q3			EME	3	1.3
Singapore	2000 Q4	2001 Q3			EME	3	1.7
Singapore	2008 Q1	2008 Q4			EME	3	2.6
Slovakia	1998 Q4	1999 Q4	Banking		EME	4	6.7
Slovakia	2008 Q3	2009 Q1			EME	2	6.4
Slovenia	2008 Q2	2009 Q3			EME	5	9.8
South Africa	1974 Q3	1975 Q1			EME	2	1.3
South Africa	1976 Q3	1977 Q2			EME	3	1.3
South Africa	1981 Q4	1983 Q1			EME	5	5.1
South Africa	1984 Q2	1985 Q3	Currency, Debt		EME	5	2.8
South Africa	1990 Q1	1992 Q4			EME	11	4.6
South Africa	1998 Q1	1998 Q3			EME	2	0.1
South Africa	2008 Q3	2009 Q2			EME	3	2.6
South Korea	1979 Q2	1980 Q2			EME	4	3.9
South Korea	1997 Q3	1998 Q2	Banking, Currency		EME	3	8.1
South Korea	2008 Q2	2008 Q4			EME	2	4.1
Spain	1974 Q4	1975 Q2			AE	2	0.6
Spain	1978 Q2	1979 Q1	Banking	Housing	AE	3	0.4
Spain	1980 Q3	1981 Q2		Housing	AE	3	0.3
Spain	1992 Q2	1993 Q2			AE	4	1.8
Spain	2008 Q1	2009 Q4			AE	7	4.9
Sweden	1973 Q1	1973 Q3			AE	2	2.1
Sweden	1976 Q4	1977 Q2			AE	2	3
Sweden	1982 Q2	1983 Q1		Housing	AE	3	0.9
Sweden	1990 Q4	1992 Q4	Banking	Housing	AE	8	5.6
Sweden	2007 Q4	2009 Q3			AE	7	7.8
Switzerland	1974 Q2	1975 Q3		Housing	AE	5	10.3
Switzerland	1977 Q3	1978 Q1			AE	2	0.6
Switzerland	1981 Q2	1982 Q2			AE	4	1.7
Switzerland	1986 Q2	1986 Q4			AE	2	0.2
Switzerland	1990 Q3	1991 Q2		Housing	AE	3	1.4
Switzerland	1992 Q1	1993 Q1		Housing	AE	4	1.5

Appendix A. (Continued)

Country	Peak	Trough	IMF	Housing	AE/EME	Duration	Depth
Switzerland	2002 Q2	2003 Q1			AE	3	0.9
Switzerland	2008 Q2	2009 Q2			AE	4	3.2
Taiwan	1974 Q1	1974 Q3			EME	2	2.3
Taiwan	2000 Q3	2001 Q3			EME	4	4.4
Taiwan	2008 Q1	2009 Q1			EME	4	9.5
Thailand	1996 Q3	1998 Q3	Banking, Currency		EME	8	14.9
Thailand	2008 Q2	2009 Q1			EME	3	7.6
Turkey	1987 Q4	1989 Q2			EME	6	4.3
Turkey	1993 Q4	1994 Q2			EME	2	11.6
Turkey	2000 Q4	2001 Q2			EME	2	7.5
Turkey	2008 Q1	2009 Q1			EME	4	13.3
United Kingdom	1973 Q1	1974 Q1		Housing	AE	4	3.3
United Kingdom	1975 Q1	1975 Q3		Housing	AE	2	1.5
United Kingdom	1979 Q4	1981 Q1			AE	5	4.4
United Kingdom	1990 Q2	1991 Q3		Housing	AE	5	2.5
United Kingdom	2008 Q1	2009 Q3			AE	6	6.6
United States	1973 Q4	1975 Q1			AE	5	3.3
United States	1980 Q1	1980 Q3			AE	2	2.2
United States	1981 Q3	1982 Q1			AE	2	2.8
United States	1990 Q3	1991 Q1			AE	2	1.2
United States	2008 Q2	2009 Q2			AE	4	5.3
Uruguay	1988 Q1	1988 Q4			EME	3	0.1
Uruguay	1994 Q3	1995 Q1			EME	2	2.2
Uruguay	1998 Q3	1999 Q4			EME	5	5.7
Uruguay	2001 Q1	2002 Q4	Banking, Currency, Debt		EME	7	19.6
Venezuela	1979 Q2	1981 Q1			EME	7	3.1
Venezuela	1982 Q2	1983 Q4	Debt		EME	6	7.6
Venezuela	1984 Q2	1985 Q1	Currency		EME	3	1.2
Venezuela	1988 Q2	1989 Q3	Currency		EME	5	11.7
Venezuela	1992 Q4	1994 Q1	Banking, Currency		EME	5	2.8
Venezuela	1995 Q4	1996 Q2			EME	2	2.6
Venezuela	2000 Q1	2000 Q3			EME	2	1.6
Venezuela	2001 Q4	2003 Q1	Currency		EME	5	28.6
Venezuela	2008 Q4	2010 Q1			EME	5	6.4

APPENDIX B. SAMPLE COUNTRIES

Country	First Value
Argentina	1970 Q1
Australia	1970 Q1
Austria	1970 Q1
Belgium	1970 Q1
Brazil	1970 Q1
Canada	1970 Q1

Country	First Value
Chile	1970 Q1
China	1970 Q1
Colombia	1970 Q1
Costa Rica	1991 Q1
Czech	1996 Q1
Denmark	1970 Q1
Estonia	1995 Q1
Finland	1970 Q1
France	1970 Q1
Germany	1970 Q1
Greece	1970 Q1
Hong Kong	1970 Q1
Hungary	1995 Q1
Iceland	1970 Q1
India	1970 Q1
Indonesia	1970 Q1
Ireland	1970 Q1
Israel	1970 Q1
Italy	1970 Q1
Japan	1970 Q1
Jordan	1992 Q1
Latvia	1992 Q1
Lithuania	1995 Q1
Luxembourg	1970 Q1
Malaysia	1970 Q1
Mexico	1970 Q1
Netherland	1970 Q1
New	1970 Q1
Norway	1970 Q1
Peru	1980 Q1
Philippine	1970 Q1
Poland	1995 Q1
Portugal	1970 Q1
Russia	1970 Q1
Singapore	1970 Q1
Slovakia	1993 Q1
Slovenia	1995 Q1
South Africa	1970 Q1
South Korea	1970 Q1
(Spain	1970 Q1
Sweden	1970 Q1
Switzerland	1970 Q1
Taiwan	1970 Q1
Thailand	1970 Q1
Turkey	1987 Q1
United Kingdom	1970 Q1
United States	1970 Q1
Uruguay	1988 Q1
Venezuela	1970 Q1

End Notes

[1] Notable exceptions being Romer and Romer (1994) and Cerra and Saxena (2008).

[2] The analysis of the U.S. data goes through the third quarter of 2011.

[3] The BBQ method identifies cyclical peaks and troughs as local maxima in the two quarters preceding and the two quarters following. It then eliminates maxima that do not alternate between peaks and troughs or do not have a long enough time span, in this case 2 quarters from a peak to trough and five quarters from a trough to peak. Once these criteria are met, recessions are defined as the time between a peak and a trough. We did not use this method because it requires at least 5 quarters of recovery, which would restrict and potentially bias our sample.

[4] This is similar to the methodology used in the IMF WEO analysis on recessions and recoveries (Terrones et al. 2009).

[5] This decline is measured as the decline in the average GDP path in our sample. Because recessions are of different duration, the average decline from peak to trough across recessions is a different and slightly higher figure.

[6] B&F recessions include Finland (1990), Iceland (1982), Italy (1982), Japan (1997), Norway (1991), Portugal (1982), Spain (1978), and Sweden (1990).

[7] Complementary to our results, Lopez-Salido and Nelson (2010) find that recoveries are not systemically slower in the aftermath of financial crises in post-war United States.

[8] Reinhart and Rogoff identify five AE recessions as banking crises. By our dating, the troughs of these recessions occur in: Finland (1992), Japan (1993), Norway (1991), Sweden (1992), and Spain (1979). Terrones et al. add Australia (1991), Denmark (1987), France (1993), Greece (1993), Italy (1993), Japan (1993), New Zealand (1987), the United Kingdom (1974), and the United Kingdom (1991), as well as a crisis in Germany around 1980 which does not correspond to a recession in our sample. In addition to the AEs, Reinhart and Rogoff also identify eight crises in the EMEs, fewer than in our sample: Argentina (2002), Colombia (1999), Hong Kong (1998), Indonesia (1998), Korea (1998), Malaysia (1998), the Philippines (1998), and Thailand (1998).

[9] Housing declines were common but not universal in the most recent recession, so are not included in this part of the analysis. Including the severe housing downturn as an explanatory variable for the pace of the U.S. recovery, the current recovery is still underperforming the model's expectation but by only one percent.

[10] Prior to the annual revision in July, the actual path of the U.S. recovery was very close to what would be predicted by the depth and duration regressions.

[11] The countries included are Australia, Austria, Canada, Finland, France, Germany, Ireland, Italy, Japan, Korea, Norway, Spain, Sweden, the UK, and the US.

[12] This section of the paper uses recession dating by the NBER in order to include the 2001 recession. The only other notable change is that NBER classifies the pre-recession peak of the Great Recession as 2007 Q3 instead of 2008 Q1.

[13] For individual recessions, we use the trend based on the average growth in the five years prior to the pre-recession peak because the four-year average two years prior to the peak introduces too much noise. Without the benefit of an average over a large sample, the results are much more difficult to interpret.

INDEX

D

E

F

G

H

I

U

V

W

Y